Your One-Minute Job Finding Coach

Your One-Minute Job Finding Coach

HOW TO FIND A JOB AND MANAGE
YOUR CAREER WHILE COPING
WITH THE HASSLES OF IT ALL

Randy Place

Place Publications
Greenwich, Connecticut
September 2015

ISBN: 0996310908

ISBN 13: 978-0-9963-109-0-1
Library of Congress Control Number: 2015951049
Place Publications, Greenwich CT

To Pudden, who made me laugh, and Ellie, who made me write.

Contents

Foreword ix
Preface xi
Acknowledgments xv

Part 1: How to Find a Job. 1
Chapter 1   What to Do When the Ax Falls 3
Chapter 2   How to Discover and Develop
             Your Hidden Talents 11
Chapter 3   Tips on Organizing Your Job Hunt 30
Chapter 4   Résumé Writing Tips 60
Chapter 5   Going to a Job Fair 84
Chapter 6   How to Use the Telephone to Get
             Meetings and Interviews 88
Chapter 7   Networking: The Quickest Way to
             Get Interviews 96
Chapter 8   How to Turn Knowledge into Power. 118
Chapter 9   Dressing for Success Isn't Just for Interviews 123
Chapter 10   How to Make a Good First Impression 128
Chapter 11   How to Turn Interviews into Job Offers 134
Chapter 12   Interview Questions-How to Answer
             the Toughies and Strategic Questions
             You Should Ask 197
Chapter 13   Secrets of Negotiating Salary and
             Getting a Raise 213

Part 2: How to Manage Your Life and Career 229

Chapter 14 Taking Care of Number One 231

Chapter 15 What to Do for an Encore Now
That You've Landed 268

Chapter 16 Getting Ahead at Headquarters
While Protecting your Hindquarters. 278

Chapter 17 When You're Sick and Tired of Being
Sick and Tired of the Corporate Rat Race 306

Chapter 18 How to Get a Job through Staffing Agencies 310

Chapter 19 Temping as a Way of Life. 317

Chapter 20 Flying Solo 330

Chapter 21 Advice for Women Only 343

Part 3: Coping with the Hassles of It All. 355

Chapter 22 It's What You Think, Stupid 357

Chapter 23 Using Your Religion as a Powerful
Job-Finding Tool 373

Chapter 24 Best Ways to Cope with Rejection 378

Chapter 25 Latest Ways to Beat Interview Anxiety
without a Prescription. 384

Chapter 26 You're Either Too Young or Too Old. 392

Chapter 27 How to Overcome Ten Job-Search Barriers 413

Chapter 28 How to Get Support for Your Search. 422

Epilogue 427

About the Author 429

Foreword

IN MY EXPERIENCE SUPERVISING CAREER counselors who worked with thousands of people, and in my own work with hundreds of people, the most successful career-counseling technique of all was to help people identify their strengths—what they were good at—and then to base a job search and a career on those strengths. Why is it so important to point this out? Isn't it obvious that our strengths and talents are what will bring success, money, achievement, and fulfillment?

As it turns out, we rarely look objectively at our strengths—we simply use them. We don't need to identify our strengths because they are right at hand, ready to be put to use whenever we need them. It's only in a job search or in a major career decision that we need to go beyond the mere use of our strengths. At such crucial junctures, we need to be able to articulate our strengths to others in order to make them aware of the value of what we can do. And at such times, we need to be able to articulate our strengths to ourselves (!) in order to go after what will be right for us in the world of work.

For most of us, that process is not easy. It involves taking an objective look at ourselves, our work history, our accomplishments, our feelings about what we have done, our fantasies and desires, our frustrations, our blocks, our latent skills and talents that might not yet have been fully developed, and how much we are able to support our own goals and aspirations. That's where Randy Place comes in.

Randy is exceptionally gifted at helping people identify their strengths and at helping people move into action to achieve their goals. I know about Randy's gifts in this regard because I supervised his career-counseling work for a very long time and saw the remarkable results he generated with clients from all walks of life and at all levels. Randy's mind is quick, flexible, and pragmatic. He is able to help people quickly identify what their next best step is, and he has the gift of putting the right words together at the right moment to help people move forward in the present.

I'm very glad to see he has put together this guide for careers and that he has written down many of the very helpful ideas he has used to help people over decades of career-counseling work.

In the book, we see Randy's warmth, his sense of humor, and his compassion for the situations of his clients. We immediately sense his ability to connect one-on-one with people, and we benefit from his generosity in giving practical advice that will be genuinely helpful. Randy is especially good at digging into the nitty-gritty of what we need to do every day to reach our potential.

I know this book will be very valuable to everyone who uses it. As Randy says, it's a book to pick up whenever a situation arises that requires a new perspective or a fresh look at what's happening at the moment. I'm quite sure many of these one-minute vignettes will have lasting impact, just as Randy himself has had a long career of making a truly important impact on the lives and careers of others.

David Rottman
Senior Vice President (retired)
Manager, Career Services
JPMorgan Chase

Preface

GOT A MINUTE? THEN READ for a minute, and learn a powerful technique you can apply to your job hunt, current job, and issues surrounding your life and career.

Your One-Minute Job-Finding Coach gives you a set of techniques and perspectives to help you launch and conduct a successful job-finding campaign. It presents a cornucopia of game-changing techniques to help you land a job faster and make money sooner.

As the title implies, you'll be coached on job-finding techniques in just one minute—that's all the time it takes. And the tactics you'll be taught to use have worked like magic for millions of job finders across all industries, job levels, and age groups in Europe and the United States for almost a century. You'll discover the techniques contained in the coaching vignettes are also shortcuts to finding a job, enhancing job performance, and managing your career.

If you're a candidate eager to jump right in to your job-finding campaign, this is the book for you. Among the many topics covered in these coachings, you'll find tips on what to do when the ax falls, how to write a résumé, how to handle mini-interviews at job fairs, how to turn interviews into job offers, and lots more.

If you're a candidate who has been putting off until tomorrow what you could be doing today or sitting at home and waiting for recruiters to call, this is the book that will motivate you to get cracking on your job campaign right now.

Either way, what you'll learn in a minute can be applied immediately to solve problems you face in your job campaign and beyond. The coachings you'll receive are about more than just finding a job. They run the gamut from discovering your hidden talents to organizing and managing your time. You'll learn how to become a star in the new job you land, how to enhance your career, how to handle personal and emotional issues like rejection and age and gender discrimination in the marketplace, and how to give your fortunes a great big boost by adjusting your attitude.

Your One-Minute Job-Finding Coach nurtures what's best in you. That's because it focuses on practical solutions to job-search and career problems, one coaching at a time. One minute at a time. This book will also complement career counseling you receive in your corporate benefits package or from state unemployment.

Furthermore, techniques you already know about finding a job and managing your career will be simplified and reinforced. Some of the processes that used to bug you—like interviewing, networking, negotiating salary, and asking for more money—will be demystified. Then you'll be able to turn them to your advantage. You'll experience many "aha moments" while learning new tips and tricks of the trade.

The idea for this book was born ten years ago when I was writing and hosting my nationally syndicated radio series. Millions of listeners across America enjoyed *Your Career Service,* which was comprised of daily sixty-second reports about how to find jobs and manage careers.

Because of the enthusiastic response I received from listeners and national advertisers, I became excited by the idea of sharing the techniques I had talked about on the air in a book. I wanted job candidates to learn in a minute's worth of reading what my radio audience was learning in a minute's worth of listening.

The result is this extraordinary book. It's packed with practical advice and tools that are tailored to job hunters and workers of all ages. The coaching vignettes have been drawn from techniques I've learned and developed over decades of experience as a career counselor and executive coach, a sales executive and sales trainer, and a broadcast journalist. And most importantly, they are drawn from my personal experiences. I successfully used these techniques in my own job hunts, career veers, and solo flights into entrepreneurial ventures. And then I taught them to thousands of job candidates for the past twenty-five years.

What makes this book special is the guidance you'll also receive from dozens of other experts whom I interviewed for my radio shows and for this book. These experts have worked across the spectrum of specialties and include some of the nation's prominent career counselors, executive coaches, and personal-success experts. The names of these awesome respondents are listed in the acknowledgments section.

It's now my privilege to share these one-minute coaching vignettes with job finders and fellow workers of all ages and in all industries who aspire to land good jobs quickly, enhance their performance on the new jobs they get, and triumph over the multitude of problems that arise daily in their careers.

You can reach those goals if you bring two things to the table: one-minute intervals for reading and motivation to translate the techniques you learn from the coachings to your job campaign.

After all, success comes from more than just reading. It's attained by your own efforts. Your endeavors will be rewarded handsomely whenever you need a tactic to solve a problem connected to your work life.

May *Your One-Minute Job-Finding Coach* guide you to finding the job you want and deserve and show you how to create a business life that's more satisfying than ever. Enjoy.

Acknowledgments

With a little help from my friends

—THE BEATTLES

ACTUALLY, I RECEIVED A LOT of help from my friends. They are my job-coaching colleagues and clients with whom it has been my pleasure to work. They are the distinguished pioneers and innovators in the fields of job finding, career management, and personal success whom I interviewed for my radio series and for this book. I'm deeply indebted to them all.

My thanks to Stephany Winston, "America's Organizational Guru," for her words of wisdom about how to organize for a job hunt. And to Camille Lavington, personal marketing consultant and author of *You've Only Got Three Seconds,* for her contribution to the chapter, "How to Make a Good First Impression." I've been privileged to share Camille's principles with many job seekers. Her tips about first impressions are by far the favorite training section in the interviewing seminars I present.

I'm deeply indebted to Stephen Cuthrell, who introduced me to the wonderful world of job-finding and career-management techniques back in the day when I retained his services as my career counselor. Steve was a special friend until the time of his passing last year. This extraordinary career strategist stimulated my interest in someday passing on the principles I learned from him to other job finders.

I'm particularly grateful to David Rottman for giving me that someday chance to become a career counselor in the department he created and managed for twenty-three years. I'm thankful for David's leadership, motivation, and friendship, and for his creating new search techniques and bringing some of the original methods up to date. David, thanks for letting the sunshine in. And thanks for your contributions to this book—and especially for the tips about how to target a job campaign that appear in the chapter, "Tips on Organizing Your Job Hunt."

Kudos to Sue Jones, the career consultant who shared her strategies for answering tough interview questions; to Jane Applegate, the small business management expert, for her input on the advantages of working for businesses owned by women; and to Jane Hodgetts, the career- and life-planning consultant who reveals how to incorporate the focusing technique into your search.

I'm most grateful to the late Don Fox, who had just turned sixty when I became his job-finding coach. Don feared that he'd "never find another job." Yet he conducted two more successful campaigns while he was in his seventies. Don was the inspiration for the chapter, "You're Either Too Young or Too Old." I also thank executive coach Bob Cuddy for sharing his views on age discrimination, and how to prepare for interviews in the same chapter.

I'm thankful to Dr. Joe Duffy, my late career-coaching colleague who I interviewed for the chapter, "Using Your Religion in the Job Search." The late seminarian practiced what he preached.

My deep appreciation to Anita Lands, who specializes in helping older workers find jobs—and in helping not-so-older ballet dancers pirouette into other fields—for providing her expertise to the chapter "Temping as a Way of Life."

Also, I recognize and sincerely thank executive coach Dr. Randy Ruppart for his contribution to the lesson about how job candidates can learn to coach themselves; Sally Skidmore for sharing how to find a job in the nonprofit sector; career psychologist Stephanie Gannon for her advice about handling stress during a job search; and Kate Wendleton, president of the Five O'clock Club and author of *Targeting the Job You Want,* for her input on getting support for your job search in the chapter, "Taking Care of Number One."

Mim Anzolut's contribution about how to conduct mini-interviews at job fairs is also much appreciated. I take my hat off to Marcia Reynolds, career coach and motivational speaker, for showing job finders how to be "in the zone" during interviews. Another tip of the hat goes to executive coach Nancy Friedburg for sharing her secrets on negotiating salary.

I'm much obliged to Jim Thompson, former news and public affairs director of WGCH, Greenwich, for his motivation and direction. Jim was instrumental in launching my radio reports about job finding on his morning news/talk shows. That resulted in the national syndication of *Your Career Service* and, ultimately, in this book.

I'm also grateful to Mitch Lebe, veteran New York radio reporter and anchor, for providing me with firsthand knowledge on job shadowing, a technique highlighted in the chapter, "Tips on Organizing Your Job Hunt."

Thanks to Bob Chazen, psychologist and psychology professor extraordinaire, for his inspiring classes at Fordham University on brief treatment. "BT" is a concept reflected in this book.

I acknowledge Kenneth Atchity, writer and author of *A Writer's Time,* for his idea about turning anxiety into productive elation. I pass this on in the chapter subtitled "Never Let Them See You Sweat."

Thanks also to career consultant Bill Roth for his contribution to research methods; to training expert Kelly Ann Foster for her input on taking courses; and to career psychologist Alan Pickman for providing the best ways to cope with rejection.

I'm indebted to Brandon Thimke, director of communication at The Reserves Network, who I interviewed for the chapter "How to Get a Job Through Staffing Agencies," and to Nickie Artese, former Reserves vice president, for sponsoring my radio series on Midwestern stations.

To conclude, I tender special thanks to Eleanore Place, my wife and collaborator, my tower of strength, and the love of my life. Ellie's creative ideas and asking, "When are you going to finish the book?" has nudged it over the finish line. Finally.

A Note to Readers

When it comes to expressing gender, I retain the use of "she" and "he" instead of the politically correct and more torturous approach of writing "she/he" or "his/her, " or even he more convoluted "s/he." I've made best efforts to alternate "he" with "she" throughout.

Part 1: How to Find a Job

What to Do When the Ax Falls

Your Pink Slip Is a Ticket to Ride

When your company cuts your job, you don't know whether to scream or go bowling. Your initial outrage is only natural. But it's not a good idea to wallow in your emotions when you're meeting people.

Your anger, projected onto personal contacts and prospective employers, can ruin relationships. You will be unsuccessful at interviews and bowl a lousy game.

That's why you need to give top priority to your psychological concerns. Admit the problem exists and is affecting your career plan. Should you be unable to shake the feelings of anger or loss, agree to consult a therapist or career counselor. Then you can move on.

Most of you will not be forced to abandon your job search while you deal with your negative feelings. But it's a good idea to slow down its pace. Just work on the self-assessment and résumé stages. Those elements take the most time anyhow, and working on them builds your self-confidence.

When you deal with emotional issues first, it eliminates psychological barriers that keep you from being at your best when talking with your personal contacts and interviewing for the job you want.

❖ ❖ ❖

Most of you feel depressed and angry after being told your services are no longer needed. When your work status has been interrupted after twenty years of loyal service, life isn't exactly a box of chocolates.

A good way to handle your emotions is to acknowledge and accept them. Then work hard to find another job. You also need to talk about your feelings. When you shut off your emotions, the result is a grouchy mood that obstructs your search.

Your emotions are released when you discuss your situation with close friends and family members. They can give you the support and encouragement you need. The process of venting your emotions clears your mind and improves your disposition. Now you can better concentrate on the job-finding campaign.

And don't even think about taking a vacation. This is the worst time to take off because it's hard to enjoy a holiday after the ax falls. Take your vacation after you've secured a new job. Then you'll be free of worry and can relax before getting back to the grind.

❖ ❖ ❖

You shouldn't feel embarrassed about losing your job. Embarrassment—that sense of being humiliated—is a disconnect between yourself and what you think you should be. You're thinking it shouldn't be you whose job has been eliminated.

Some feelings like anger are useful to hold because it can drive you to victory. But embarrassment is an emotion not worth holding. It makes you feel degraded. You can cast out embarrassment by presenting this alternate model to yourself:

There is dignity in struggling with a difficult situation. And because you are one of the multitudes whose jobs have been eliminated during the past year alone, getting the axe is not your fault.

Yet some interviewers will want to know why your job, and not someone else's, was cut. That interview question is best answered by looking your prospect straight in the eye as you explain it was a business decision to eliminate your position and you were told it had nothing to do with your performance.

Because this explanation most likely describes your situation, there's no need to feel embarrassed over getting a pink slip. Cutbacks are a way of life these days.

❖ ❖ ❖

It's a kick in the head to lose your job. Matter of fact, you experience one of life's biggest blows when you're thrown out on the street. A job loss caused by a merger or downsizing can erode your self-confidence. Even though you were a smashing success at work, when your job is yanked away, you start to forget how proficient you were.

An important part of your search is trying to remember all of the good things you accomplished on the job. Then you'll recover that feeling of self-esteem and hold on to it.

The best way to remember your accomplishments is to write a résumé. That's because a résumé not only compels you to recall your achievements, but it also becomes your self-marketing tool. Then you'll begin to restore your self-respect. While writing the résumé, you'll be pleasantly surprised to rediscover how much you've accomplished. Then you can practice thinking about how to present your success stories at interviews.

When you're convinced how proficient you are, you'll have all the self-confidence you need to present your skills in the job market.

❖ ❖ ❖

Your emotional state can bewilder you after losing a job. Your anger and loss of self-confidence can bring confusion. Yet you still have to cope with the problem of landing a job. "You become filled with anxiety and fear when you plant the thought in your mind that losing a job implies personal failure," said Dr. Claire Weekes, a pioneer in the study of anxiety.

"You must start to rebuild your self-confidence," Weekes advised in her book, *Peace From Nervous Suffering.* "The best of all remedies is to accept your feelings as quite natural under the circumstances." Otherwise brooding can make you so sick that you'll have no desire to begin your job hunt.

You can go into an emotional tailspin after losing a job. Emotions might run the gamut from feeling angry and depressed to confused, indecisive, or loss of confidence. Because your confusing thoughts are grooved in a compulsive way, the resulting brain fatigue can play tricks on you by slowing down your thinking.

When you understand the reason for your loss of self-confidence, its return will be automatic. Then you can look at your job-finding problem more calmly and rationally.

❖ ❖ ❖

The surest path to finding your next job is to stop complaining about your situation and face the music. Your job is gone—period. You now have a responsibility to yourself to waste no time in finding another position, pronto.

By facing the music, you stop indulging your fears of interviewing or networking with idle chatter about how you were screwed. It becomes idle chatter once you've performed the necessary task of venting your feelings of anger and anxiety to people who know you well. Idle chatter about why you were dismissed gives you emotional support, all right, but not the job you need.

When emotions overwhelm you, talk to friends and family members who you think will provide support. You can also vent to a mental health professional or a career counselor, or to your priest, minister, rabbi, or Zen master.

Facing the music best supports your emotions. When the ax falls, face and accept your loss. Then get on with your career by starting your job hunt.

❖ ❖ ❖

After you've lost a job, you must keep moving ahead. You need to start looking around immediately so you don't lose momentum. The concept of momentum is a crucial element to help you succeed in any endeavor. That's because momentum enables you to power through a job search, and, in the process, to advance your career.

A pink slip is also a ticket to ride on an exciting journey to fulfill your dreams. When you get booted, it could be the boot you've needed to get out of a comfortable rut. American industrialist Henry Ford put it this way: "Habit conduces to a certain inertia, and any disturbance of it affects the mind like trouble."

But opportunities are often disguised as troubling situations like getting the ax. In his book *My Life and My Work*, Ford wrote, "Life, as I see it, is not a location, but a journey. Even the man who most feels himself settled is not settled – he is probably sagging back." Ford believed life is meant to be in flux.

So when the ax falls, keep moving ahead and building momentum by getting your job-finding act together and taking it on the road.

❖ ❖ ❖

It's not losing your job that'll do you in. There are jobs out there in any economy. All you need to do is fill one of them. It's the loss of momentum after being terminated that can do you in. You can come to a standstill when you don't climb back on the bicycle after a pink slip pushes you off of it. That's the time to continue to pedal and move forward.

The reason not searching right away causes a loss of momentum is because you become stagnant. When your personal productivity decreases, you become frustrated and angry as you lose balance and fall off the job-search bike. Remember that you build momentum by moving forward toward your job search goal. Then your campaign takes on a life of its own.

As momentum builds, you can ease up a bit on the pedaling and take time to enjoy the scenery. This is an occasion, after all, to think about what you have always enjoyed doing the most and to decide what job or career will satisfy you the most. Then go for it.

The key word in building momentum is "go." Otherwise, it's like paying tennis with a hockey stick. You can do it. But just imagine what your serve will be like.

❖ ❖ ❖

After losing your job, don't isolate yourself. Stress is the consequence you suffer from being alone. You need the support of people. And you lost that support when you lost your job. The remedy is to start your job hunt right after you've been dismissed.

Only a job campaign lets you reunite with the world of work. You reconnect by talking with your contacts who are employed. That means attending job fairs and seminars and joining a job-finding support group.

You reconnect by grabbing the outplacement package provided by the company that kicked you out, especially if it includes career counseling. Most job candidates benefit from working with a career counselor while letting their former employers pay for phone, fax, and postage costs. But when you find yourself on the beach without a package, that's the time to join a job-finding support group.

Any method you choose to reconnect with others will beat isolating yourself. Isolation equals anxiety. The downside of isolating after being downsized is brought into focus by Spanish novelist Miguel de Unamuno, who wrote, "Isolation is the worst possible counselor."

❖ ❖ ❖

When you assume losing your job is an opportunity to take an extended vacation, you risk losing your working edge. And you'll be faced with having to answer one of the thorniest interview questions, which is the question about what you've been doing since you stopped working. You are not going to knock interviewers' socks off by describing your trip. Who wants to hire somebody who's a live commercial for the joys of not having to work?

The best time to begin your job hunt is before the ink has dried on your termination notice. Why? Because you're still in a working mode. But if you're hell-bent on taking a trip, call it a sabbatical. That's a paid leave college professors get to study or travel. When you label your time-out a sabbatical, at least it sounds like you were nurturing your career.

When you're paid to look for work with a severance or unemployment package, it's much like a sabbatical—especially if you attend classes to acquire new skills. And calling your time out a sabbatical sounds an awful lot better than flaunting a trip to Europe.

❖ ❖ ❖

Unless your vacation was planned months ago and you'd lose the cost of your tickets, start your job campaign at once. The quickest way to land is to keep your working momentum going.

When you had a job, your activities were disciplined as you structured your time. You got up at 7:00 a.m., showered, shaved or put on your makeup, ate breakfast, and commuted to work. You organized the rest of the day in the same way. This lifetime of good work habits will continue to operate for you when you launch a job-finding campaign lickety-split.

But terminated employees who decide to take trips or to stay home awhile to catch up on chores find that their working momentum has decreased, and it's hard to gear up again to kick off a job-finding campaign.

If you're tempted to think losing your job is an opportunity to sit on the sidelines because you have free time, appreciate the fact that you already have a job—the full-time job of looking for a job. In any line of work, you can't just hang out. You need to hit the ground running.

❖ ❖ ❖

You have just learned your job has been cut and have picked up the phone to call a few people who popped into your mind. Then you wonder what to do next. It would be uncool to pick up the phone just yet.

You need to plan your work before working your plan. You'll start your job-finding plan by simply writing down the names of those people you were going to call. This list will be used later for the networking step of your job-finding plan.

For the time being, lay your list aside until you decide what kind of job you want. That's the first step. Ask yourself what parts of your previous positions you enjoyed doing most. That will help you to list your skills from which to select a job target. And it will help you to determine an objective for the top of your résumé. When you've finished writing the résumé, you'll have something to show the personal contacts you put on your list.

Now it's time to call your contacts. Some of you will have a short list. Not to worry. As your job hunt unfolds, you'll think of more names to add to your network list. Today you've started to plan your work. Tomorrow, begin working your plan.

❖ ❖ ❖

CHAPTER 2

How to Discover and Develop Your Hidden Talents

GETTING TO KNOW YOU

> He's gotten to the top of the ladder and finds it's against the wrong wall.
> —JOSEPH CAMPBELL

DON'T LET ANYONE TELL YOU IQ tests can help decide your next career move. "Intelligence tests cannot predict your business and personal success," said psychologist Robert Sternberg.

IQ tests measure only a narrow range of abilities. They don't indicate if you'll be satisfied with a particular job. And test results can be distorted by not getting enough sleep, a head cold, or a hangover.

"Successful intelligence is measured by your ability to think in ways that will help you develop personal excellence at work," says Sternberg in a printed report.

The former professor of management and psychology at Yale University says personal excellence is reflected in the strengths you already possess. They can be uncovered by simply recognizing your pattern of strengths and weaknesses.

You can identify your strengths by asking yourself what you do well. Then you can improve those skills by using them more frequently. After picking out your weaknesses, stop using them or find ways to work around what you lack.

Because a career or job search is not predictable, it's what you want to do that counts. So the secret of achieving success has nothing to do with your IQ. It's all about identifying and using your strengths.

When it comes to discovering your assets, the best assessment is a self-assessment.

❖ ❖ ❖

A useful technique to uncover your strengths is to study past achievements. You pulled off those accomplishments by using your strengths. And what you achieved before with satisfying results can be repeated anytime with equally satisfying results. That's because you have already demonstrated you can do it.

The first step to uncovering your strengths is to write down one-line descriptions of some of your achievements. Organize the list by jotting down several achievements in each of these five periods of your life:

1. During the past four years at work
2. During your high school and college years
3. During the next four years after graduation
4. During the four years after that
5. And during each four year segment that follows up to your past four years at work

Before you begin, let's agree to work with this definition of "achievement":

An achievement is a personal triumph. It's something you did well, enjoyed doing, and were proud of regardless of what anyone else thought, whether you got paid for doing it, and whether the achievement was associated with work, family, or community.

You can apply this definition to the exercise by listing the skills that enabled you to perform each achievement. You'll notice a pattern of skills—things you did well—that enabled you to triumph each time.

Now you're ready to look for a job where you can use those skills to triumph over and over again. In order to be happy in the present, you need to study your past.

❖ ❖ ❖

There is hardly a more important decision to make than what you want to do for the rest of your life. When you're undecided about what your dream job or career looks like, there are assessment tools that can help verify your interests and what you like doing. They're available on the Internet.

The Strong Interest Inventory is one of the most popular career assessment tools. It can provide an insightful look into your interests and preferences to help you decide on the right career and job choice.

Your interest in a particular endeavor indicates that you probably have the aptitude and abilities to succeed in it. That's the theory behind the Strong Interest Inventory and other career assessment instruments.

As already mentioned in this chapter, you can also test yourself. That's what most job finders do. The following list describes a three-step self-assessment technique for uncovering your interests:

1. Ask yourself what you want most in the world. Without stopping to think, write down the first thing that comes into your head. Then record a couple of more ideas that pop into your mind. After reading your thoughts, put the paper away.
2. Repeat this exercise the same time the next week—and then during the following two weeks.
3. On the fifth week, take out your list and study all of your answers.

Notice how your desires form a pattern. The responses that repeat themselves can be highlighted—they are the job goals you need to investigate.

❖ ❖ ❖

Your job hunt needs a message. You can begin to think about your message while getting to know yourself through writing a résumé.

You can uncover the right message by asking yourself what skills you need in order to land the job you want. Those skills are listed in your résumé.

When you talk about them at interviews, you're delivering a message about your ability to perform the job you're applying for. And by adding several values to each skill, you're bound to leave a great impression.

Values are things in life you're automatically drawn to. They can be that you are energetic and a hard worker who knows how to get results. After determining your values, write a few lines about them for the "Summary" section of your résumé.

When it comes to interviewing, predetermine two things: how those skills and values match the specifications of the job you're interviewing for, and how you'll position your message within each interview so you can repeat it several times.

Your chances of getting hired escalate when you create a message for your campaign.

❖ ❖ ❖

The key to a successful career is to do what you love and to stop doing what you dislike. When you think back, didn't your peak performances happen when your strengths—skills that came easily to you—were used? Your energies need to be focused on using those strengths while recognizing your weaknesses. That's because it's easier to improve a skill than to fix a weakness.

You can recognize your pattern of strengths and weaknesses by determining two things:

First, know what activities you do well. Skills used to accomplish those tasks are your assets. Using them more often can strengthen them.

Second, know what activities you don't do well. Skills used in doing them are your liabilities. You'll need to find a way to either work around your weaknesses, delegate those tasks to others, or stop doing them altogether.

Once you've identified your strengths, you're ready to talk about them at interviews by focusing on how your favorite skills fit the description of the job you're interviewing for.

As you'll learn in the chapter titled "Tips on Interviewing," it's best not to mention your blemishes at all unless you're asked about them. A nice way to respond is to admit everyone has weaknesses. Then explain how you've always focused on your strengths in order to give them more power.

You will be a smash hit at interviews and work by soaring with your strengths.

❖ ❖ ❖

When it comes to getting ahead, you must learn about your best, not your worst, and use that knowledge about your best to succeed and to overcome your problems. The more you concentrate on problems and mistakes, the more you encourage that garbage to wind up in your affairs.

You can uncover your best by focusing on experiences in your life that paid off—even if they were small. That's how Thomas Edison succeeded. The inventor developed the commercial use of electricity not by scratching his head over mistakes but by focusing on what had gone well in his experiments.

There are many experiences in life that make you feel that you've done something well. These are your achievements. What others thought doesn't count. An achievement is anything you enjoyed doing and are proud of.

If you neglect to pay attention to your achievements, why should anyone else? You present your past achievements or successes, not your failures, at interviews.

Make a list of your achievements from high school up to the present as interview preparation. Yes, it is a chore to dig up all of your triumphs. But as Thomas Edison said, "There is no substitute for hard work."

❖ ❖ ❖

You need to sell yourself to get a job. And the first rule of selling anything is to know your product.

Why do you think product knowledge is important in your job-finding campaign? Because you are the product. That's the reason that getting to know you is the first step in your job hunt.

Before you determine your strongest selling points, it's not possible to talk confidently about yourself. Your unique selling points can be uncovered in five easy steps:

1. Make a list of the seven things you do best.
2. Reflect on the skills that went into accomplishing those achievements. Did you plan? Write? Manage?
3. Make a second list of things you did that turned you on. This step usually identifies a special quality that lets you handle a situation or solve a problem better than anyone else.
4. Choose your main selling points from the combined lists and include them in your résumé.
5. Practice talking about your job-search selling points as you prepare for upcoming interviews.

Your product knowledge will be used in all aspects of your campaign—from writing a résumé, phoning to request meetings, and writing cover letters and e-mails to making brief introductions at networking meetings and job fairs and selling yourself at interviews.

Knowing yourself makes you enthusiastic and gives you courage because knowing about yourself as the product will reduce your anxiety. And it helps you talk about why a prospective employer should see and hire you.

❖ ❖ ❖

What do you want to be when you grow up? Many of you still ask that question even after working for many years. In today's climate of cutting jobs, now is a good time to answer that question by doing some career planning.

An excellent method for planning ahead is to perform a personal self-assessment by examining your skills and looking at various fields and occupations where they can be used. A self-assessment lets you look at change as an opportunity to reinvent yourself.

Career makeovers are do-it-yourself projects. There are no tests or computer programs that will spit out the answer to your life's work. Answers lie within you.

What follows are two steps that will enable you to uncover answers that apply to your situation. You may choose to work through either or both of them.

The first step is to reflect on your favorite achievements in your life. Perhaps you've written an article or built and installed kitchen cabinets. You can polish up those skills and find out if there's a job out there where you can use them.

The second step is to ask yourself what you'd do if you had a million dollars. Would you go to law school? Or buy more expensive tools for your hobby?

Maybe those million-dollar interests are skills you already have or would love to learn. Then you won't need a million bucks—just a little imagination.

❖ ❖ ❖

Being notified that your services are no longer needed is enough to make grown people cry. News of your termination can come as a bolt from the blue even if you had expected to be let go after hearing your company was going to downsize.

If you're still in denial, snap out of it. The time has long passed when firms guaranteed you a job until retirement. You'll stop reminiscing about the way you wish things were when you understand your job was terminated because of changes in the company beyond your control.

So raise your right hand and shout, "It's not my fault!" Feel better now? Then get on with it by taking an inventory of the skills you enjoy using the most. You can market them in your field or in other areas.

For example, lawyers are trained in analytical thinking. That's a broad skill they can apply in many areas of business to negotiate, persuade, and write clearly.

A smart way to assess your skills is to analyze a recent working day. List your tasks in simple sentences beginning with past-tense action verbs: wrote, developed, performed, researched, sold, marketed, created. These statements speak to your skills—and are the basis for bulleted contribution statements on your résumé.

Your ability to understand your skills and to practice talking about them will determine whether you are selected.

❖ ❖ ❖

Although many roads can lead to your success, your career might be overcrowded or no longer there. If that describes your predicament, select a new destination by studying your past achievements. They're the signs that point toward new paths that will guide you to achieve greater success.

An achievement is an experience that makes you feel you've done something well. What others think doesn't count as long as you enjoyed doing it and are proud of what you've done.

If you can't think of even one achievement offhand, remember that there are at least some things in life that turned you on. They'll come to mind when you put on your thinking cap and reflect awhile. That's because your achievements started when you were a toddler.

But the achievements to list are those that happened during your high school years up to the present. Circle or highlight those achievements that outshine the rest. They are your successes.

The skills you used to produce those successful experiences should be listed next to them. They will lead you to future successes because one achievement leads to another.

Isn't that reason enough to study your lifetime achievements? They are the aids that help you create a new path to success.

❖ ❖ ❖

You dislike awakening and going to the job you detest. Chances are you aren't using your favorite skills at this job you love to hate. A job will feel right only when you enjoy what you do.

There ought to be a job out there where you can do what you love. You'll find the right slot after you think about your past achievements and then determine the skills you used to make those accomplishments happen.

The easiest way to list performances that gave you the most satisfaction on or off the job is to take a little time each day to jot them down. By week's end, you'll have listed over twenty accomplishments.

The next step is to select a half -dozen of your favorites. A set of skills went into making each success story possible. Those skills will jump off the page when you ask yourself what you enjoyed doing as you worked toward each particular achievement.

Did you enjoy working with your hands? Or was it the written or verbal communications that excited you? And did you get turned on when you sold on commission and earned bug bucks?

You were born with those special skills. Your bag of tricks can be taken anywhere to repeat those victories. The right position is the job that allows you to use four or more of your preferred skills.

❖ ❖ ❖

Getting to know yourself is the first step to landing a job because you are a product that needs to be marketed and sold—and product knowledge is the most important ingredient when it comes to selling any product or service. This includes your services.

There is no need to even start thinking about interviewing until you determine your strongest selling points. An easy way to do it is by making a list of six things you do best. You can then ask yourself what skills went into accomplishing those achievements. Planning, managing, writing, manual dexterity, and verbal or written communications are some examples.

The next step is to make a second list of assignments that turned you on and to determine which skills you used to accomplish those tasks. This usually identifies a special quality that lets you handle a situation or solve a problem better than anyone else.

Be sure to include your major skills or selling points on your résumé. And practice talking about them. You'll use this product knowledge not only to sell yourself at interviews, but also during the self-marketing aspects of your job campaign: during networking, telephoning to request meetings, and writing cover letters.

You'll present yourself with enthusiasm and confidence by getting to know yourself as the product.

❖ ❖ ❖

When you have an aptitude for something, it means you were born with the ability to do it. Aptitudes are those natural abilities inherited from your parents.

When choosing a career or job, choose one that uses as many of your aptitudes as possible. Mental abilities that go unused not only go to waste but also often cause you to be confused and distracted because your brain is not focused on your strengths—those things you like to do.

You probably won't be able to use all of your aptitudes in a career. But knowing your God-given abilities will help you to make informed career decisions.

An easy way to rate your interests is to list a number of occupations that appeal to you. Opposite each career, assign a number from one to five. That expresses your degree of interest. Occupations receiving the highest ratings can be selected for initial investigation.

Analyze each selection in terms of how your aptitudes would be helpful in doing the work of that occupation. You will have the most success in using a strong aptitude when you combine it with other aptitudes.

❖ ❖ ❖

Bishop Fulton J. Sheen, who is known for his inspirational books and television broadcasts, was asked why he never used notes or cue cards during his weekly hour-long TV lectures of the 1950s. Bishop Sheen explained that before you can sell anything to others, you must first make it your own.

The late Catholic bishop made talks his own by committing them to memory. Likewise, you can make an interview sales pitch your own by becoming thoroughly familiar with its contents. Only then will you be able to communicate ideas to your audience of potential employers in a way that convinces them that you have what it takes to do a particular job.

To make stuff your own is part of the getting-to-know-you process that begins with discovering your strongest points. Just make a list of a half dozen thing you do best. Then ask yourself three key questions:

1. What skills do you bring to a job—planning, working hands on, or managing?
2. What are your interests—do you enjoy writing, or do you prefer crunching numbers, training, or selling?
3. What is your work style—are you methodical or creative?

Finally, make a list of assignments that turned you on. That will identify a special quality in you that lets you handle situations better than anyone else.

In order to make this sales pitch your own, rehearse it a lot. Now you're ready to sell it to others.

❖ ❖ ❖

There is a superior way to find work other than just sending out résumés, responding to ads on the Internet and in newspapers, or going to job fairs, employment agencies, and executive recruiters. That's what most of you are tempted to do after being canned—go after the hot jobs by twisting yourself into a shape that fits them.

When you become a pretzel, you guarantee discontent. You may not be blessed with the skills or interests such work demands. For that reason, the best place to begin a job-finding campaign is with you.

Career expert Richard Bolles, quoted in a printed report, says "God has already outlined the work He wants you to do while on this earth." The author of *What Color Is Your Parachute,* believes it's a unique work only you can do. And you are born with the very gifts you need to do that work.

You can begin by asking yourself what talents, aptitudes, skills, or gifts God has given to you. Then look for work that matches them.

❖ ❖ ❖

Money is hard to earn when you're doing what you hate. When you do what you love, the money eventually follows. But you need a plan for determining what it is you would love to do for a living.

Unfortunately, most of you spend more time planning your vacations than thinking about your vocations. You should start your career plan by fleshing out your interests and finding a career that links up to them.

Another exercise to analyze what turns you on is to study job sites on the Internet along with help-wanted ads in newspapers each week. Classifieds are like windows that allow you to see the opportunities out there.

When something grabs your interest, determine if you qualify for it. More training or education might be necessary to help you land the job you see yourself doing.

The key is seeing. It's helpful to see your daydreams and to remember your night dreams. What you're doing in them indicates what your role in life can be.

Awareness of your daydreams is especially important. As motivational speaker Earl Nightingale said, "What you should be doing in life is what you daydream about all day."

❖ ❖ ❖

It's never too late to do what you've always dreamed about. Instead of working at a dream job, most of you are plodding away at whatever it is you do with little or no thought about why you're doing it. Then you wonder why you are unhappy at work

Unhappiness can be interpreted as a signal that motivates you to reevaluate your situation. Dreams come true after reexamining what you would love to do and then trying to find a career and job to match. Here are four steps that can help you focus on your interests:

1. Jot down the titles of articles and books you've read.
2. List the kind of TV shows you watch.
3. While watching the boob tube, observe any fictional roles characters play that you relate to for a job or career. Many college students were turned on to study law by watching legal TV shows like *LA Law* and *Law and Order.*
4. Put your daily lists away without reading them for a couple of months. Then study your inventory of reading and TV material.

You'll see patterns of interests you might not have realized before. They could lead you to a job and a career that makes sense.

It's never too late to do what you've always dreamed about.

❖ ❖ ❖

Yes, you can have it all—but not all at once. If you have too many interests and cannot settle on one, you might be suffering from "the Smart Person's Disease."

To cure SPD, paint yourself a corner. This means to list your interests, and then weed them out until you're left with a single option. Start the process by making a list of your favorite achievements that are related to your career, family, or social life. Those should be the things that you enjoyed doing the most.

Where to begin? In high school, by jotting down a few of your favorite achievements during that four-year period. Do the same for the next four years, whether you went to college, joined the military, or started working.

Finally, note several achievements for each four-year period after that…right up to the present.

Your favorite successes or projects you've listed involved the use of skills that came easily to you. You couldn't have written that impressive article without good writing and organizational skills, for example.

The rest of the process can be completed in three easy steps. First, whittle away all but one of your successes—your favorite. Second, list options in the workplace that would make the best use of your major skills. And third, eliminate all possibilities but the one you really want.

Now that the SPD has been cured, you are free to pursue your choice of a job or career with a mind that is focused and clear.

❖ ❖ ❖

You'll have it made at interviews when you know what your strengths are. A technique to analyze your strong points is to list a half dozen of your favorite accomplishments. They might include writing and delivering your commencement speech—or the presentation you wrote and delivered that resulted in a really big sale.

Next, filter out the skills you used to achieve each success and list them separately. Those skills might be writing, speaking, and customer service.

Finally, circle the most predominant strengths on your list. You'll find they pop up in almost all of your accomplishments. That's an indication that the strengths you circled are the principle skills that make you tick.

This procedure will enable you to name several of your dominant skills when you answer the question usually asked at interviews: "What are your strengths?"

The interviewer is hoping to hear that your major skills match the needs for the job. You'll tell them what they want to hear by highlighting several of your strong points and illustrating how they were applied at work.

A prospective employer also wants to see if your presentation is confident, sincere, and honest. Those qualities will be front and center when you know what makes you tick.

❖ ❖ ❖

You can also uncover the talents you need to cultivate by getting some feedback on yourself from close friends and business associates.

This technique for self-directed feedback is accomplished in two steps. Make a list of what you perceive to be your strengths and weaknesses. Then ask some of your contacts to rate you on a scale of one to ten. Their answers will inform you about what other people are thinking and saying about you

Their opinions will go into your plan for self-development. And that plan will become the basis for self-improvement strategies available to you from reading books and buying CDs to taking courses and getting hands-on experience for the talents you want to cultivate.

The difference between this tactic for improving or developing a skill and self-help is getting the input of others.

The results will be gratifying. You'll discover you have many more strengths than areas that need to be developed. That is a wonderful understanding to have both on the job and when searching for one.

Either way, information gathered from self-directed feedback lets you build from your strengths.

❖ ❖ ❖

There is another reason it makes sense to check with your friends before deciding on a program for self-improvement. You might think you know which skills you need to improve, but people who know you well might disagree. Here's an example:

Because you believe listening to others and acknowledging the points they make is one of your strong skills, you decide your listening skill needs no improvement. On the other hand, you believe the way you respond to colleagues and prospective employers could be upgraded and decide that that's the skill that needs to be polished.

You're in for a big surprise. When you ask a bunch of friends for feedback, they say you're not as good of a listener as you think. Your contacts believe what you're told goes in one ear and out the other.

This feedback has tremendous value. It informs you about how you're really coming across and which skills needed to be developed.

That's why it makes sense to share your perception of yourself with some friends, family members, and colleagues and ask them to comment. Use the self-directed feedback technique described in the previous coaching vignette.

❖ ❖ ❖

When you are bewildered about the kind of work you want to do next, let your index finger point the way.

A job hunting client of mine from Brooklyn, New York, discovered this technique after being baffled for many months about what to do next. Jeff Goldstein lost his self-confidence after his job was cut—and depression blocked his ability to make a decision.

As the job hunter was reading a newspaper one morning, he decided to run his index finger down the columns of classified ads until he felt something resonate. Goldstein stopped when he saw jobs for investigators.

Jeff's feeling of excitement escalated when he realized the previous jobs he had loved the most in the financial industry had required him to examine and investigate people and to write reports about what he saw. "I used my inner gut feeling," Goldstein told me.

The job candidate's search became focused on finding a position that would make use of his investigative and reporting skills. A position in a related field was offered to Jeff. He accepted a position as an auditor and inspector for an insurance company, almost doubling his previous salary.

When you see an ad that excites you, it's a positive sign. The job supports your "inner gut feeling" about something you like and want to do.

❖ ❖ ❖

You will be happy in your work only when you "keep your eyes on the prize."[1] When you don't have a prize—something you desire to do—you need to decide on a vocation.

Finding your prize is a giant first step that will lead to selective perception. That means that once your mind has focused on an object, you'll begin seeing that object everywhere and be led to attain it.

When you work toward a goal by keeping your eyes on the prize, this four-step process will naturally happen. After selecting an object, which is the field of your choice, you'll start to read articles about it, and then you'll seek out people who work in that field to learn what their jobs are like. Next you'll notice you're not doing anything about getting your job campaign going to enter the field, so you'll feel pressure building to go out and do it.

For centuries, wise men have spoken about the idea of keeping your eyes on the prize. In the third volume of "The Philokalia," Saint Peter of Damaskos wrote, "Where a resolute disposition and desire are lacking, even easy things appear difficult, though the reverse is true as well." The reverse of Saint Peter's statement holds the key to your success: when desire exists, even difficult things appear effortless.

The work you desire, no matter how difficult it is to break into it, can become effortless when you keep your eye on the prize.

❖ ❖ ❖

When you have many interests and cannot settle on one, you suffer from the Smart Person's Disease (SPD) mentioned earlier.

---

1 Title of a popular folk song during the Civil Rights movement in America. A stanza urged blacks to "Keep you eyes on the prize, hold on."

You know it's impossible to use all of your talents in a single career. Yet you refuse to give anything up. Shame on you! When you try to do everything and capture every opportunity, your energy becomes scattered.

The cure for SPD is to focus down—that means giving up interests not related to what you want to do in life. When deciding what career to choose and what skills to lose, focus your energies by considering one area at a time.

It's like the experiment you performed in grammar school with a magnifying glass held over a piece of paper on a sunny day. The glass focused the sun's rays into a tiny dot that burned a hole through the paper.

It's okay to experiment in your career as long as you perform one experiment at a time. Oprah Winfrey understood the concept of focusing when she said, "You can have it all. Just not all at once."

❖ ❖ ❖

Just because your career has come to a screeching halt and you're caught between jobs doesn't mean you are without choices.

One technique that will help you to generate the best possible choice is to ask yourself what you would do if you knew you could not fail. The answer that comes to mind will be something that motivates you to succeed.

Chances are you've already thought about lots of things you would rather be doing. After you lose your job, you have a wonderful opportunity to explore them and to discover what you are motivated to do.

Motivation is the key to your success. Anyone who has tried and failed and then learned and mastered a sport, a musical instrument, or a field of study knows that failures are the foundation for success. The reason you kept on keeping on? You were motivated to do it.

The price you pay for success is long dedication to a job, a career, or a craft. Success is easier to achieve when you have a motive.

Motivation manifests itself when you feel so strongly about something that you're driven to take action. And what could motivate you more than doing something you know you'll succeed at?

❖ ❖ ❖

When you're having trouble figuring out your next career move, try a method called Focusing. "It's a way to tap into your mind-body and be with something that's not clear," says career consultant Jane Hodgetts.

For example, you might be a teacher who has thought about moving into either law or real estate but can't decide which path to take. "When you cannot make up your mind," says the Boston-based consultant, "you've smashed into an action block that needs to be dissolved."

Focusing can empower you to do just that. When you need to break down that block of indecision, Focusing teaches you to pause during the decision-making process in order to discover new possibilities.

First, you focus on each choice, one at a time, to get a sense of what it would be like to teach and to be a lawyer. Picture yourself doing each. Second, expect some new meaning and information to come to mind that wasn't on your list of pros and cons.

In a nutshell, Focusing is a process that helps to resolve problems and allows the decision that feels right for you to unfold. To learn more about the process, visit The Focusing Institute at www.focusinginstitute.org.

But focusing alone won't help you decide. You must first use traditional approaches of gathering information about each field. When you feel at a loss about what to do with this information, then use Focusing.

❖ ❖ ❖

CHAPTER 3

Tips on Organizing Your Job Hunt

GET YOUR ACT TOGETHER BEFORE TAKING IT ON THE ROAD

AN EFFECTIVE JOB-FINDING CAMPAIGN IS an organized one. When your search is structured, you're able to keep track of activities surrounding it. You can't keep it all in your head. So the first step is to decide whether you prefer to organize yourself on paper or by using technology.

When it comes to paper, look for an appointment book that has a calendar and a to-do list so you can enter all of your job-hunting activities. The best bet is an organizer that displays a day or a week at a time. That's because it gives you more room to enter tasks, brief notes, appointments, and reminders to follow up.

If you want to use technology, consider a personal digital assistant (PDA), a lightweight package that slips into your pocket or purse. That usually means a cell phone or "smartphone." Many offer the same organizing features that an organizer offers, along with other kinds of applications (apps). Either way, make sure the system you choose lets you schedule appointments and write a to-do list.

Because we're so used to using complex technology programs to do our bidding, perhaps you've forgotten about the simple index card. A card file is the easiest, most economical organizer of all. You can use a card for each contact and list the contact's company address, e-mail address, along with phone and fax numbers. Any time you contact somebody—in writing, in person, or by phone—write down the date of that communication and a brief note about what was said.

You will do away with much of the stress associated with your campaign by being organized.

❖ ❖ ❖

An interesting way to deal with feeling upset about an event is to ask yourself these two questions: What would you need to change in order to feel better? And what's preventing you from changing right now?

Sometimes the loss of a job makes you feel so hurt that you cannot begin a job hunt. It's normal to feel emotional pain. But when you promise to start a job-finding campaign "one of these days," it means none of these days—unless you act.

Let's consider the two questions. What you need to change in order to feel better is to get yourself into the job market today. What's preventing you from doing so, or from changing right now, are your emotions. When feelings run high, they can block you from taking action.

It's easy to chop through an emotional block by associating pleasure with beginning your search and pain with not beginning it. The feelings of working on a job campaign are far more pleasant than just sitting there and stewing in your own juices.

If you had some job prospects right now, you would feel much better, and you know it. You will find potential opportunities by placing all of your energy behind your goal of finding work. Only then will you be motivated to start.

❖ ❖ ❖

Finding a job is not difficult, because all you need is one. But finding that one job is not for lazy candidates. It takes lots of effort to bring about change of any kind.

When you've lost or decided to leave a job, the change you're going through is extra large because you have also lost the support of your position, title, associates, and paycheck, along with your office environment.

The first step in beginning to cope with this change in your life is to get into a job-finding mode by using the same good work habits that have served you well during your career.

You can work through emotions that are blocking from you from making this start by understanding that modifying your lifestyle is like getting in shape. Or getting sober. You need to wake up some morning and decide to just do it. And do it now.

Your deciding to make this effort will give you two megabenefits— a sense of purpose and a feeling of accomplishment. To launch your job campaign into orbit, select the kind of job or career you want. Then make the effort to get it.

Only the decision to do it now stands between you and that one job you need.

❖ ❖ ❖

There are no excuses to procrastinate your job hunt. The feeling of wanting to delay your campaign does not mean you cannot get started. It's possible to overcome the lethargy of your brain by just making yourself do it. And the simplest method is to command your muscles to act.

In his book, *Mental Health through Will Training* Dr. Abraham Low wrote, "The sense of hopelessness in the brain [can create] an attitude of helplessness in the muscles." So when your brain is crippled from fear, your muscles can become sluggish and inactive. Neuropsychiatrist Low contends the way to get rid of anxious fears is to "make muscles do what the brain can't do."

So whenever your brain tells you that now is not the time to look for a job, tell it to shut up! Then command your leg muscles to walk in front of a computer and your finger muscles to start writing a résumé; then command your arm muscles to pick up the phone, your finger muscles to dial numbers of personal contacts, and your vocal muscles to speak to them.

Muscles can be made to mold to mental activity when you practice commanding your muscles to act. Muscles will demonstrate their ability to restore self-confidence to your brain.

Then it becomes easier to get started, even when you don't feel like it.

❖ ❖ ❖

Successful job-finding campaigns are conducted by creating challenges for yourself and setting time limits to accomplish them. It's essential to make your own challenges. That's because a job hunt is an ambiguous project.

The challenge of finding a job stimulates you to take action while arousing your interest in competing in the job marketplace. Some challenges you can initiate include giving yourself three days to develop a résumé, a day to draw up a list of contacts, an hour or so each Sunday to review the classifieds, and an hour daily to survey job postings on the Internet.

It will be easier to deal with challenging yourself when you understand that your job hunt, like running a business, is not a smooth ride. We're not talking serenity here. You will develop the momentum necessary to carry you over the bumps by setting time limits even when none exist. This technique of setting deadlines will get your adrenaline going, which will stimulate you to move forward.

When you have a job, challenges are built into it. However, you need to create your own challenges in the ambiguous job hunt. Richard Crashaw, the English poet who lived over two hundred years ago, expressed the value of challenge when he wrote

Life that dares send
A challenge to his end,
And when it comes, say, Welcome Friend!

❖ ❖ ❖

There are three rules for running successful job-finding campaigns: initiate, initiate, initiate. This means start getting your act together right now instead of taking time off to catch up on work around the house or to take a vacation. You lose momentum that way.

The best time to initiate your job-finding campaign is while you're still in working mode. You can use the energy generated by your desire to get even in the service of your job search. The best revenge is to get a better job than the one you lost.

You can start the ball rolling with this two-step process: initiate your search at once, and then establish a routine. Then, when you arise each morning, you'll have the structure that was lost when your job expired.

Because part of that structure was an office environment, take advantage of office resources provided by an outplacement vendor if your severance package includes the support of an outplacement firm. If you're doing a solo job hunt, turn the corner of your dining room into an office.

Job opportunities seldom ring once, much less twice. Nobody ever enjoyed waiting for the phone to ring. And you won't have to when you initiate, initiate, initiate.

❖ ❖ ❖

Prospective employers don't send you engraved invitations to attend job interviews. So what are you waiting for?

Maybe the thought of starting your job hunt makes you feel frightened. If that's the case, think back to a time when you hesitated to jump into the water because you thought it would be tool cold. Then a friend said, "Jump in, the water's fine." And it was.

Now is as good a time as any to jump into your search. While you'll discover the process is easier than you think, nobody can teach you how to conduct a job search. Career counselors, self-help books, and job-finding seminars only point the way. You master a job hunt the same way you mastered bicycling, bowling, and driving. You learned by doing.

As you search, switch your thinking from "I must get a job," which creates too much anxiety, to thinking of your job hunt as a process that ends with one or more job offers.

So at interviews, make your goal just to get the next interview. Your search, like any other project, is a one-step-at-a-time deal. It's like eating a meal. You wouldn't think of shoving it all into your mouth at once. You finish lunch one bite at a time.

❖ ❖ ❖

A good way to drive yourself nuts is to think "I've gotta get that next job." Give yourself a break. Your search will be less of a hassle when you understand the theory of steps.

Conducting your job hunt is like taking a trip or starting any other business venture. It's a series of steps, and projects always begin with the first step. For that reason, your job while you're finding a job is to pay attention to just one step at a time, one day at a time.

The bottom step is to decide what you want to do. The next step can be determining which strategies or job-finding techniques to use, such as creating a résumé, developing a personal network, responding to ads in the papers and on the Internet, and starting a system for tracking résumés and letters you sent out.

Not everyone will start on the same step. That will be the case if you already know the direction in which you're headed and just need to update your résumé.

The theory of steps in a nutshell: Find the step you're on. Then activate it. And stay there until the step—or problem within the step—is solved.

Being aware of the phases contained in the steps that compose your self-marketing campaign will give it direction and momentum. With this knowledge, you'll intuitively know when each step has been completed and the next step you need to take.

❖ ❖ ❖

Your job-finding campaign, like taking a trip, begins with the first step. It's helpful to think of your search as a process of steps where you find the next step and activate it. The method is easy to use:

Should you find yourself stymied about how to go about finding a job or career, you have found the first step, which is determining what you want to do. You'll activate this step by exploring career options and defining goals.

After solving that problem, you're ready to stand on the second step, which is preparation of a résumé and other job-search tools. You'll activate the step by selecting job-finding tools you want to use, starting with a résumé. The third step is deciding where to present it.

Other steps typical in a job campaign include developing your network of personal contacts; attending meetings of business, industry, community, or religious organizations to gain visibility; expanding your network; and practicing interviewing skills.

You'll take the next steps that are right for you based on your ability to make decisions. You have already demonstrated the ability to make the right choices in the past. So you're simply applying to your search the proven capacity to make smart decisions.

Now you can step out in faith, knowing that you are taking the right steps to find the right job.

❖ ❖ ❖

Instead of stumbling into a career or job, why not at least try to have a plan? Planning means arranging the various parts of your venture from beginning to end.

When it comes to your job-finding venture, for example, break down your campaign into simple steps: determine your skills, assess what you want to do, and write a résumé that reflects your employment target.

Then you'll have a plan you can activate step by step. It'll be a doable plan because you'll get to concentrate on the small parts that make up the big picture.

The smart way to kick off your campaign is to put each step on a calendar. You'll be sure to complete each step by a certain date because the calendar will direct your campaign or project.

The next step is to take action. Attack your job campaign. Because you have reduced the task to achievable daily proportions, there will be no need to worry about anything except working the plan.

Be sure to build periods of time into your calendar for the purpose of evaluating your progress. You need to have a plan in order to give life to any project. After all, a happy birth is a planned birth.

❖ ❖ ❖

Well, look what they've done to you now. After years of loyal service, you got dumped. The only way to get even—and to feel better about yourself—is to find another job. That means you need to begin your job campaign this instant. The first step is to decide what you want to do, where you want to do it, and for how much money.

Target the job by identifying the kind of work you want. Then concentrate your energies only on that area of the job market. To establish where you want to do it, select the towns or cities where you choose to live and work. Find out how much you want by researching what the industry pays for the kind of job you're looking for.

It's not necessary to spend all of your time scrounging for openings. Instead, use your detective skills. There are people out there doing the kind of work you're aiming for. You'll find them by uncovering the organizations where they work. Try to meet some of those people. They might tell you more about their job function, the best locations to work, and starting pay, and they could even provide information about future openings.

Even if they don't provide all of the needed information, your detective work should uncover some clues about getting into the field.

❖ ❖ ❖

Your chances of getting a job quickly are increased when your job-finding campaign is efficient. The way to make it so is by not limiting your planning time.

The best time to work on your schedule is the first thing in the morning. After awakening, your mind is clear, and there are fewer disturbances from extraneous thoughts. Setting a daily agenda is no sweat when you follow four steps:

First, think about what you want to accomplish today. You'll have a number of items on your plate that might include responding to ads in the papers or on the Internet, initiating or returning phone calls, and writing thank-you letters and e-mails.

Second, determine your objective by selecting the main goal you hope to accomplish today. Highlight or circle it.

Third, with your objective in mind, select other items that need to be accomplished this day.

And fourth, decide the best way to work those tasks around today's scheduled appointments.

Outside meetings are the key. The only way you'll be offered a job is by attending meetings and interviews. Let's consider the difference between meetings and interviews. Meetings are face-to-face conversations with employment agencies, executive recruiters, and personal contacts on your network list. Interviews are meetings with prospective employers. And mini-interviews are conversations with recruiters at job fairs.

The more people you see, the sooner you'll land. You need to bounce in and out of your job-search office as a rubber ball bounces out of a barrel.

❖ ❖ ❖

An organized job hunt begins with buying a notebook. If you're technically inclined, a laptop, tablet, or smartphone will also do nicely. That's some advice from Stephanie Winston, a self-organization strategist.

"Notebooks and computers allow you to keep records and notes in one place," says Winston, who also suggests "you think of your system as a central operations resource." Transfer things to be done today or by a certain date to a calendar (or the calendar in your system).

Should you decide to use a notebook, "buy one in a distinctive color. Then you can just glance and say, "Okay, this is my career-search notebook." A notebook can also be a loose-leaf binder divided into sections.

Once your system is operative, sit down and brainstorm all of the places you can think of from which a job could come. Your list can include newspaper classifieds, job sites on the Internet and within your company, and your college alumni office. Should you belong to a club or an organization, tell people you're looking for a job. Finally, after brainstorming opportunities for your search, explore them one at a time.

A job hunt is organized like any project. "It's a question of marshaling your resources, then setting about dealing with them systematically." Stephanie Winston has written several books including *Best Organizing Tips.*

❖ ❖ ❖

The best way to keep control of your job search is to organize yourself. There are three aspects of the search you need to keep track of: appointments, contacts, and interviews.

For the first, you'll need an appointment book with a calendar. It makes it a lot easier to schedule interviews, phone calls, and follow-up activities.

It's easy to keep track of contacts with a three-by-five card file. On the top of each card, write the name of your friend or prospective employer along with his company, phone number, e-mail address, and fax numbers. Every time you contact that person, enter the date and a summary of your communication.

You can keep control of interviews and networking meetings on a larger piece of paper. A pad will do nicely. Immediately after each interview, make notes that cover five areas:

1. Who said what
2. What went well and what didn't
3. Your plan for following up (the most important area)
4. Any referrals you obtained
5. The date for your next interview

Why make notes after interviews? Because you you'll use this information in a follow-up letter and during your next interview with the same prospect or the person she refers you to.

❖ ❖ ❖

When you're trying to find a job, there's so much to do and so little time to do it. So what's the secret to getting more done in less time? Keep a list of things to do. And prioritize it.

Write down each task you want to accomplish today. Then go back and assign priorities to your to do list. Give urgent matters an *A*. Important matters that are not urgent are assigned a *B*. And items that can wait until tomorrow are marked with a *C*.

Most people work on the *A*s until they're completed. Then all of your urgent matters will be finished. Your list should focus on the stuff that's going to help you get a job.

But hey, you also have a life. And the way to keep it balanced is by not sacrificing what's important to you—family and friends, church or synagogue activities, and your exercise program. Those items should also get top priority because they support your career. And they'll continue to do so when you sequence the to-do list.

Job hunting is a job in itself. You'll accomplish each day's important tasks by keeping your organizing system as simple as *A*, *B*, *C*s.

❖ ❖ ❖

Some of you still spend more time fussing with your organizing system than it takes to complete the projects you enter in to it. You used to lug bulky organizers around, entering the same item on various pages to see how it looked from different views.

Although many companies that sell those cumbersome systems also offer compact electronic counterparts, before putting money into one, you would be wise to heed this ancient Latin proverb: *caveat emptor*—let the buyer beware.

The folks who sell organizers are part of a huge industry that makes billions of dollars suggesting you can control time. That's nonsense. Time is not a commodity you can hold, manage, bottle, or box. Time is fluid. You cannot lose it, because what goes around comes around. That's time. You get the same amount of it back again tomorrow. That's the reason there's a calendar—and why you get second chances.

You cannot manage time. Only yourself. For that, all you need is a calendar and a piece of paper. Enter appointment times on your calendar, and list a half dozen tasks you want to do today on paper or on the back of an envelope.

This method of managing yourself is simple. It lets you accomplish more and costs next to nothing. Think about that when you consider investing in an organizing system. Caveat emptor!

❖ ❖ ❖

The penalty you pay for not organizing your day is being disappointed. In the case of finding a job, your penalty is a longer job hunt.

Although you might be an enthusiastic person who is good at selling yourself, if you lack the ability to get organized, you will lack the opportunities to sell yourself at interviews. If you lose momentum or schedule poorly, it can take you all day just to do a couple of hours of work.

As for your job search, the problem is how to make more contacts. You'll solve this problem by determining what your job campaign is all about. Write down what you think you're supposed to do, and discover a way to organize your time and to work in order to get more meetings and interviews.

So organize yourself today. It isn't that you don't know how. You just haven't done it. But organize in a way that makes your life well rounded. A schedule must allow you to exercise, to have a social life, and to take courses you need to succeed.

❖ ❖ ❖

It's important to take control of the clutter in your work environment so the clutter doesn't take control of you. Clutter controls you because it reduces your effectiveness by slowing you down. You can take control of clutter by using one of four ways to get rid of the things scattered around your office:

1. Throw it away
2. Give it away
3. Sell it on eBay
4. Keep it in a place of its own

Before you begin, close your eyes and visualize what you want your office to look like when it becomes neat and orderly. You can believe it's possible to get order into your life when you make a commitment to have your workplace look exactly like you've just visualized it. Write down what you saw. And make a plan for getting organized.

Save newspaper, magazine articles, and computer printouts and file them in a folder marked "To Read." Folders can be placed in cardboard or metal files, or you can create an enclosure from a box or a grocery carton.

You already know what to do with those newspaper or magazine articles and other unnecessary items you can do without. Throw them out. And when you buy a book, give away a book. Then you'll always have room on your bookshelves.

You need to keep in mind that it could take half of a year to clear away all that mess. It took a long time to accumulate it. However long it takes, promise yourself to take control of the clutter so the clutter doesn't take control of you.

❖ ❖ ❖

When it feels you can't take it anymore because you have too much to do, use a technique I call "easily moving forward." When you're feeling anxious, the wrong approach is rushing into things. Hurried work causes more anxiety.

The correct approach is to easily move forward by making a list of all that stuff you have to do and numbering it in order of importance. But please have no more than five items on your list each day. That amount is doable, while longer lists will intimidate you.

When one of your items is a big project, break it down into small steps. That will make easily moving forward possible.

As a matter of fact, using the easily moving forward philosophy in all aspects of your life is a powerful defense against feeling depressed and anxious. Your morale gets a boost. That's because it allows you to achieve something each day, even if it's only a single thing or a single step done well.

It's a paradox, but you'll get more done this way. The expression "less is best" applies here as well. And so does "easy does it." But do it while easily moving forward.

❖ ❖ ❖

You have just learned your job has been cut and have picked up the phone to call a few people who popped into mind. But then you wonder what to do next. Before you do anything, remember this slogan: plan your work, and work your plan.

You need to resist the temptation to pick up the phone just yet. The very first task is to write down the names of those people you were going to all. Now congratulate yourself. You have started a job-hunting plan with your personal networking section.

The network list can be laid aside until you decide the kind of job you want. You'll uncover a target by asking yourself what parts of your previous positions you enjoyed doing the most.

You should determine the skills you used to make those favorite activities happen. Your target is a job where those skills can be used. They will become the objective for your résumé.

A résumé demonstrates how you can perform the goal or objective you've selected. When the résumé has been completed, you'll have something to show your contacts. Now is the time to call them.

As your job hunt unfolds, so will the rest of your plan. You'll think of more names for your network list, and maybe you'll decide to attend job fairs, respond to ads in newspapers and on Internet job sites, and research industries that interest you.

Today, you've started to plan your work. Tomorrow, begin to work your plan.

❖ ❖ ❖

Starting your job campaign is no different than launching a new business. You start by writing a business plan. You'll begin to write your job-finding plan as you answer five questions critical to your campaign.

First, what's your objective? Before you're able to tell a prospective employer what you can do for him, you must know exactly what it is you're offering. To put it another way, what do you want to do?

Second, will the job marketplace accept you as you are? Maybe not. Perhaps you need to develop some new skills by taking courses.

Third, what aspects of yourself will you present in order to show you're a good match for the job in question? Understanding the skills and achievements you need to show will give you poise and self-assurance.

Fourth, how do you plan to bring yourself to the attention of potential employers? Here, you decide how to approach the job market and choose from tactics like networking, answering classifieds and posting on Internet job sites, attending job fairs, and targeting companies you want to work for.

And fifth, how long can you survive without income after your severance and unemployment insurance run out? The answer to this question lets you set a deadline for getting back to work

A business plan for job hunters is like a blueprint for builders.

❖ ❖ ❖

When you want to get ahead, it's wise to fantasize. Your fantasy about what you want to do will become the plan for your business, career, or job hunt.

Because we're talking about fantasizing, do not start by writing your plan. Begin by dreaming. Your dream develops in your mind as a picture begins to develop when placed in a chemical solution. Only after you've given your fantasy time to develop are you ready to write about what you see as your dream.

That dream defined—and spelled out on paper as a plan—

becomes your goal. All you need now are the steps required to get there. You'll manage this by breaking down your goal into a series of steps that can be accomplished easily.

So daydream away until the picture of your goal emerges. It's necessary to have goals. When your mind has focused on an object, you'll begin to see that object everywhere.

It's like falling in love. Wherever you are, you cannot get that person out of your mind. The picture of what you would love to do puts pressure on you to think and to take action. After that happens, watch the momentum build.

❖ ❖ ❖

When big firms lay off most of your colleagues and competitors in the job market, it's the small companies that hire you back, according to the O-I Partners Work Reemployment study. The New Jersey–based outplacement company tracked the job campaigns of five hundred terminated executives.

The study showed that nearly half of those candidates had been laid off by large firms and that small companies with one thousand or fewer workers had hired three-quarters of them. A little more than a quarter of the candidates landed at companies with fifty or fewer people on staff.

The study also illustrates the wisdom of showing off your years of experience. The more experienced employees had less difficulty finding new jobs. More than half of the job hunters surveyed had had sixteen years of experience. Seasoned workers who have gotten the ax might keep that in mind and consider making big plans to find small companies to work for.

Any time the economy cools and the hiring doors slam shut due to layoffs and hiring freezes, focus your search on small and midsized companies that are still hiring. In that way, you can take advantage of the new supply of labor that would have commanded premiums in better times.

❖ ❖ ❖

A key ingredient in life is having goals. That's what Dr. Milton Erickson taught. Setting goals was the prominent psychiatrist's favorite prescription to help people enjoy life—and even to prolong it. "Always look to a real goal in the near future," Erickson said. "It's not necessary to have a reason for your goal. But it is critical you set goals that are immediate and easy to achieve."

Take Dr. Erickson's prescription as you start getting your act together. Your goal is to have an objective. It will be uncovered when you define the job you're looking for.

Perhaps you're not sure what it looks like. If that's the case, then talk to people who are doing the kind of work that interests you. When you have a clear picture of your objective, write down the steps necessary to achieve it.

Some goal setters break down the steps by drawing an inverted pyramid and working backward. Your goal, or job objective, should sit on top of the upside-down triangle. Work backward by beginning with the last step on the pyramid—the one right under your goal—and then list the steps before that down to the very first step at the pyramid's base. That's the step you can take today.

Be sure to assign a completion date for each step. As Dr. Erickson put it, "A goal without a date is just a dream."

❖ ❖ ❖

You can uncover your job objective in two easy steps. Target the kind of work that interests you, and then find people you can talk to who do that work.

When you find people willing to assist you, begin by asking two questions: "How do you like your job?" and "How would you describe a typical work day?" If their answers turn you on, ask if you can spend a day with them in the office or in the field.

This technique of tracking someone for a day in order to observe and later reflect that work is called "shadowing." "By looking over someone's shoulder," said legendary career consultant Saul Gruner, "you can learn in five minutes what it took that person years to master."

This author took Gruner's advice and looked over the shoulder of a seasoned and popular broadcast journalist who worked for a competing radio station. Reporter Mitch Lebe granted my request to shadow him in the field as he covered a New York City subway strike.

From observing Mitch at work and listening to his comments, I learned how to cover a story from recording and editing to writing and getting it on the air. Because Mitch generously shared his time and exquisite talents, I gained more income from adding reporting to my repertoire.

When you talk with or shadow people who do the work you're considering, you generate options. "If you want to know something yourself," said an ancient sage, " just look how others do it."

❖ ❖ ❖

When interviewers ask job hunters what kind of job they want, some job hunters reply, "I'll take anything." Taking that approach to your search is not only stupid but could also be the reason you still haven't found anything after a half year of searching.

How can you say you'll take anything when washing windows, mopping floors, or polishing brass is not what you had in mind? Until you have a job objective in mind, you'll confuse the job market and receive blank stares from prospective employers.

So go figure out what it is you want to do. Then and only then will your job-finding campaign begin to take off. With an objective before you, it'll be easier to explain the kind of assistance you need to your network of personal contacts. And based on that objective, you can target and respond to help-wanted postings on the Internet and classifieds in newspapers.

It's important to notice the key words in job descriptions. Your résumé and cover letters need to use those words to describe your experience in a way that matches the job requirements. You'll write short anecdotes describing what you did and the results.

But until you know exactly what it is you want to do, postpone marketing and selling yourself and instead focus on the assessment part of your campaign.

❖ ❖ ❖

In order to be selected for interviews, you must get the attention of prospective employers. Targeting your job campaign does that. "It's a well-established fact among those who help people find jobs that the more targeted you are, the more successful you are," says career consultant and therapist David Rottman, in an interview with this author.

There's an important reason you must conduct a search that's targeted, especially when there are fewer jobs around: companies are more selective. "So you must become that needle in the haystack employers are looking for by targeting your sales material to the employer's business needs," Rottman said.

Targeting begins with your objective. Yet most résumé objectives are too generic. For example, imagine you're seeking a position with a major bank.

"You can have a tremendous advantage over other job hunters," says the therapist, "when you write a targeted objective like this:

> Seeking position with a major banking institution where my five years of experience developing demographic profiles of small companies can be used to build customer relations, increase market share, and improve the corporation's position among lenders to small business."

The employer who looks at a targeted objective like this will not only understand where you want to go but will also be impressed because you grasp how the job fits into the overall scheme of the company and business.

❖ ❖ ❖

The most important factor in a job search is weather you have an idea of the business needs of the employer with whom you're seeking a position.

To uncover those needs is a piece of cake when you follow three simple steps:

1. Perform Internet and/or library research. "Just make sure you come up with articles that discuss trends of your particular business," advises David Rottman, the therapist and career counselor.

2. Write a trial objective that's based on your research. Then you can show it to some of your networking contacts and ask if it's a good fit for the company you're going to see.

3. Write two or more objectives, or targets, to match the different job categories you plan to pursue—sales, teaching, hands on technology, for example. That will allow you to have several résumés with different objectives for each category.

A targeted objective gives you a tremendous advantage over job hunters who write feeble, generic ones.

Discovering the needs of prospective employers enables you to target your résumé and cover letter. "And the work you do in order to target your résumé and cover letter gives you confidence." says the New York City–based therapist. "Targeting your job search is where it's at these days,"

❖ ❖ ❖

The more specific you are in your job search, the more successful your campaign will be. Being specific means you need to have a particular job objective, but not the lame kind of objective that appear on most résumés.

For example, imagine if your objective simply said "seeking a job in broadcasting."

Why is that a lame, impotent job objective? Because it omits what the candidate for a broadcasting job wants to do in the broadcasting industry.

A more specific job objective would tell prospective employers the three *W*s:

1. What you want to do
2. Why you can do it
3. Where you fit into the overall needs of the organization

With the three *W*s, the ineffective objective blossoms into this persuasive job target:

> Seeking position as news anchor/reporter with major market news/ talk radio station where my ten years experience as an award-winning broadcast journalist can help improve ratings and maintain the prestige of a news department.

You can determine a company's needs by finding out what's going on in the industries you're looking at. Friends and networking contacts can supply this information. When you're new to an industry, discover the areas and learn the buzzwords the industry uses. That kind of information can be found by reading trade magazines in a business library.

The information you get should be incorporated into your approach to the job market.

❖ ❖ ❖

With staffs cut to the bone, companies have become extraordinarily selective. Because managers are looking for just the right skills from an evergrowing pool of qualified candidates, you need to target your job campaign. It's the only way to stand out from other candidates in a competitive job market.

When it comes to targeting, think of your search as archery practice. Arrows represent the skills you offer for a specific job. The targets are the companies you're aiming at. Your goal is not just to hit the target, but also to score a bull's-eye—the job's requirements—each time.

When those flying arrows carry your skills that match the job requirements of the target, you'll always hit smack dab in the middle of the bull's-eye. Guaranteed.

Along with interviewing, feel free to target other areas of your search. You can network with friends and business associates by asking if they know people who work for companies or are in the industries you've targeted—and your responses to job listings will get immediate attention when you target your reply to match what a company is looking for.

As you may have gathered, mass mailing résumés and cover letters is not targeting. It's wasting time. People do not have time to read material they haven't solicited.

When you reach into your quiver for just the right skills, aim for the bull's-eye—the requirements of the job—and let the arrow fly. That's targeting.

The more targeted you are, the more job offers you'll get.

❖ ❖ ❖

When you're trying to select a job target or to decide what kind of business to start, it pays to look before you leap. But lots of you leap before you look. While that makes sense, too, you must choose the method that works best for you.

On one hand, people who look before they leap have a dream they want to create. To realize that dream, you must prepare. The looker does that by visualizing the outcome. If you are a looker, check to see if the results are matching your dream as the job-search progresses.

On the other hand, people who leap before they look also have a target but leap immediately to see what other options emerge. The leaper discovers possibilities and then moves on to a more desirable prospect. If you're a leaper, check back to make sure you haven't missed your target during the leap.

When it comes down to conventional wisdom about looking before you leap, listen to what the English poet Samuel Butler had to say several hundred years ago:

"And look before you ere you leap;
For as you sow, ye are like to reap."

❖ ❖ ❖

You'll become a champion in the job market when you apply some advice from the late boxing manager Cus D'Amato. He taught champion boxers like Floyd Patterson and Mike Tyson to apply his lessons to their lives as well as in the ring.

D'Amato taught "the will to win is more crucial than the skills to win." The will to win in your job hunt and career means selecting a target and not letting anything get in the way of reaching it. You can always pick up the skills to win either on the job, by attending classes, or through self-help books and videos.

Lessons learned in the boxing ring can be applied to the business arena. "He who trains harder, fights harder, is more focused, and wants the victory more can often overcome an opponent's superior skills," D'Amato said.

Consider for a moment how this advice from the boxing manager applies to your search. The job applicant who communicates the best at interviews usually beats out the candidate with superior skills.

You can train yourself to win as a prizefighter does. The punches you deliver are your achievements. Learn to talk about them. Then deliver your knockout blows by matching those saccomplishments to the job.

❖ ❖ ❖

It's a terrible feeling to agonize over lacking the skills necessary to apply for another job, especially when the job you held has become obsolete. You know you need to study. But how can you tell which skills you need to succeed?

"It's kind of a game," explains Kelly Foster, a training manager at JPMorgan Chase. One of the ways you can play it is to look at some classifieds and postings on the Internet to see what skills are required for people at your level. "Then take classes to help fill those needs even before you need them," says Foster.

Another way to play the game is to identify the direction your company is moving in and to learn new skills while you're still employed. Then you'll always be prepared for when you need to make a change. Consider yourself fortunate if the corporation you work for offers in-house training programs.

When you're looking for a new position, you'll find lots of vendors who offer classes every day on many subjects. Many are not that expensive. Community colleges are probably the least costly, and they offer classes over a period of several weeks. You might also find the right course in your community's continuing education or recreational programs.

The training manager contends that you need to look at training and education as an ongoing process. "It's not something you do when you're worried about losing your job within the next few weeks."

Lifelong learning is something you commit to for the rest of your career.

❖ ❖ ❖

To uncover and develop a skill you need for your next job, you can use a method called Self-Directed Development.

Begin the process by asking your business associates and friends to answer questions about what you perceive to be your strengths and weaknesses.

"The feedback can sharpen your focus and help you get an understanding of how you're really coming across with other people," says executive coach Randy Ruppart. "You can then determine where, in your judgment and theirs, you can use further development."

Opinions received from others should go into your self-development plan. Now you're ready to take a look at the self-improvement strategies available to you. They can include reading a book, buying CDs, or taking a course about what you need to improve.

There is a difference between self-help and self-directed development. It's getting feedback. "Constructive and positive feedback from others is very uplifting," says the executive coach. "Do you know what most people discover? They have far more strengths then they do development needs," says Ruppart. And this is a good outlook to have on the job or when searching for one."

Whether you have a job or are searching for one, information uncovered from Self-Directed Development will let you build on your strengths and increase your skills even further.

❖ ❖ ❖

Job hunters can pick up the skills they need to get up to speed by taking courses. But after acquiring a new skill and hitting the job market again, it's the same old story: interviewers say you still don't have experience using the new skill on a job.

"The situation is a tricky one but can be handled easily," says Kelly Anne Foster. "As you take the course," says Foster, "try to find a way to incorporate that new skill." Make an effort to use it on the job. Or you can offer that skill at no charge to a volunteer organization, to your place of worship, or to a friend.

List the newfound experience on your résumé. "You'll find a lot of employers are just looking for a little bit of experience that says you have the ability to do the job," says the training manager.

The best time to develop new skills is before your company dumps you. So evaluate the job skills you need right now and the skills you'll need down the line, and then take courses to pick up those talents.

While a lot of jobs aren't considered technical, most of them have technical aspects. So if you don't have basic computer skills, acquire them. "It's one of the easiest ways you can bring yourself up to speed."

❖ ❖ ❖

Many of you face the problem of not being able to find another position like the one you lost. So you steal time away from your job search to take courses. You were told that would help you get a job in another field.

But a former employee who worked with computers found out the hard way that getting a new career was not as easy as it had been trumped up to be. "He figured with all of his prior experience, having a Novell Administrator and engineer certificate under his belt would make him a shoo-in," said that job-hunter's career consultant Steve Cuthrell. "Novell people are highly wanted."

But after receiving his certification, Cuthrell's job-finding client ran into a big problem. Interviewers agreed the candidate performed well in passing his courses, but he had no experience as a Novell Administrator or Novell Engineer.

It not only took the job hunter a year to land, but he also had to relocate down South and settle for a lot less money than he had expected. And it was five years before the job candidate began to overcome the difference in the pay he received and the pay he had been accustomed to.

"You have to be careful when someone sells you a bill of goods," said Cuthrell. "When you're told taking a course is an open sesame to a whole new life, you gotta take it with a grain of salt."

❖ ❖ ❖

If you're a middle-aged job seeker and computer technology still leaves you scratching your head, you will not get ahead in the job market. You must offer technical skills for practically any job you go after, because every walk of life has entered the technical age.

Take the mechanic at your local garage. In order to keep his job, the old grease monkey needed to learn some technology—like how to diagnose a problem using a computer—before he could begin to work on your car.

The more technical skills you offer, the quicker you'll land. You need to learn, at the very least, how to operate both PCs and Macs. Some basic software programs you need to know include Microsoft Word for writing documents and Excel, a spreadsheet application. A working knowledge of graphics and desktop publishing is also a plus, even if it's not a job requirement.

Many corporations offer free courses to employees. You can also check out your outplacement facility and local unemployment office for free computer training.

If you fail to master the technical skills needed to get ahead in your field, you will be left far behind.

❖ ❖ ❖

If you become freaked out by the thought of learning computers during middle age, it's likely you have a case of cyberphobia. It's obvious that you need to treat this condition in order to advance in the position you hold or to get the kind of job you want and deserve.

Even with all of the experience you gained during twenty-five years of successful employment, you are not prepared for the modern workforce if you don't know technology. At interviews, you'll be asked about your computer skills. Wouldn't it be nice to answer something other than "duh"?

Unfortunately, you're in the same boat as many other people. According to a Pew Internet and American Life Project report, one-fifth of All Americans either don't own computers, don't know how to send emails, or are clueless about how to use the Internet.

Those Americans are older and less educated, according to The US Bureau of Labor Statistics. That is the demographic of those suffering from the fastest rises in unemployment. Older workers, for whom unemployment rates are at sixty-year highs, are hit the hardest by the demand for computer skills.

Be that as it may, the treatment for cyberphobia is easier than you think. You need to go back to school. Then you'll cease to be freaked out by computers, and you'll learn very basic technical skills.

In fact, learning your way around computers is a cinch once you get the hang of it. And you'll learn how to do it by taking courses

❖ ❖ ❖

Like anything you own, a job can be taken away from you. But nobody can take away your skills. You own them forever, and your talents can be transferred to other occupations. Sometimes you have no other choice.

Workers of all ages who get bounced often find either the job they did will never come back, or the demand for the profession they've trained for has dwindled.

While searching for another kind of job in the same or different industry, remember this: a career is not your last job title. It's a combination of your skills that can be repackaged and offered to other employers.

The process of learning how to present yourself in a new way can be easily broken down into three manageable steps:

1. Identify your bag of tricks—the skills you offer to prospective employers.
2. Separate those skills into three categories, people, data, and things.
3. Determine if your abilities and achievements relate to working with people, handling information, or working with objects like tools and machines.

It makes sense to repackage and transfer your skills from one business to another only when you present yourself on the basis of those skills—and not on your former job's duties.

Now you're able to look at your pink slip as a blessing in disguise and a challenge to discover what you really want to do.

❖ ❖ ❖

It's a big mistake to think your skills can be used only in your current job. What if you're planning to retire from one career—let's say military service—to enter another field?

You can transfer many of your current skills to a wide variety of other fields and positions. In order to do that, you need to evaluate which of your skills can be transferred. Well, don't just sit there—make a list.

Practically every job under the sun has transferrable skills. How to uncover and present yours? It's a piece of cake after you break down the process into five easy steps:

1. Decide on the new career or job you want to enter.
2. Read over the list of transferrable skills you've just made.
3. Select those skills you believe are the most important in the new role you want to play.
4. Go figure out how to show those transferrable skills on your résumé.
5. Before each interview, rehearse how you'll match your skills to the needs of each prospective employer.

So when you need to enter another field or industry, there's no need to throw away all of the valuable experience you've accumulated or to start from scratch.

The skills you've pickled up in various jobs, volunteer work, and hobbies are your transferrable skills. You can take them from one job or career to another.

❖ ❖ ❖

As a job hunter, you need to have choices. When you try to follow a single career path, it locks you into just one choice for a job. That limits your chances of being hired. You'll increase those chances by expanding your thinking about directions worth pursuing.

You can uncover options by taking a look at the skills you now offer. Your talents might be a big plus in industries other than the one you're now in or have just left.

Determine if those skills and interests are transferrable to another field you're interested in exploring by talking to people who have already made that career change. Ask what skills they offered that made their current employers willing to hire them.

Now check to see if you can offer those skills, or if you need to take courses in order to obtain them.

After you get your ducks in a row, generate multiple job choices to explore. That is where your choices come in. Then you won't have to put all your eggs in the one basket that might go out of fashion.

❖ ❖ ❖

Lots of job hunters want to try something different. After spending many years with the same company doing the same boring job, you want to try something unrelated.

Radical change may seem sexy. But hey—get real. Just because you'd like to do something new doesn't mean a company is going to train you.

In today's job market, employers want to hire candidates who are out of the box. That's "business speak" for already having the skills a job requires.

This is why your expertise—what you already know how to do—is your career currency. It's invested most wisely in the industry where you acquired it. Your skills can be transferred to other jobs within your industry at the salary you're used to making.

The quickest way to land is to stick to your knitting. Apply for jobs that look like the position you left or are pretty close to it. An interviewer doesn't want to hear you say, "With a little training, I could learn this job." Prospective employers want you to be ready right now.

❖ ❖ ❖

CHAPTER 4

Résumé Writing Tips

What You should Know About Writing Convincing Résumés, Cover Letters, Memos, and E-Mails

A RÉSUMÉ ADVANCES YOU TO the next level, the interview, and is intended to be a marketing tool that opens doors and gets employers interested in meeting you.

The résumé also opens doors to your network of personal contacts—business associates, friends, and family members—who might pass your document along to their contacts.

But you as a person, not a piece of paper, will be asked to talk about yourself while you're interviewing for a job. A résumé helps you do that. It becomes your basic selling tool and suggests the words you'll use to present yourself in writing and at interviews.

The process of writing a résumé helps you sell yourself to you. That's its most important function because writing it helps you assess your skills and achievements. That is an affirmation of your positive qualities.

Accordingly, a résumé is a reflection of you. It reflects your career's direction while presenting your past. It also reflects your strengths while informing an employer that what you have achieved in the past is an indication of what you can do in the future.

But keep in mind that your résumé has only half of a minute to make an impression. For that reason, the top half of your résumé is the hot zone—the part of the document that receives the most attention.

❖ ❖ ❖

You are having trouble starting a résumé because you want it to be perfect, and you are not interviewing yet because you don't think you're ready to knock 'em dead. That's called procrastination. You think you must do it all so perfectly that you're putting off doing your job campaign at all. It's your thinking that's got you stuck.

So let your thinking be guided by the advice of psychologists who say that trying to do things perfectly means you're scared you might bomb. As a consequence, you avoid change until success is guaranteed.

There are no guarantees in life. And nobody is perfect. So what are you waiting for? A happy landing doesn't depend on writing a perfect résumé. You can revise it later. And understand that interviews improve with practice. The only way to practice is to get out there and do it.

❖ ❖ ❖

So you think your résumé will get you a job. Wrong. You'll probably get a job eventually without a résumé or even with an inferior one. That's because you are hired on the basis of interviews, and prospective employers use résumés to decide which applicants to see and which to screen out.

It helps to think of your résumé and cover letter as marketing tools designed to convince employers that you are worth seeing—and make sure your résumé is about an employers needs, and not yours. Who cares about your hobbies, height, or weight? That information has no place on your résumé.

And don't copy parts of your résumé—like a summary or objective—from books about how to write them. You could end with a lame objective like, **"Seeking challenging opportunity where I can apply my skills with a company that offers me an opportunity for continuous growth."**

What's wrong with that objective? You are out of work, yet you have the nerve to tell a company what you need. The idea is to talk about a company's needs. A better objective would be something like, **" Seeking position as copywriter where I can use my background for creating broadcast**

and print advertising to help an advertising agency maintain and attract clients."

A first-class résumé communicates what you do and want to do. It's the headline at the top of your document—the objective and/or summary—that motivates people to continue reading.

❖ ❖ ❖

When it comes to writing a résumé, do it yourself instead of having it done by someone else or copying portions from a book.

A handful of candidates decide to take this shortcut because, after all, résumé writing is the grungiest part of a job campaign. Yet it's the most important part. The résumé becomes your major selling tool because the material and language you communicate to prospective employers, both in writing and during interviews, is adapted from your résumé.

So beware of shortcuts. English writer J.R.R. Tolkien had it right when he wrote, "Short cuts make long delays." A job-finding candidate I know learned this the hard way.

The first draft of Stewart's résumé was filled with clichés. He admitted to lifting much of it and his job description from a résumé-writing book. That shortcut delayed Stewart's campaign because he needed to start again from scratch.

When Stewart showed me the revision, he expressed amazement that during the writing process he had remembered managing the Y2K project for his department. That was a huge achievement, yet it hadn't appeared in the plagiarized version.

So writing a résumé is a do-it-yourself project that enables you to recall past achievements long forgotten. And the better you know yourself, the more convincing you will be.

That's why a résumé must come out of your own head—not someone else's.

❖ ❖ ❖

While a résumé opens doors to meetings and interviews, its most important function is that it sells yourself to you. The process of writing a résumé serves as a self-assessment tool that reminds you of all the good things you have accomplished on the job and during your career. What a boost to your self-confidence!

Let me tell you about the experiences of two job-finding clients I coached. Their episodes illustrate why making use of résumé writing as a self-assessment tool is vital to the success of your job campaign.

The first is Stewart, who I mentioned earlier in this chapter. His résumé failed to include one of his major achievements—managing a department's Y2K project—because he had someone else write the résumé for him. When Stewart wrote the next document himself, he recalled that and other successes that made his résumé considerably more marketable.

The second job hunter is Francis, who benefitted from a similar experience. He, too, had someone else write his document before deciding to do it himself and remembering important achievements that he had omitted the first time around. "As time goes by, what you do fades from memory," he said. "I completely forgot how I planned and tested disaster recovery procedures for my department."

Writing the résumé is a self-evaluation process that triggers your memory and boosts your self-esteem while reducing any trauma surrounding the loss of your job.

❖ ❖ ❖

You must write a résumé and cover letter to get a job. Résumés are a tradition in job-finding campaigns. But as with any other kind of ritual, there are false beliefs surrounding the customs of résumé writing.

Sometimes you get false information from your friends and relatives. An example of that is when you try to squeeze the résumé onto one page because someone told you that nobody would read a longer document.

A single page is okay only if you're applying for your first job out of college. If that's the case, there's not a heck of a lot more you can put on a srésumé. But when you've been working for a number of years, you don't want to come off as a recent graduate. Besides, you cannot possibly do justice to your years of experience on just one page.

You'll need a couple of pages to describe all the things you did and their results. However, there are exceptions, like when you're applying for an academic or international position. In those cases, a half dozen pages or more might be in order. For most job seekers, two-page résumés will do nicely.

❖ ❖ ❖

Your name is printed at the top of your résumé in such tiny letters that prospective employers need to squint in order to read it.

What are you ashamed of? As a product that needs to be marketed and sold, your name is your trademark, so you need to display it prominently. Then you'll stand out as a job candidate and empower future employers to remember you.

Because the information that tops your résumé is so important, print your name in capital letters in as big a typeface as you are comfortable with. State your full professional name. You should avoid abbreviations like B.J. Galloway unless your name really is B.J. And it's ill-advised to stick a Mr., Mrs., Ms., or Md. in front of your name, or a PhD after the moniker. It makes you look stuffy.

Your home address should follow your name in a smaller font, but avoid using post office box numbers. If you lack a corporate address, don't worry about it. The purpose of your address is to get the mail to you quickly, not to indicate where you are from.

Under the address, list the telephone numbers where you can be reached during the day and evening. Finally, position your e-mail address under the telephone numbers.

Because information you put at the top of your résumé is important, be sure to get the right stuff up there—especially your name in big, bold block letters.

❖ ❖ ❖

Psychological barriers can surround various aspects of a job-finding campaign. Trying to get a résumé started might be one of your stumbling blocks.

Perhaps you're concerned the résumé will not look impressive. Why? Maybe you think you don't have much to say because you haven't done a heck of a lot, or you lack necessary skills to put on a résumé. Both of those concerns are poppycock.

Everybody has accomplished tasks in their jobs and has used certain skills to achieve them. Although you are no exception, you might not have a clue about what they are. Getting some outside perspective to help you uncover your successes solves this résumé dilemma.

Books about résumés provide techniques for presenting your strengths. You can also get feedback from friends and colleagues or by working with a career counselor.

Another barrier might be a concern that putting something down in writing is like setting it in stone. No writing is set in concrete, and you need to you realize it can be changed, revised, and edited as your job search unfolds.

It's always a good idea to revise a résumé along the way. As you search for a job, you'll get a clearer idea of what you're looking for and what you need to present in order to get there.

❖ ❖ ❖

Although you bristle at the thought of writing a résumé, it's easier than you think. Even you can follow instructions about how to write a résumé in one of those books written for "dummies" or "idiots."

In the meantime, here's a successful way to format your résumé, no sweat:

Many résumés begin with an objective, which is a specific statement about the kind of job you want. A good example of an objective is, **"Seeking position as customer service representative."**

Those seven words tell a hiring manager what you have to offer.

A bad example is, **"Looking for position that will provide me with opportunities for growth."** That's brazen! Here you are, out of work, and yet you're telling a company what you want it to do for you.

Remember that an objective tells an employer what you offer and helps you create a résumé that matches your job target. The rest of the document proves you can perform the job you seek.

When you've finished writing the first draft, add a summary under the objective. It tells, in a few lines or paragraphs, how you can perform the job you want. A summary features your résumé's highlights. For example, **"Over ten years successful experience as a customer service representative. Background includes problem solving, research, and writing reports."**

Most prospective employers won't read your entire document, so you want to catch your reader's attention at the start—with an objective and a summary.

If you do, prospective employers will be interested in reading the rest, which will be about your work experience.

❖ ❖ ❖

When you write an objective at the top of your résumé, think of it as a newspaper headline. A headline summarizes the story that follows and persuades you to read it.

An objective highlights what you want to achieve. You can write your employment objective as a one-liner and use it to describe the job you want or the type of work you do.

A number of job candidates have asked me why they should bother writing an objective. Unless you have a target, don't even think about writing the rest of the résumé. The entire document is based on the objective you wish to achieve, and you need to back it up by proving in the document's body that you have the experience to do the work. Besides, if you don't know what kind of work you want, how will readers catch the drift?

After your résumé has been completed, write a summary. It's a short paragraph that follows the objective, highlighting the main points in your résumé.

Prospective employers only read your sales document for about twenty seconds before deciding if they're interested in you. So your objective and summary informs them whether to bother rereading the rest.

You'll find examples of an objective and a summary in the previous coaching vignette.

❖ ❖ ❖

It's a lame idea to write a résumé that includes everything but the kitchen sink. Too much information tells the interviewer you are older than Methuselah, that biblical character who lived to be over nine hundred years old.

The idea is to write a résumé that won't reflect your age. When you give the year you graduated from college, it's like shouting, "Hey, I'm sixty years old!" The decision to hire you is based on many factors. Age is only one of them. While you need to include the years you worked for each employer, you can drop the years you attended college.

It's crucial to write a résumé that's oriented around your performance because you need to sell employers on your capabilities. So instead of presenting your entire background, just include the parts that are important to the job you're applying for.

Employers are mostly interested in what you did on your last job. That's because skills fade after about a dozen years of not using them. A reverse chronological résumé highlights your most recent experiences. It begins with your last or current position and works backward.

So if the first ten years of experience date you, cut them out.

❖ ❖ ❖

It's not so much how you write, but how you spell. When you misspell words in your résumé or in cover letters, readers get the impression you are sloppy.

Your résumé is tossed on the screened-out pile and you're not invited for an interview.

You need to be sure the spelling is right before you e-mail, snail mail, or fax written work. This is what proofreading is all about. But you don't catch spelling errors simply by reading through your written work. Your brain tends to focus on the information and ideas communicated in your writing while your eye moves quickly past résumé headings to the paragraph that follows.

Professional editors often check for spelling and typographical errors by reading written work backward. They look at each word from the last one in the document to the first word in its beginning. Words not spelled correctly stick out like sore thumbs.

When you want to check writing for content and flow, read your copy aloud. Because if it sounds right, it probably is.

But why sweat the spelling when your spellchecker is just a mouse click away? Chances are it won't catch homonyms—two or more words that are spelled alike but have different meanings. Examples are "wood" and "would," "they're" and "their," and "your" and "you're."

Marvels of technology aside, just remember the easiest way to catch misspelled words before your reader does is to read your piece backward.

❖ ❖ ❖

You hate to express yourself in writing for the wrong reasons. While you worry about grammar and are afraid of what your readers will think, you need to concern yourself only with typographical errors and spelling.

A staffing service conducted a survey that showed that over 75 percent of executives polled said they would not hire job candidates who had a typo in their résumé or cover letter. Even when you have a strong background, one little typo or misspelled word can kill a deal. Remember that those little buggers not spelled correctly give the impression that you are a careless person.

And you must not rely on your computer's spell checking program to proofread for you. As explained in the previous coaching vignette, programs do not catch words that are omitted or used incorrectly. Computers lack the ability to flag nuances between certain words such as "be" and "bee," for example.

When it comes to writing, just sweat the small stuff. Look out for typos. And get the spelling right.

❖ ❖ ❖

A letter written carelessly represents a job candidate who is careless. Misspelled words convey the impression that you couldn't care less about the outcome. Before you send a résumé, cover letter, or e-mail, check your spelling.

You also want to make sure you don't write business letters the old-fashioned way by using lots of hackneyed business phrases. You wouldn't enter a businessperson's office and say, "Yours of the ninth received and contents noted." Nor would you end a meeting with, "Hoping to see you again. I remain yours truly." Then why do it in writing?

Those stale business phrases are relics of the days when business writing tried to be clumsily legal. So get with it. When you write, use a friendly approach. Today's business is built upon courtesy and customer service. Stereotyped expressions make you come across as an unfriendly person and takes all the spirit out of what you have to say.

You'll write effective business correspondence when you write it as you would say it.

❖ ❖ ❖

When you make writing your résumé, e-mails, and letters part and parcel of interviewing, it's like the effect caused by snapping a whip—a sharp, explosive sound. You'll get more "bang for your buck" by using the complete communications package: researching, writing, and speaking. It's the most effective way to convince prospective employers and customers to do what you ask—to grant meetings and interviews.

John Adams, the second president of the United States, put this another way when he wrote, "Let us dare to read, think, speak, and write....

...Let every sluice of knowledge be opened and set a-flowing."

Opening your memory while writing your résumé sets your knowledge "a-flowing" in a way that not only reminds you about past accomplishments but also enables you to explain your job function to prospective employers. You'd be surprised to know how many of my job-coaching clients could not do this. Because those job hunters knew what they did, they took it for granted that everyone else would also know. Not so.

When asked to describe their duties and responsibilities, those job candidates would respond with puzzled looks or blank stares accompanied by head scratching. As one exasperated job hunter put it, "Well...I know what I did. I did it for twenty years but never had to explain it."

Prospective employers won't know what you did until you show them in a résumé and tell them at interviews.

❖ ❖ ❖

The best way to land interviews and to get offers is to write letters and e-mails. Cover letters or e-mails need to accompany your résumés even if they weren't requested, and follow-up letters need to be written after interviews. It's job-search etiquette.

But your letters need not be boilerplate. For example, you don't need to write, "I'm responding to your ad in the *Times*." Instead, the first sentence in your business or cover letter should grab your reader's attention. You could write, "Our mutual friend, Eleanore Vent, said you might be looking for customer service reps and suggested I contact you."

After catching a reader's attention in the opening, zero in on your qualifications that match the job description. However, you won't hook your audience into reading the rest of your document by summarizing your résumé.

That defeats the purpose of a cover or sales letter, which is to focus on what you bring to the table.

You'll accomplish that purpose by writing about the contributions you made to previous companies. That information will appear in your résumé where you can paraphrase pertinent material.

The middle part of your communication should also state what information you're enclosing or attaching, whether it's a résumé, samples of your work, or endorsements from customers.

You should end your letter by indicating the next steps. Should you plan to follow up with a phone call, state when you expect to do it. When you want your reader to contact you, say "I'm looking forward to hearing from you," and give your contact information—home address, phone and fax numbers, and e-mail.

You'll write convincing letters when you give them a snappy beginning, middle, and end.

❖ ❖ ❖

The best tools for getting your ideas across are letters, e-mails, and memos. Written material holds a reader's attention and dishes out your concept. If you just call up someone with a new idea, you might not get a chance to tell her all the details. Because your call could come as a surprise, there's a good chance your listener won't be receptive.

However, when you put it in writing, it's not enough just to know your objective—the reason why you're writing. You must also understand your audience. A message can accomplish your objective but fail to consider the feelings of the person receiving it.

Imagine how you would feel after seeing a memo from your boss that read, "The Acme Software Company is downsizing, and you're out of here." You want to light a fire under your readers, not torch them!

You won't trample on the emotions of your audience when you write in the most positive light. Use positive words, and tell them what your offer will do for a company, not what you want a company to do for you.

With this in mind, jot down your thoughts, researching material, and facts. Your notes can be organized into some kind of a format. A beginning, middle, and end will do the trick.

Now you're ready to write in the most positive light and to be clear with regard to both your purpose and who your reader is.

❖ ❖ ❖

Because a cover letter becomes your personality on paper, avoid hackneyed phrases and write as you speak. So instead of writing "I would suggest…" and "please find enclosed…," say "I suggest that…" and "I enclose…"

Likewise, it's wrong to conclude your letter or e-mail with participial phrases such as "hoping to meet you again," or "I remain yours truly," says Professor David Lambuth in *The Golden Book on Writing*.

"The last sentence in a letter is the place for a clear-cut, effective statement," says the professor. "Not a dying-out phrase."

And you need to avoid cluttering the opening words of your first sentence with routine details like, "I received yours of the seventeenth." Instead, begin with a personal message that grabs the reader's attention. Then bring in the rest of your facts.

Writing is like interviewing in that it's the first personal impression you make. Remember that it's the first impression that counts.

So strike out all the old-fogeyish mechanical phrases that have lost their punch, and write as you would talk with someone face-to-face.

❖ ❖ ❖

You waste time by sending cover letters that say, "Dear Sir or Madam, I'm enclosing my résumé for your review." Who cares? Nobody asked for it. Because executives don't have time to read unsolicited résumés, they toss them out.

But there is a way to write a cover letter to a company where you hope to get your foot in the door. Cover letters result in interviews when they reflect knowledge of the company and state the reason for your interest. You can produce that kind of cover letter when you take time to research a company.

This research will both uncover information about companies and provide names for you to contact. Then and only then will you be empowered to write a personal letter with the salutation of "Dear Eleanore" or "Dear Fred."

An opening paragraph that grabs your readers' attention is next:

"Because you have introduced several new products this quarter, I'm interested in discussing your future needs and how I might help. I specialize in designing customer-friendly websites and have developed a new way to assess website performance."

That paragraph will motivate a prospect to read the résumé you've attached. But only doing your homework can empower you to write an opening designed to grab a reader's attention.

❖ ❖ ❖

Most job hunters think a cover letter covers all prospective employers. They are mistaken. When the same letter is sent to everyone, it's called a "boilerplate."

When you think about it, there are no cover interviews or cover phone calls. Employers are just like you. They are unique people with separate requirements. So they hire on the basis of their individual needs.

Presenting your materials the same way to everyone is a boo-boo. A sales pitch that impresses one prospect may not work with the next, even if they're both in the same business.

So custom-tailor all of the elements of your job search—writing, phoning, and interviewing—by anticipating the needs of each prospective employer and then telling them what they want to hear.

You'll learn about individual needs by looking at the job specifications and matching your qualifications to those requirements. That's what custom-tailoring means: building according to individual needs.

When you think of a cover letter as a custom-tailored letter, you'll make each reader feel you are a perfect fit for her needs, and it will enhance your chances of getting interviews.

❖ ❖ ❖

You always give three interviews: the interview you rehearsed, the interview you gave, and the interview you wish you had given.

The interview you wished for can be delivered in your follow-up letter. Remember that interview protocol requires you to create a thank-you letter or e-mail after each meeting.

Letters are an important part of the interview process because interviewers are just like you. When we converse, our minds wander every now and then. It's impossible to pay attention 100 percent of the time. But whenever a prospective employer reads your letter, you have his full attention.

You should begin your follow-up letter or e-mail by thanking your interviewer for her time and interest. Then express your appreciation for the opportunity to meet him.

The body of your letter should repeat some of the interview's positive points—especially how your skills match the job specifications. If you forgot to mention one of your strengths or an accomplishment as it relates to the position, now is the time to do it in writing. You can also clear up misunderstandings or negatives that came up during your meeting.

End your follow-up letter by telling the reader you want the job and explaining why. Correspondence should be sent within several days after each interview.

Nobody gives a perfect interview. But writing a follow-up letter gives you a chance to improve the one you gave.

❖ ❖ ❖

After each interview, sit right down and write your prospect a thank-you letter. You can also think of it as an interview follow-up letter. Either way, keep in mind that it's job-search etiquette to follow up in writing—and to do so within several days after each interview.

Your letter should be based on the notes you take right after the interview. Key phrases and buzzwords used by your interviewer can also be jotted down.

The best way to draft a letter is to link your material to the subjects you and the interviewer discussed. Parts of the interview that were a hit should be included along with new ideas that popped into your mind since the meeting.

You can also support parts of the presentation you considered weak. The interview you wish you had given will then be presented in writing.

A thank-you letter gives you another chance to show excitement for the position and to say you want the job. Studies show that many job hunters are rejected because they don't seem interested.

By the way, when you interview at the company where you work, it's okay to e-mail your letter. But when you interview at another company, a hard copy letter is the most appropriate because it will stand out from the rest of the applicants' letters.

❖ ❖ ❖

When you pay attention to your sentences, your cover letters, follow-up letters, and sales letters will attract more attention. You can think of a sentence as a unit for one idea. It's a good idea to limit each sentence to about thirty-five words.

After you've finished writing a first draft of your letter, count the words in each sentence. When units are more than thirty-five words, make them shorter by cutting out words you don't need. You can also break a long sentence into two.

It's also effective to vary the length of each sentence. A short sentence can be followed by a long one, and then a short sentence can be followed by a medium-sized one. Varying the length of sentences is like the effect of cracking a whip. It gives your letter more bounce to the ounce.

The most important part of a sentence goes last. Instead of writing, "I saved a million dollars by implementing a new system for the Blue Sky Company," write, "At the Blue Sky Company, I implemented a new system that saved the company a million dollars." You want the reader to remember the important part of that sentence, which is how much money you saved and how you did it—not the name of the company.

You can make your letters look even more exquisite by writing good paragraphs, which is the topic of the next coaching vignette.

❖ ❖ ❖

Your letters are more likely to be read and remembered when you make them look attractive. You can make them attractive with good graphics, or by displaying your writing in an interesting way.

Writing that is good-looking invites your reader's eye onto the page. Another technique guaranteed to make your letters look cool is varying the lengths of your paragraphs.

Whereas a sentence is a unit for an idea, a paragraph is a unit for a group of ideas that compose a thought. Paragraphs start with the most important point you want to make, and that point should be followed with less compelling information in a logical order.

Your longest paragraph should be seven or eight lines—no more. After all, if letters consisted of only seven line graphs, all your readers would see would be black walls of type, and they would be discouraged from reading your work. How short can a graph be? From one to several lines.

As I stated earlier, in order to score interviews and land the position you want and deserve, job-search writing needs to be read and remembered. That's why your letters and e-mails require good looks along with good writing.

❖ ❖ ❖

Your chances of being accepted as a salesperson or a job candidate increase when you use positive words. You'll accentuate the positive when you avoid using the words "no" and "not."

William Strunk and EB White, the authors of *The Elements of Style*, understood the value of putting statements in positive form. "Consciously or unconsciously the reader feels dissatisfied with being told only what is not; he wishes to be told what is."

So instead of writing, "I hope you will not find my résumé lacking in experience," rewrite the statement to read, "I trust you'll find my résumé contains the background you're looking for."

"As a rule, it's better to express even a negative in positive form," say the authors who advise that instead of writing "not honest," try "dishonest." "Not important" should be "trifling," "did not remember" should be "forgot," and "did not pay any attention to" should "ignored."

While you practice using positive words in business and job-hunting correspondence, you'll also begin to speak more positively.

❖ ❖ ❖

Fax it, schmax it. Your fax machine might be the quickest service for same-day delivery of your job-search materials, but faxing is not foolproof. And you're foolish if you don't back up what you fax the old-fashioned way—by mailing it.

The person who asks you to fax a copy of your résumé and cover letter is minutes away from receiving it only if his fax machine is not being used. If it is, you'll get busy signals. When your fax goes through, there's no guarantee it will arrive intact or be delivered to its intended receiver.

It's also important to drop hard copies in the mail when you do not get a confirmation your fax was transmitted or when you get documentation of a poor line connection. While you can try faxing again the next day, mail your hard copies right away.

Not only do you make an extra sales impression, but mailing your documents also adds a touch of class. Your word-processed copies look much neater than messy faxed pages.

❖ ❖ ❖

It's easy to keep track of letters you're required to write for your job campaign when you organize your writing and keep it simple. The celebrated author Thomas Mann wrote in *Buddenbrooks*, "Order and simplification are the first steps toward the mastery of a subject."

You can achieve order by putting your finished correspondence in a file or a three-ring binder and keeping it on top of your desk. You can also add letters you receive.

When you need to look up something you've written to a prospective employer or to a personal contact, open your binder, which will also be a chronological file. You can easily find the letter you're looking for when your folder's organized by date.

Simplification is thus accomplished by keeping a file of your job-search writing. This is a simple way to create more letters. Just rephrase what you've written to someone else in a similar situation. There's no need to reinvent the wheel each time.

Remember that business letters are not written in one sitting. The key to effective writing is revising—and the letters you write build upon each other and get better and better.

The chronological file of letters you've written for your job search or business is now your own personal reference guide.

❖ ❖ ❖

You really can judge a book by its cover. Books are marketed with nice book jackets to present the work and sell it, so consider presenting your next letter to a perspective employer in a special cover.

You have a handful of choices. Priority mail is one. The post office can give you attractive red, white, and blue envelopes and address labels. They're free. And your prospect will get the letter a little faster than if you had sent it first class, which is another inexpensive option.

Both options are less pricey than the postal service's express mail or FedEx. But they're both faster because they use next-day service, and they also give your letter a distinctive cover.

And if your job target is nearby, put your letter in a flat envelope and deliver it yourself. On the lower left-hand corner of the envelope, write "delivered by hand." You can hand it to the receptionist or ask the receptionist to give it to target's secretary or administrative assistant.

Regardless of how you do it, packaging your letters will make you stand out from the competition. Who knows? A letter in a special cover might even nudge your name to the top of the list.

❖ ❖ ❖

Before you send someone a letter or a résumé by mail or e-mail, you had better ask, "May I?" Many of your prospective employers and networking contacts are on information overload. They might not welcome correspondence from you.

When permission is granted, check the recipient's e-mail address. Then make sure your correspondence is professionally written. Because most of you have a tendency to get sloppy with e-mail, its important to treat the medium like any other kind of written correspondence and make your notes polished, short, and to the point, with correct spelling.

Misspelled words give prospective employers the impression that you are sloppy. In that case, the target won't take time to consider you for employment—or waste time accepting your follow-up call.

E-mail is a fantastic job-hunting tool when it's used correctly. That's because e-mail is private. And your correspondence does not get screened out as do letters and résumés when they're sent by regular mail.

❖ ❖ ❖

People don't have time to read your long memo. So keep it short. Your clear ideas can be laid down in single-page memorandums or letters with your objective stated quickly and simply.

The objective is the reason why you're writing in the first place, and the rest of the communication should support your objective.

The place to make your point is in the first couple of sentences. American theatrical producer David Belasco said, "If you can't write your idea on the back of my calling card, you don't have a clear idea." Consequently, if you cannot state your objective clearly on the back of your calling card, spend more time thinking it through.

When you write a final draft, use the words "I" and "you." They will let you write in the active voice, which is always the key in memo writing because it's stronger and more direct.

You also need to send your memo to the right party—to the person who is in a position to take action on your idea.

The principles of powerful memo writing chronicled in this coaching vignette are the same for writing either hard copy or e-mails.

❖ ❖ ❖

If you can say it, you can write it. The next time you need to write something, say it to your paper or keyboard. The first step is simply to speak your thoughts on paper in the form of notes.

It's also a good idea to carry a small pad. When an idea comes, write it down, or you'll lose it. It's those first thoughts that are the most important in writing. That's why you want to capture your original thoughts on paper. You'll organize, outline, edit, and polish them later.

You will obtain the best results when you write down those ideas as you would speak them. Be loosey-goosey, and have fun.

When it comes time to editing, get rid of big words when simple ones will do. As you select just the right words, use action nouns and verbs.

Remember that the most important part of your sentence comes last and that the beginning and end of each paragraph are the most consequential.

Your first sentence tells the reader what the graph is about. The ending can either summarize it or segue into the next graph.

The good news is that you need not worry about grammar, punctuation, or style. You'll make the writing clear during the editing process.

You can apply these suggestions to any piece of writing whether it is for job finding, business, or personal correspondence.

One last word of advice: don't try to impress. When you write it as you would speak it, your writing will come across as friendly and sincere instead of stiff and pompous.

❖ ❖ ❖

"There's nothing to writing at all," said Sportswriter Red Smith. "All you have to do is sit down at the computer and open up a vein."

Nobody said writing is easy. But you'll bleed less when you write letters, e-mails, and memos for your job or job hunt by applying this precept: if you can talk it, you can write it.

The next time you're required to write business correspondence, just chill out and talk on paper or to your computer. If you feel silly talking to a piece of paper, talk to a recorder instead. Either way, use everyday speech when you write.

You should talk to your paper or keyboard as you would talk to a friend. That's how to avoid sounding phony. When you try to adopt a business or literary style, you're inventing a new language, and you'll turn off your readers. After all, you wouldn't speak that way.

Sometimes your first draft turns out to be okay as it is. But most times, you'll need to edit. When you write and edit, remember to use your standard speaking style.

❖ ❖ ❖

As you write a résumé, keep this motto in mind: when in doubt, leave it out.

Your résumé is a promotion piece—an advertisement of you. It's like a magazine ad that highlights a product and says, "For more details, call this number."

When the highlights of your résumé grab a reader's attention, you will be called and invited to interview. That's the time to provide more details about your background.

Even when a résumé is printed on two pages, space is limited. You can omit an education section unless you have graduated from college. In that case, leave out the year you graduated unless you want them to guess your age. It's not necessary to include the name of the high school you attended. Nobody cares.

When you're over fifty, it's acceptable to disregard your earliest jobs. The dates you started and ended those positions will date you. Besides, the last ten years of your experience are the most relevant.

Another item to leave off is the phrase "references available upon request." References are your important contacts. You don't want them bothered until you and a prospective employer have mutually agreed you are the one.

And leave out anything you don't want to be questioned about or have to defend. Your résumé is also an interviewing tool for a recruiter or hiring manager.

❖ ❖ ❖

When you're entering a new field, consider writing a consultant résumé. It's written around a list of your skills and services rather than specific work experience.

A consultant résumé differs from the chronological format. Consultants and workers entering new fields emphasize special skills and describe client assignments rather than listing names of former employers in reverse order as the chronological format does.

When it comes to consulting, people often ask, "What do new consultants with no client experience put on their résumés?" The answer is to put forward your prior employment until your client list grows. Then you can keep updating the résumé by adding names of new clients while eliminating previous nonconsulting employment.

Creating a format for your consultant résumé can be as easy as one, two, three:

1. Start by listing areas of special service performed as an employee. Examples are **writing, project management,** and **financial planning.** That tells prospective clients what you can do to help them.
2. List your clients and name several former employers.
3. Finish by listing your education credentials.

Your consultant résumé needs to be easy to read and kept short. As already mentioned, you'll keep it short by deleting less important assignments as you add the more significant ones.

❖ ❖ ❖

CHAPTER 5

Going to a Job Fair

TECHNIQUES FOR HANDLING MINI-INTERVIEWS

JOB FAIRS PLAY A KEY role in a company's effort to recruit. Recruiters come to the fair to meet you and other job hunters who get the opportunity to meet face-to-face with dozens of them.

"Job fairs are indeed mini-interviews," says Mim Anzolut, the former director of the job development program at JPMorgan Chase. "Unlike the interview model, you only have a few minutes to sell yourself."

Companies are impressed with candidates who look and sound professional and who know something about the company. So dress in business attire, rehearse how you'll introduce yourself, and remember to send a follow-up note to thank recruiters you saw for meetings. It's another opportunity to sell yourself.

It makes sense to attend job fairs even when you have a good job. Longevity isn't what it used to be. You can never tell when your company will start swinging the ax. A New York City executive in the finance industry found this to be true the hard way.

John turned down a job offer because he liked the one he had. His company dumped him a week later. "That's true but sad," comments the job development director. "Where does loyalty go? Out the window."

❖ ❖ ❖

When you go to a job fair or to a networking affair, your objective is to make contacts. You are given three-minute opportunities to get names and phone numbers in order to extend your network. That's a good reason to show up early and to stay until the end. The longer you stay, the more contacts you'll make, and the more contacts you make, the more meetings you'll get that can lead to interviews.

But don't leave home without preplanning the event. When you learn whose going to be there, you can determine your purpose for attending. And be sure to bring the right amount of business cards for networking meetings and résumés for job fairs. If you attend with a friend, split up. You waste time talking with anybody but new contacts.

Have your introduction down pat. That means you should be able to give your name, tell what you do, and mention a benefit you offer in ten seconds or less. When the person with whom you've just met is not a good prospect, move on to the next. But be polite while making your exit.

Above all, you need to make an effort to be happy, outgoing, enthusiastic, and positive. People want to do business with a winner. Not a whiner.

❖ ❖ ❖

You stutter and stammer at job fairs while rummaging around your mind for something to say because you don't know what your message is going to be. That message should be contained in your opening line and should give a brief summary of who you are and what you do.

So before going to a fair, prepare your opening. You want to have a good meeting with each representative without appearing to be rushed—which is a tough job when you are limited by time.

The wrong way to introduce yourself is by shoving a résumé in the company representative's face and delivering a long speech about who you are. The correct approach is to offer a firm handshake while giving a ten-second introduction. Proffer your résumé after the introductions are over.

Your opening line ought to focus more on what you do than who you are, because what you do is what you're selling. Practice delivering your introduction until it sounds spontaneous. Remember to smile, to speak slowly, and to make eye contact.

Rehearsal is the only way to overcome any stuttering and stammering. The more you drill on the introduction, the more natural you'll appear.

❖ ❖ ❖

The way to be remembered is to give an unforgettable introduction. Let's face it. Your competitors perform the same function as you do. So recruiters, interviewers, or buyers of your product cannot keep in mind all of the people they meet. But you need them to remember you.

When you meet a prospective employer or customer, giving your name and the business you're in is a good start. You'll make your ten-second introduction unforgettable when you add a benefit of what you do. For example, you could say **"Hi, I'm Randy Place, a career coach who helps people find jobs." Or "I'm Joel Taylor, a broadcast time salesperson who helps stations increase sales and profits."**

These are more lively introductions than just saying, "I'm a career counselor," because people will recall your name when you include a benefit with your introduction.

The strongest impression is the one made in the shortest amount time. You can make your introductions simple and direct in less than ten seconds by telling who you are and what you do and stating a benefit of your work, service, or product.

❖ ❖ ❖

Sometimes you're required to wear a name tag at job fairs or networking meetings. Name tags should be worn correctly on the level of your collar. Why? Because it looks odd to see everyone bending over, reading each other's chests.

Name tags should also be stuck on your right-hand side. Then you'll be able to sneak a quick look at somebody's name as you shake hands, make eye contact, while pretending to have remembered the person's name.

An effective way to remember a name is to repeat it at least a couple of times during a conversation. This is also the best way to make friends. In his best-selling classic, *How To Win Friends and Influence People*, Dale Carnegie advised readers to "remember that a man's name is to him the sweetest and most important sound in any language."

You need to offer a firm grip when you meet someone. Nobody wants to shake hands with a dead fish! And smokers shouldn't light up before working a room. Nobody wants to speak with somebody who smells like a cigarette. Also, it's a bad idea to eat just before meeting people. You want to be free to talk without spitting food.

❖ ❖ ❖

CHAPTER 6

How to Use the Telephone to Get Meetings and Interviews

TELEPHONE TECHNIQUES FOR JOB CANDIDATES

TELEPHONES.

Sometimes it's hard to live with them. But job hunters cannot live without them—no matter how much you hate to use the phone. The telephone is your primary tool for getting networking meetings and interviews. You'll be unable to get them without picking up the phone. And without interviews, you can forget about getting job offers.

You'll make picking up the phone less frustrating when you apply four telephoning techniques:

1. Recognize your phone as a tool for obtaining meetings and interviews.
2. Decide to prepare for each telephone call as carefully as you would for a meeting or interview.
3. Accomplish telephone prep by having a purpose for each call. When you know why you're calling, you can decide what you want the result of your telephone communication to be, whether that's setting up a network meeting, sending a follow-up a letter, or scoring an interview.
4. Know what you are going to say and how you'll sound delivering the message. You'll sound more polished after you jot down the ideas you want to communicate. Or, write a telephone script and rehearse it several times before placing your call.

Remember that the telephone is your tool for getting face-to-face meetings and interviews. The more meetings you get, the sooner you'll land. It's easier to get those meetings when your telephone communications are on track.

❖ ❖ ❖

If you despise the way you sound on a tape recording, how do you think you come across on a prospective employer's voice mail? A good way to find out is to leave a message on your own answering device. Then you'll hear how you sound to others.

You can improve the delivery of your voice messages by practicing this three-step telephone technique:

First, write a script or make an outline about what you intend to say. Then pick up the phone and call it into your answering gizmo.

Second, you need to keep rehearsing until you get it right. A job hunter in New York City who used this technique said he tried leaving a message to himself a dozen times before it sounded okay to him.

And third, when you start to sound right, practice communicating your script in half of a minute or less.

Now your voice messages will sound professional, and prospective employers will be motivated to return your calls.

Although you'll no longer be talking to a machine when contacts pick up the phone, you'll be prepared to deliver the same message live. It's important that you practice delivering your telephone message several times before you reach out and touch someone.

❖ ❖ ❖

You will sound friendlier over the telephone when you smile while you dial. A smile lifts your mood. That helps you come across as an enthusiastic person on the phone.

At interviews, where prospective employers can see your facial expression, a smile says, "I like you and am glad I'm here." And on the line, although you lack visual input, a smile conveys the same impression through your voice. That is why radio disc jockeys are always smiling when they're on mic. It comes across to their listeners.

Research shows that the expression on your face can influence the way you feel. American philosopher and psychologist William James first advanced this idea almost a century ago. "The facial expressions are not just the visible sign of an emotion," James wrote, "but actually contribute to the feeling itself."

The brain receives sensory information from facial muscles and skin. So the expression on your face can tell you what to feel instead of being a reflection of your feelings.

Go ahead and try it. Smile, and you'll feel happier. Pout, and you'll feel down. A smile is a quick fix to get you through a phone call or an interview.

What to do when you just don't feel like smiling? Smile anyway. You'll sound a whole lot friendlier to your listener. The words from Louis Armstrong's hit are right on target: "Oh when you're smilin' keep on smiling. The whole world smiles with you..."

❖ ❖ ❖

Voice mail is a system that bugs most job hunters. That is as it should be. Telephones provide the most direct way for you to speak with your contacts, but sometimes you have no other choice than to leave a voice message.

But you need to make an effort to get through to your party first. So each time Mr. Machine answers, hang up. You can vary the times of day you call in order to increase your chances of getting through to the target. Frustrating, isn't it? That's why you should make only half of a dozen attempts. After that, you'll know it's time to leave a voice message.

The technique for doing so is the same as for recording a commercial. You are selling someone the benefits of taking some kind of action. In this case, it's calling you back.

Before you pick up the phone, write a script you can deliver in a half of a minute or less. Explain who you are and why you're calling. Then invite your listener to call you back, give him the best time to reach you by phone, and leave your number, repeating it slowly a second time. Finally, it helps to rehearse your script or outline four times.

Voice mail can be a pain in the…phone. But the technology has one advantage: no person can take as accurate and detailed a message as a machine.

❖ ❖ ❖

A small number of job hunters do not own answering machines or do not have messaging services on their landlines and cell phones. That's a no-no. Employment agencies or companies who call you in response to your having sent a résumé or letter are not going to keep trying until they happen to catch you in. Nether will networking contacts who return your call.

That's why it's critical to invest in a high-quality answering machine or a mobile phone that comes with an answering device. When it comes to recording an outgoing message, there are some dos and don'ts.

Don't record a cute announcement and have your child say, "My mommy and daddy aren't home right now."

It's almost worse to use the computer-generated outgoing message when your new machine or service provides it as an option. Callers need to hear a real voice—not a robot's.

And it's in poor taste to invite your callers to leave the day and the time of their call or to "wait for the tone." Callers know the drill.

Do keep your outgoing message simple. "Hi, I'm Randy Place on tape. Please leave a message, and I'll return your call shortly." Most voice devices allow you to time the beep so it comes right after your last word.

Record your own message. Even when you dislike the sound of your voice, it sounds a heck of a lot better than a droid's! Those of you who are microphone shy can ask your spouse or a friend with a clear voice to do the recording.

❖ ❖ ❖

Some job hunters and telemarketers haven't the foggiest idea about how to use voice mail to their advantage. You might think it's better to be brief, but there's no need to worry about how long your message takes. Why? Your listener needs to be motivated to return your call.

You can use voice mail to you advantage by first understanding the benefits the tool offers and then by following a five-step telephone technique for motivating people to return your calls.

Voice mail guarantees your message will get through the way you want it to be heard instead of being filtered through an assistant. That's why you need to include the same information you would say if you were speaking to an assistant or a secretary.

The five-step technique for recording your voice message is easy to follow:

1. Use your listener's first name, followed by yours. When someone has referred you to her, include the name of the person who suggested you call.
2. State the day and time of your call.
3. Explain why you're calling—whether it's to follow up on a letter or to request an appointment—and the reason why you want to meet.
4. Give your phone number and the times you can be reached.
5. Thank your listener and say, "I'll be listening for your response." If this is your second voice message, mention that you'll keep following up.

Now watch how fast you'll be called back.

❖ ❖ ❖

You waste too much time playing telephone tag. Unless you stop doing it, you might as well leave a message on a contact's voice machine and say, "Phone tag…you're it!'

Of course I'm being facetious. But there are a couple of alternatives to playing the losing game of phone tag.

You can create an outgoing message on your answering device asking callers to leave a message along with the best time for you to call them back. Also, give callers your cell phone number so they can return your call at once.

When you speak to a secretary or an assistant, try not to leave word, or you will initiate the game of phone tag. When asked if you would care to leave word, explain that because you'll be in and out of the office all day, it's probably best if you call back later. Then inquire about the best time to call back. After getting that information, be sure to inquire about what time your prospect arrives at work each morning.

Many hiring managers are in their offices between 7:15 and 8:45 a.m. So when it comes to calling people, those are a job hunter's golden hours.

❖ ❖ ❖

"Who are you and what do you want!" Isn't that what you feel like barking into the telephone after a telemarketer greets you by saying, "Hello Ms. Williams, how are you today?" When making a cold call, you can turn listeners off by introducing yourself in a presumptuous way.

A person's need to know underlies every contact. When it's romantic, you wonder if the person is for real or is just playing around. And when it comes to business, you're curious about what kind of hidden agenda could come up. So when you make a call, it's only natural to want something from the telephone communication.

You need to think about what you want from the listener before picking up the phone. Then you can introduce yourself by telling the prospect who you are and what you want. People, especially strangers, will like you more. That's because your listeners will relax and be open to accept what you say when you express who you are, what you want, and what you expect to happen.

That makes you a more attractive job candidate or salesperson because it puts your listeners at ease. And when you remember the two magic words ("who" and "what") you'll be more likely to get what you want—more meetings and job interviews.

❖ ❖ ❖

Some of you equate disconnecting your telephone with deviant behavior. Your behavior is only deviant when you allow constant incoming calls to interrupt your work.

The problem annoys you the most when you're working out of your house and you're interrupted by calls from home improvement, carpet cleaning, and credit card salespeople during intense moments of writing business correspondence.

There are times you need to make interruptions impossible—or at least postponable. So whenever you want peace and quiet, go ahead and turn off your cell phone and disconnect the landline. It's your phone. You, not the telephone, are in charge. You can use it as you want.

If you do not have answering devices at home or on the mobile phone, get them. You can turn off the devices when you require an uninterrupted block of time. When it comes to answering devices at home, you can also turn down the volume in order to avoid hearing incoming calls.

You will save time by not returning calls from strangers who haven't stated their business—and that's a good way to discourage those peddlers who are trying to sell something else you don't need.

❖ ❖ ❖

It's not what you say on the telephone, but how you say it.

Job hunters must speak professionally to get meetings and interviews that result in job offers. That's the reason for practicing your phone approach before dialing. The approach involves both speaking and listening.

When you speak, the idea is to sound competent and professional instead of pushy or too excited. And when it comes to listening, just hearing the person on the other end of the line is not good enough. You need to understand what's being said, or you'll miss important clues.

To that end, it helps to take notes. Notes will help you to focus you on the speaker and will prevent you from interrupting. And you can use your notes later at interviews and sales presentations that result from your telephone communication.

Should you not understand something the speaker said, ask for clarification. Some job candidates don't ask questions for fear of sounding stupid. That's nonsense. Questions make you sound intelligent and prepared, so always have a list of them at the bottom of your telephone script or outline.

❖ ❖ ❖

CHAPTER 7

Networking: The Quickest Way to Get Interviews

IT'S WHO YOU KNOW, STUPID

NETWORKING IS NOTHING NEW. THE concept of getting referrals, which is still your best bet for finding a job, has been around for years. Only the name has changed.

The concept began years ago in the insurance industry when hooking up with people was called "radiation." Insurance salesmen asked prospects for the names of several friends, and sales possibilities radiated out.

Over fifty years ago, career consultant Bernard Haldane coined the phrase "remembrance and referral," a roundabout approach where you ask contacts to review your résumé so they'll remember you when they have an opening and in the meantime will refer you to some of their contacts.

The names for networking have changed over the years, but the rules haven't. You network by talking to your list of personal contacts who'll refer you to their friends and contacts. That is how you'll be guided to job openings.

After you get a referral from networking with somebody, try to get two more. You can say, "Thanks for the lead, Mary. And while you're in your address book, are there any other names you can think of?"

As you network to be remembered and referred, job possibilities will radiate out.

❖ ❖ ❖

Networking becomes less mysterious when you consider it an opportunity to develop contacts. The technique of using family members, friends, and associates to get introductions to others is a basic sales approach. It doesn't involve going to your acquaintances with your hat in your hand.

Networking is based not on asking your contacts for a job, but on asking them for advice and referrals. You take your listener off the hook by saying, "I know you probably don't have a job for me. But perhaps you can look at my résumé and give me some advice about which direction you think I should take."

Networking has been called different names over the years. Napoleon Hill, in his classic *Think and Grow Rich*, called the tactic "developing a mastermind alliance." That means getting together with two or more people you respect who can provide suggestions for your project.

Whatever you call it, networking means that two heads are better than one. A Fordham University professor said you need the help of others to accomplish any venture. In the professor's words, "Alone stinks."

❖ ❖ ❖

Here's a slogan to paste on your wall: "It's who you know, stupid." The quickest way to land a job is with a little help from your friends. That includes your business associates, customers, and family members.

The first step in networking is to make a list of people you know. In the process, you'll discover you're acquainted with more folks than you think. You can be upfront with your personal contacts by telling them you are out of a job, but make it clear you do not expect them to know of any openings. Just ask whom they know that you should be talking to.

That's how you get leads to other people who might be in a position to either offer you a job or to introduce you to someone they know who can help.

When it comes to getting a job in the shortest possible time, networking for referrals is where it's at. Companies get thousands of résumés, and bosses feel safer hiring candidates who have been recommended by people they know.

When a mutual acquaintance endorses you, an interviewer might overlook a soft spot on your résumé and give you a break with some on-the-job training. You won't be treated like that when you walk in cold.

So approach people you know in order to get to know people you ought to know. They can all help you land. In other words, it's who you know, stupid.

❖ ❖ ❖

Because the quickest way to find a job is with the help of others, your initial step is to make a list of your contacts.

At first you may think, "Gee, I don't know that many people." But you'll be surprised by how many names you can come up with. You'll find them in your address book or Rolodex. How about those business cards in your wallet?

Next, begin to develop your list by noting after each name whether the person could be very helpful, helpful, or not so hot.

You won't experience a dose of rejection when you contact the "very helpful" category first. They're the most likely to lend a hand. Write them a letter or e-mail and follow up with a phone call. When you know somebody well, just pick up the phone and call. In either case, you want to schedule appointments.

Your meetings will go a lot smoother when you give them structure—a beginning, a middle, and an end. Begin by expressing appreciation for your prospect's time and interest.

In the middle, request advice about your résumé and job search. The kind of support you'll ask for will be determined by your job objective or career goal.

End the meeting by asking for referrals to other people who can help. Even if you decide to contact only twenty people on the list, your inventory of names can explode as you're referred on to others.

So match up your experience to your ambition, and then decide on the kind of help you need through the cooperation of others.

❖ ❖ ❖

It's not what you know, but who you know. This familiar phrase is especially true when you're looking for a job. That's because you'll have a better chance of being hired when you know someone who works for a company you're applying to. Your inside contact can vouch for you.

The reason you'll find it easier to get an interview and to land a job when you know someone who can recommend you is elementary, my dear Watson. Executives fear making hiring decisions. They're afraid the person they hire might turn out to be a dud. Then guess who will be held accountable?

On the other hand, hiring managers also believe they will not be criticized for employing a candidate who does not work out when the employee was recommended by another party.

Even when answering a help-wanted ad, ask yourself two questions: Do I know anyone who works for the company? And who do I know that might have a contact there?

You can look at the expression "it's not what you know, but who you know" this way: What you know qualifies you to apply for a job. And who you know improves your chances of landing it.

The fact is that the easiest way to get a job is to know someone who can recommend you.

❖ ❖ ❖

The most effective way to land a job is to know the right person or to know someone else who knows the right person. After all, you can never tell where you'll bump into someone who can help. It could be an acquaintance or even a stranger with whom you strike up a conversation.

So whether you're in a business setting or have the day off, be appropriately dressed and well groomed—and never leave home without résumés and business cards.

You'll get to know the right people who can help you land by telling everyone you know—your associates, your friends, your relatives, and your dentist—that you're looking for a job.

You can expand your network by attending meetings of your alumni association and by joining professional groups and serving on committees.

When anyone along your network chain helps you by providing advice or a referral, be sure to write a thank-you note. And when you're hired, thank your contact again. It's common courtesy to let contacts know the role they played in helping you make a landing.

Whether you give networking heavy emphasis or just let it happen, learn to use it. Networking is your most powerful tool for finding jobs and changing careers.

❖ ❖ ❖

You need visibility to find your next job. That means getting noticed by people who can help you achieve your objective of getting reemployed.

The coolest way to become more visible is by networking. It's cool because you're not putting pressure on your contacts by asking them for a job. You're simply letting them know you're out looking and telling them the kind of job you want.

The idea is to get advice and information. That will help you focus your campaign. The networking process gets you introductions to others who can lead you to future interviews.

The first step to getting visibility is to make a network list of people you know—colleagues, associates, friends, and relatives. You might even want to list your former bosses and favorite high school and college teachers. And while you're at it, write down your college alumni association.

When you begin to contact people on the list, make it clear to everyone that you're not asking them for a job—just for guidance and information.

Remember that you are a product to be marketed. No product is sold until it develops visibility in the marketplace. Networking enables you to achieve that visibility.

❖ ❖ ❖

The time to network is before your head gets chopped, not just when you need a job or have to change careers. Your network of personal contacts should be in place when your career is humming along.

Networking is no big deal when you think of it as a process of collecting contacts. After all is said and done, your network is another support system. You're building a community that will enrich your personal and business affairs. When you need a new job or want to change careers, you can ask network members for advice and referrals.

Building your network before hearing that jobs in your department are being transferred to Calcutta is an everyday process of putting yourself where the people are. That would be in business, community, and religious organizations. You'll also meet people in classes and support groups.

Sometimes you're able to help others. Look for those opportunities because networking is a two-way street. This teaching is summed up in the Golden Rule: "And as ye would that men should do to you, do ye also to them likewise." (Luke 6:31.)

However, you need to do for yourself first by being proactive in meeting new people.

❖ ❖ ❖

Job hunting can be compared to catching fish. The wider the net you cast, the more fish you'll catch, so you need to enclose lots of fish in your net in order to have a successful job-finding campaign.

The fish you need to catch are as many networking contacts as possible, and you also need to increase your level of job-hunting activity. It's helpful to have at least a half dozen search activities going at once. Remember that job hunting is a numbers game.

So you need to cast your net wide in order to fish for the most people. You'll accomplish that by putting less emphasis on answering ads, posting on Internet job sites, and using employment agencies—and more emphasis on networking.

When you meet with friends, associates, and people they introduce you to, adopt the consultant's approach. Then you can go in with the idea not of trying to land a job, but of asking questions in order to discover needs and how you can help. Only by uncovering a need do you earn the right to offer your expertise by making a more direct approach.

And don't tell yourself you'll look into a job or career opportunity with a networking contact just because you need a job. It's better to look at any networking situation as an opportunity to meet new people and to develop new relationships that can then be added to your network.

Then you'll have created a platform of networking contacts with whom you can keep in touch on an ongoing basis.

❖ ❖ ❖

Networking is your most powerful job-finding tool, but some of you have problems using it. On the one hand, you think networking is like begging for something, or you just don't like asking for help.

But on the other hand, there are many people out there who want to help you. And you won't be going hat in hand when you realize a networking meeting is a two-way street. You can give back.

Offer to share some of the information you've been learning about the job marketplace. You can also give back by keeping in touch with your networking contacts to let them know how your job hunt is going. That will make your friends and associates feel they've made important contributions to your life.

You'll also be more willing to try networking if you keep in mind that there's an important information-gathering process you need to do before you're ready to present yourself as a candidate. So you can think of networking as a legitimate way to request the information you need to conduct a campaign for finding a job. It will let you become clear about the kinds of jobs to which you want to apply.

You won't feel like you're using others when you remember that networking is like the Golden Rule. You can give back to others what they have given to you.

❖ ❖ ❖

Many people who prefer working alone hate to network. You would rather do it all yourself than ask somebody you know for help or advice. Get over it.

Your job campaign is not a do-it-yourself project. As in most life situations, you need the help of others.

When you would rather die than ask for help, discover at least one person with whom you can talk—preferably someone who shares your values and brings out the best in you.

From that comfortable relationship, others will follow. Networking is like any project you dread starting. It becomes easier as you get into it.

You can develop other safe contacts by making lists of alternate occupations and then thinking of people you know who might lead you into those trades.

Safe contacts to put on your list could include members of your church or synagogue, people in business and professional organizations to which you belong, school and college friends, and folks on your Christmas card list.

That's how to slide into networking the easy way. The emphasis here is on the word "easy." Networking becomes easier as you get into it.

❖ ❖ ❖

You equate networking to begging for something. That's why you have problems doing it. Maybe you're not comfortable reaching out for help. Get over it. There are many people you know who want to help you. Networking is simply giving them an opportunity to do it.

When you ask for suggestions about your résumé and advice surrounding your situation, contacts are motivated to refer you to people they know who might want to meet you.

You won't be going to those contacts with hat in hand when you understand a networking meeting is a two-way street. You can give back. Offer to share information you've been learning about the marketplace, and keep in touch with your contacts to tell them how your search is going. That will make contacts feel they've made an important contribution to your life.

You'll also be more willing to try networking when you keep in mind that it's important to gather information through networking before you present yourself as a candidate.

So think of networking as a legitimate way to request the information you need in order to conduct a job campaign. That will let you become clear about the kinds of jobs you want to apply for.

Remember that networking is your most powerful job-finding tool.

❖ ❖ ❖

Although you've been reading that networking is the quickest way to land, you still shy away from it. Your timidness might result from one of several causes.

You might feel that networking is using other people. Or you might equate asking for help to having a tooth pulled. Or perhaps you think others are too busy and won't take time to see you.

While some of the people you know are too concerned with their own lives to lend a helping hand, you can take heart that others are willing and able to be of use—but not when you think that networking is just about notifying people you're looking for work.

On the contrary, networking is actually about skillfully managing brief meetings with your contacts and the folks they refer you to in order to elicit some information what will help you to clarify your goals. It's also about obtaining some additional names of people to network with.

It becomes easier to ask for information and advice when you understand the concept of networking as a two-way street. You can share information gathered through your networking process.

Most of you network but fail to inform your contacts about your progress. That's an oversight. Your helpers want to know how they played a part in your life.

So if you're concerned about feeling you're using others, be mindful of the fact that networking is a two-way street. You can give back.

❖ ❖ ❖

A good way to turn off your network of personal contacts is to communicate with them only when you need a job. People want to help friends—not needy job hunters. That's the reason why networking is about building friendships, not asking for work.

Because friends who want to help will volunteer to introduce you to their contacts, you'll be led to prospective employers as the networking process unfolds.

The beauty about networking is not having to ask for a job. Introductions happen naturally when you learn the science of networking and turn it into an art.

The first rule for managing network relationships is to not get caught selling. That's when you sound like a job hunter. Instead, establish common ground by turning contacts into friendships. When you both like tennis, for example, you have something in common. That will draw you closer.

The second rule is to have a good time while networking. Do you have a sense of humor? Then show it. If you can make people laugh, you can get them to help you. Laughter implies approval, and tacit approval leads to acceptance as a friend.

Networking comes down to what was stated earlier—people want to help friends.

❖ ❖ ❖

There is a reason your crusade to find a job is taking so long. Like most candidates, you don't know as much as you think you do about job hunting. So you make mistakes, like spending all of your time answering want ads in print and online. That's where many job hunters think the action is.

But the "posted job market" represents only 20 percent of all of the available jobs out there. The majority of them—a whopping 80 percent—are not advertised, according to a study by Harvard sociologist Mark Granovetter. You'll find them in what's called the hidden job market.

Why are those jobs hidden from view? Because most employers fill them by either hiring from within their own companies or by asking friends and business associates if they know people who are suitable for the positions.

That is why it makes sense to spend 80 percent of your efforts tapping into this hidden job market by reaching out to your network. Touch base with everyone you know, and develop relationships with new acquaintances.

The fastest way to get a job is to have someone recommend you. The more power that person has, the better.

❖ ❖ ❖

How do most job hunters go about finding new positions? This question is easy to answer. It's by responding to want ads, posting résumés on the Internet, networking, and contacting employment agencies and executive recruiters.

But here's a fact that will surprise you: Only a small percentage of all available jobs are found this way. A Harvard sociologist investigated how people get jobs. Mark Granovetter concluded a whopping 80 percent of all positions are found through networking.

The remaining 20 percent of all available jobs are uncovered through the traditional strategies mentioned in the first paragraph. That is why your personal contacts are vital to the success of your search.

You need to ask your friends and business associates if they know of any openings or if they can introduce you to people they know who might steer you in the right direction. That's how you'll discover better jobs.

That doesn't mean you should ignore some of the traditional job-finding methods. Just spend less time doing them and put most of your effort into networking, which is where 80 percent of the action is. The percentages are in your favor.

❖ ❖ ❖

Another study confirms that job seekers should spend less time answering ads, mass mailing résumés, or applying for openings on the Internet.

The survey, which was conducted by a group of New Jersey–based outplacement firms, authenticated the value of spending more time speaking with personal contacts through networking. It's the technique that always works best.

The O-I Partners Work Reemployment Study tracked five hundred job hunters who received outplacement counseling. Almost 90 percent of that group found new jobs, and over 60 percent of those candidates landed through networking.

Compare those figures with the figures about jobs obtained by answering ads and contacting recruiters. They trailed in effectiveness by a wide margin: Job hunters who found jobs through classifieds were under 20 percent, and those who landed through search firms, only 12 percent.

It's worth repeating that this and other surveys don't indicate that you should forget about responding to published ads, posting résumés on the Internet, and contacting staffing services. You need to cover all of your bases.

Just make sure you spend well over half your time networking.

❖ ❖ ❖

People who succeed in sales work from a prospect list. You need to work from a personal networking list in order for your job-finding campaign to triumph.

Most new job hunters make a common mistake. When you decide to go out to talk to people, a few acquaintances pop into your mind. You phone them without writing their names on a list. That is a mistake for a couple of reasons.

First, it's unwise to call valuable contacts when your mind is in a state of confusion after being dumped. Second, you'll run out of names to call within five minutes.

The right way is to make your complete network list before calling. Wouldn't it be a pleasant surprise to discover you have more contacts than you think? You'll experience that surprise when you use the following five steps to create and grow your networking list:

1. List those few people who first come to mind.
2. Add other folks you know on a first-name basis by going through your address book and business cards.

3. Now ask yourself, "Who else do I know through my work, children, interests, and hobbies?" Write them down.
4. Show the list to close friends and family members. They'll help you generate names you haven't thought of.
5. Review the list and put check marks next to the names of people you think are most likely to help and provide leads.

It's time to congratulate yourself. You've created a long list of prospects from which to network. It's also the time to pick up the phone and start calling them.

❖ ❖ ❖

If you really want to get married, you gotta pop the question. You also must pop the question if you want to get referrals from networking contacts. They are business associates, friends, and family.

The name of the game in networking is "referrals"—being referred to others who might be in a position to either hire you or to provide introductions to their contacts.

While many of your contacts will be happy to oblige, sometimes even good friends will be reluctant to come up with introductions. That's when you need to speak up and pop the question.

The time to do so is toward the end of a networking meeting when no referrals have been offered. The thought of asking a friend for something might feel awkward at first. However, with a little preparation and rehearsal, asking for referrals will become second nature.

The nicest way to pop the question is to simply ask your friend, "Who do you know that I should be talking to?" But what if she responds, "I can't think of anybody"? Then you can say, "I'm sure you don't have names on the tip of your tongue. So let me call you in a couple of weeks after you've had time to think about it."

Another way to handle the situation with a contact who hesitates to help is to ask for the names of professional people your friend knows in his field. You might suggest it by saying, "You would introduce me to your accountant or lawyer, wouldn't you? You pay them to work for you, so they would see me."

In a nutshell, your networking objective is to be referred to another prospect. Several are even better. But when names aren't forthcoming, you need to pop the question: "Who do you know that I should be talking to?"

❖ ❖ ❖

People who buy your product or service need to remember who you are. As a job candidate selling a service, who are you?

Let's face it. Your competitors perform the same function as you do. Interviewers are unable to keep in mind all of the job candidates they meet. That's why you need to be remembered. A way to separate yourself from the pack is to give an unforgettable introduction. Let's look at a handy way of doing it.

When you meet a prospective employer at a job fair, networking meeting, or while introducing yourself for the first time on the phone, give your name and tell her what you do. Then mention a benefit of your service. I've listed three examples:

- "Hi, I'm Randy Place, a career management consultant who helps people find jobs and manage their careers."
- "I'm Eleanor Vent. I sell broadcast time and help TV stations increase sales and profits."
- "I'm John Harrison, an experienced customer service representative who helps keep customers happy."

These are livelier than just saying, "I'm Sam Vitter, a career counselor." Or, "Hi, I'm Sue Sullivan, a customer service representative." People will recall your name when you include a benefit of your service with your introduction.

It's a fact—the strongest impression is the one made in the shortest amount time. And when you use this technique for being remembered, you'll perform introductions in fewer than ten seconds.

So when you have an opportunity to introduce yourself, apply this simple and direct formula for making a lasting impression:

Your name + what you do + a benefit = remembrance.

❖ ❖ ❖

A career change is an exciting process when you do it right. You'll be on solid ground when you can support your decision for entering a new kind of employment.

That's accomplished when you explore the new kind of employment you're considering and make contacts in the field. You want to talk to people there in order solicit information and advice.

Personal meetings, which are sometimes called informational interviews, are a critical part of your career shift. Up to 80 percent of all of the available positions are filled through personal contacts.

Informational interviews are the reverse of job interviews because you are the interviewer who asks the questions in order to obtain information and guidance for your career choice.

When you request appointments to gather intelligence and ask for advice, there's something you need to make crystal clear: you want to talk about the field, not ask for a job. You'll be led to one eventually without having to ask.

When it comes to changing careers, the typical job-hunting methods of responding to ads, posting your résumé, contacting recruiters, and mass résumé mailings are not your best bets.

You need to focus on information interviews. It's the process that will eventually lead you to a new trade.

❖ ❖ ❖

The best card game in town used to be presenting your engraved business or personal card. The custom of handing out business cards barely survives these days.

But it's still a tool used by business people and job finders who want to give their names to new contacts in a more formal way than a name tag reading, "Hi, I'm Jim Thompson."

When people ask if you have a card, it's good business to accommodate them. You lack business sense if you don't have a card to return.

People are proud of their business cards. That's why you should treat any card you're handed with respect. When you take someone's business card, it's improper to slip it into your jacket pocket or even into a wallet that ends up in your back pocket. Read and acknowledge the card, and hold it until the end of your meeting. Then put it in your pocket.

Most job candidates wait until they have a job before printing business cards. So why not get a leg up on them by printing cards for your search right now? It's another self-marketing tool to add to your arsenal.

You never can tell when you'll bump into someone who might have a lead or job—or ask if you have a business card.

❖ ❖ ❖

As you look for a job, think of yourself as a professional. Doctors, lawyers, and accountants get business for their professional services through referrals.

Even professional blue-collar workers, like carpenters and electricians, get business through recommendations from their satisfied customers. Likewise, prospects for your services are comfortable getting recommendations from people they know.

Prospective employers feel the same way. If someone vouches for you, it makes you a safe bet. Your satisfied customers are former bosses, clients, and business associates. They already know how terrific you are, so they'll feel free to recommend you to their contacts who either know of openings or can introduce you to others.

This process is called "networking," and many of you fail to network properly. That's because you fail to keep in touch with your network after obtaining referrals. That's not nice.

Contacts who provided help have invested time in your career, so they deserve to know the role they played in your success.

That being the case, it's important to keep in touch by letting them know how your search is going—and especially how it ends.

❖ ❖ ❖

Job hunters have discovered networking beats the Net. This, According to a workplace-consulting firm that surveyed over seven thousand executives who switched jobs.

The study by Drake Beam Morin showed that only 4 percent of job seekers found their positions on the Internet. Compare that to the stupendous 65 percent of people who got jobs the old-fashioned way—by networking.

Another survey by Forrester Research indicated that the majority of people who used job-finding sites were generally dissatisfied with the quality of the jobs that were advertised. Companies and recruiters advertise jobs online because it's such a cost-effective way to reach applicants.

As a result, top Internet job-finding sites like Monster, Indeed, and CareerBuilder have doubled their users because millions of you have spent most of your time searching the Internet. Yet networking and referrals from networking remain the primary methods that job candidates use to actually find work.

Should you find yourself outside of the networking arena, climb into the ring and score a big win during the early rounds of your job campaign with a one-two punch: become fully aware that your full-time job of finding a job is to network like crazy, and spend less than 10 percent of your time answering ads and posting your résumé on the Net.

Then you'll experience how networking beats the Net.

❖ ❖ ❖

It's not easy to get a job from a stranger. That's why your best bet is to go to the people who are most familiar with you and your work—friends, colleagues, and family members—because they can give you information about companies and careers along with job leads.

This approach to landing a job is called "networking." You develop a list of people you know who have some contact with businesses in your field. That's how most jobs get filled—by word of mouth and through the influence of friends and relatives.

The labor department estimates that two-thirds of the jobs available to you are found in the unpublished section of the job market. Networking provides the structure for tapping into it and increases your odds of landing in the shortest amount of time.

The beauty of networking is your ability to get a job without having to ask for it. Instead you can ask for information or advice about your résumé, suggestions about entering a field, or advice about problems surrounding your job search.

Remember that each of your contacts is a source of information about jobs and industries. They can also introduce you to a job prospect or three.

Getting referrals, which is the byproduct of requesting information or advice, is your primary goal while networking.

❖ ❖ ❖

The easiest way to find a new job is by to talk to your contacts. If you're like most job hunters, you think only of the people you know—of your network of business associates, friends, and relatives. But you can also create new contacts. Doing so will enhance your campaign.

You can create new contacts by selecting a number of companies in your target job market and then asking your contacts if they know anyone who works at the companies you've targeted. That is an excellent use of your personal network.

While getting referrals is the best way to meet new people, let's consider how to approach companies you've targeted where you don't know anyone.

You need to find the name of the executive who would hire you if there were a job. You'll uncover the appropriate names on the Internet and in directories found in the business section at your local library.

Then you can write or call these people to request a brief meeting. However, you need to make it clear that while you're not going to ask for a position, you do want to talk about your background and the company's future needs for your services.

While the best and easiest way to find a job is through personal contacts, you can land even faster when you expand your personal network list by creating new prospects.

❖ ❖ ❖

It's not always possible to make networking the main event in your job hunt. Perhaps you don't know that many people, or the contacts you have are too worried about their jobs to help you.

If that describes your predicament, consider manufacturing a network. The concept is to list companies you want to work for and then get the names of people inside those outfits who could hire you if there were a job.

There are four steps to creating a network from scratch. You can remember them easily by remembering the acronym CRAW (**c**ontact, **r**esearch, **ar**ticle hunt, **w**rite).

1. Contact the companies you want to crack to determine the person in charge of your area of interest. Or, even better, call your personal contacts and ask them to introduce you to people they know who work there.
2. Research your local newspaper and industry trade magazine. You'll learn about companies that are expanding, moving into your community, or creating new divisions. That's where the new jobs are.
3. Article hunt by continuing your research on the Internet.
4. Write to people mentioned in your basic research and article hunt. You can explain where you got their name and request a brief meeting to discuss your background and to see if it fits with the future needs of a company.

Job finding depends on connections. And you never can tell where you'll meet a new connection—maybe you'll even share an elevator or bump into someone you know who knows someone you should know.

❖ ❖ ❖

The way to build your network of personal contacts is to start conversations with people you meet.

You can draw anyone into a discussion by introducing yourself with conversations that are open ended. That means asking questions that permit your listener to give spontaneous responses. Here are a few examples:

"What made you decide to come tonight?"

"What do you know about the speaker?"

"How long have you belonged to this organization?"

The trick is to collect contacts for your network on an ongoing basis. The way to organize for this task is to create a file so you can keep track of each conversation. You'll want to include each person's phone number, e-mail, and company address. Each time you contact someone, write down the date of the communication along with a brief note about what was said.

You'll progress in networking by keeping in touch with everybody on your expanding network list. There are various ways to do so.

You can pick up the phone now and then, write notes and e-mails, mail or e-mail articles of interest, send a Christmas or Hanukkah card, and connect with people at the next meeting of your organization, class, or support group.

Let's face it. You bump into people all day, and you have countless opportunities to start conversations.

Building your network can be a picnic when you look at networking as a challenge that enhances your life and career.

❖ ❖ ❖

When it comes to finding a job, it's who you know, stupid. A new study shows how true this is.

A survey of several thousand people who applied for job openings in a large bank showed that only a little over 25 percent of the applicants who did not have referrals from inside the company made it to the interview stage. Among the job hunters who did have referrals from bank employees, 40 percent got job offers.

When human resources recruiters run short of applicants, they ask their own employees if they know anyone who can fill the opening. That's why it's a good idea to make a list of people you know who work for various companies when you're starting your job campaign. Then ask them if they know of any openings.

The phrase "do you know of any openings inside your company?" is important to remember. When a contact can vouch for you, you'll have a much better chance of getting the interview and landing the job.

❖ ❖ ❖

Now that you've landed, what do you do for an encore? Stop congratulating yourself and begin looking for your next position by keeping your network green.

When you got your current job, you probably allowed personal contacts to help and advise you. Some provided referrals. Perhaps such a lead helped you to land the new job

So the network that guided you to a happy landing can assist you again the next time you need help. There are two steps for keeping your network green.

The first is to thank each person on your network list after you accept an offer. Either pick up the phone or write an e-mail or letter to explain how your search turned out and the role everyone played in your success. Because networking is about people wanting to serve their fellow man, your contacts want to know how they helped you.

The second step is to keep your network activated. You'll accomplish this by finding opportunities to drop a line or make a call—even if it's just sending a Christmas or Hanukkah card once a year.

You keep your network green by letting people know you value them.

❖ ❖ ❖

CHAPTER 8

How to Turn Knowledge into Power

Research Methods that Work Best for Your Search

You believe your job search is stuck but you are unable to put your finger on the reason why. A job campaign can lose its momentum when you fail to perform the one job-search element that most candidates detest: research.

It's critical to learn about industries and companies before going on job or information interviews. Research is the key to successful interviews. You need to take this basic step for two reasons.

First, research helps you sound like an insider. And second, it enables you to give an interview that is more intelligent.

You can save time and end your anguish surrounding research issues by simply using the Internet. Hey, it's the best doohickey for quickly researching an industry that interests you or a company you are about to interview.

An easy way to generate interviews is to post your résumé on major job boards such as Careerbuilder.com, Indeed.com, Jobing.com, Jobcentral.com, and Monster.com.

You can learn about companies by visiting their home pages. Also, AltaVista. com provides information about companies, industries, products, and much more

In a nutshell, the best way to prepare for a successful interview is by doing your homework.

❖ ❖ ❖

The Internet has removed much of the drudgery of researching companies. Prior to the Net, job hunters considered library research to be the yuckiest part of the search process. Nevertheless, research has always been the key to giving better interviews, developing job prospects, and learning about industries of interest.

The information superhighway eliminates the need to sit in a library for several hours. However, there are times when you'll require resources such as directories and other reference items that only a library can provide.

In most instances, you will accomplish the task of research much faster when you sit in front of a computer in your home or office. You will get the most power from using the Internet when you understand that it's more about finding information than finding jobs.

You cannot expect to get invitations to lots of interviews by distributing résumés to thousands of hiring managers by e-mail or snail mail or by posting on the Internet. Broadcasting résumés has always been an inadequate technique for getting interviews.

But as a research tool, the Internet lets you get up to speed quickly on industries, employment trends, companies and their management.

❖ ❖ ❖

If you think you're unable to give a knock-'em-dead interview, it's because you've failed to do your homework. The two traditional ways of preparing— meaning getting information about companies—are getting information from people and from printed materials.

You can obtain information from people by identifying personal contacts on your network list who can tell you more about a particular company; and it's even better when one of your contacts can refer you to someone who works there. You can tell the insider that you are being considered for a job or that you're interested in applying for one and want to know about the climate and culture of their organization.

Information from printed material is readily available in annual reports, newsletters, and magazines and online. When you read what the companies say about themselves, you'll be able to turn their words to your advantage. That's because you'll be prepared not only to tell the interviewer that you want to work there, but also to give reasons why you do.

Homework builds your self-confidence. In turn, that empowers you to give winning interviews. After uncovering how much ability or background an interviewer is looking for, you will often discover the job requires less experience than you had thought.

And you can demonstrate that you already have what it takes by matching your experience to the requirements of a job.

❖ ❖ ❖

Knowledge is power only when you use it. The most important knowledge you need for an interview is the job's requirements. Don't leave home without it. Or if you don't have job specifications, don't open your mouth at an interview before you get them.

Only when you know what the requirements are for a particular position can you talk about how you can fit the bill. Then instead of saying, "Gee, I'd like to work here," you'll able to give specific reasons why you want to work for that company.

Here are four straightforward techniques for uncovering a job's requirements:

1. When an agency or a recruiter sets up an interview, ask your contact for the job specifications.
2. When somebody from a company calls with an invitation to interview, ask that person to tell you more about the job and what it requires.
3. As you study job postings in the newspapers and on the web, you'll notice that some of the larger postings list the qualifications the company is looking for.
4. Should you still lack this information when you sit down to interview, ask your prospective employer to describe the job or the ideal candidate for the job. You need to pop the question as soon as you're seated—before you're asked to speak.

After a prospective employer tells you what she's looking for, you'll have the ammunition necessary to match your skills and abilities to the job's requirements. And that's what interviewing is all about.

❖ ❖ ❖

Talented people will not accept just any job. They go beyond traditional Internet and library research to discover what it's really like to work for a company.

Serious job hunters must become sleuths for this kind of research. So before interviewing at a company or accepting a position, sit in a company's parking lot to observe the organization's dress code and how employees interact.

Do they greet each other by shaking hands, and do they seem to enjoy going to work? Or do you see personnel hanging their heads while shuffling to the front door, looking like they dread the start of another workday? The answers to those questions will inform you about the company's culture and whether you'd be happy in that particular environment.

Other important clues to recognize are the times people arrive at work and if there's reserved parking. When you see employees arrive at seven every morning, you know it's got to be a workaholic environment, and reserved parking could mean your stature in the company will be measured by how far away from the entrance you get to park.

Many of you go to great lengths to analyze work environments. That's because surveys agree that ambiance, corporate culture, and surroundings are the most important considerations for job candidates.

❖ ❖ ❖

Sometimes you can talk your way through the process of researching a company with whom you plan to interview. That's the word from Bill Roth, an executive coach based in Norwalk, Connecticut. "It's accomplished by networking your way into talking with someone who is already employed there," says Roth.

You can explain that you're being considered as a candidate for a job and would like to know a little more from an employee's perspective. "Just ask them if they can tell you about the climate and culture of their company."

When you cannot talk with someone inside the company, you need to rely on standard research techniques such as reading business magazines, a company's 10-K report, or its annual report to shareholders, or on visiting a company's website.

Nobody needs to explain that you should do this research before going to a company. "So when the interviewer says, 'What do you know about our company?' you don't just sit there and say, 'Duh...not very much,'" Roth said.

In a nutshell, you are responsible to learn as much as you can about a company before interviewing.

❖ ❖ ❖

CHAPTER 9

Dressing for Success Isn't Just for Interviews

DRESS WELL AND MORE OPPORTUNITIES WILL COME YOUR WAY

THE CLOTHES YOU WEAR ARE like the cover of a book. Sometimes, you can judge a book by its cover. Because a book jacket is attractive, you might be motivated to buy the book.   Your cover is the outfit you wear. It enhances the first impression you make and helps an interviewer determine whether or not he wants to hire you.

But dressing for success isn't just for job interviews. Whether you're conducting a job campaign from home or an outplacement office, always dress as if you were going to an interview. You could be invited to meet a job prospect today. And if you bump into someone you know, that person will be more likely to refer you to another contact when you are dressed for business.

You need to always look like you mean business. This is especially true when you're between jobs. Business clothes—or the clean, well-tailored outfit of your trade—ought to be worn most of the time. You'll feel better about yourself because dressing for success boosts your morale.

Wearing nice clothes is a constant reminder that even job hunters have a job—the full-time job of finding a job.

So when you're out of work, don't dress like a jerk. Always look your best, and you'll stay in touch with success.

❖ ❖ ❖

An employee or interviewee is an actor on a business stage, so you need to dress for the part by wearing the right costume for what you do. Regardless of the message you are trying to express, the clothes you wear are part of your package.

When you consider the investment you've already made in your career—the time you've spent, your education, and your postgraduate business training—spending money for well-made outfits just makes sense. Now is not the time to skimp on clothes. That doesn't mean women should run out and plunk down a lot of money for designer suits. You can either buy well-made knock-offs or a designer suit on sale.

Men who cannot afford a custom-made suit can also play it safe by selecting one from a well-known men's store that carries quality brands. You might be tempted to buy off-price suits at discounts. But when a suit does not fit just right, it's no bargain.

Remember to dress well, and more opportunities will come your way.

❖ ❖ ❖

You must be well dressed from the bottom up—from your shoes to your hair. That's because your top and bottom are what prospects notice first.

Hairstyles have evolved from the wigs of the Renaissance to the curly hairstyles and pompadours of the 1940s, the long and unruly hair of the 70s, and finally to the streamlined haircuts of the computer age. People who want to be taken seriously in business today are cutting their hair short. Your hair is your crowning glory. Or if you shave it, your head is.

The shoes you wear to impress a prospective employer or client should send a message that you care about yourself and buy only the best quality. If you're a man, regardless of whether you choose Italian or tasseled loafers or a cap-toed lace-up style, your shoes must be comfortable to walk in.

Women should wear shoes that look conservative and new. But before selecting your shoe styles, look around to see what other women in your company are wearing. You'll notice stiletto heels are passé while pumps are in vogue.

Your hair and shoes speak volumes about you because they are the first parts of you that people notice as soon as you enter a room.

❖ ❖ ❖

Even though business has accepted more casual dress, it's incorrect to dress down for interviews. Employees who work at the company to which you're applying might wear blue jeans and a shirt. But when you're interviewing, dressing for success usually means a dark-blue business suit for men and women.

However, it's not necessary to plunk down thousands of dollars for a designer or tailored suit. Well-made suits can be purchased on sale at department stores.

Your clothing is part of your personal presentation. Even before you open your mouth, a prospective employer has already judged you by your looks. Dressing well allows you to make that important first impression.

Additionally, a proper interview outfit helps build a common bond between you and a prospective employer. You dress as a sign of respect for others and for the positions they hold, not for your comfort or self-expression. The right interview costume also shows you can conform when necessary.

Most job hunters focus on job-search techniques but give little thought to the most important tool of all—their personal appearance.

❖ ❖ ❖

Dressing casually on dress-down days does not mean wearing your Mickey Mouse sweatshirt with a pair of torn dungarees, athletic shoes, and a baseball cap worn backward. Your company has not abolished its dress code. Anything that looks wash and wear is tacky. You should save the khaki for the company picnic.

Dress-down days are not to be taken literally, or you'll confuse "informal" with "sloppy." That's the reason why grabbing just anything from your closet is taboo.

When your company has an informal dress code, feel free to wear more comfortable and less confining—not less stylish—clothes. Coordinated colors, a proper fit, and quality fabrics are still important.

Should your organization lack guidelines for dress-down days, pay attention to what others wear, or copy your supervisor's dressed-down outfits. This is important because dress-down Fridays have become less in vogue since business attire has started making a comeback.

The fashion trends in business right now are button-down oxford shirts; close-fitting dresses, or "sheath dresses," without belts; and pencil skirts. Tailored jackets are popular with men and women.

This should inform you that even on days you can dress casually, you still have to look polished.

❖ ❖ ❖

After the days of World War II—the era of Rosie the Riveter—only blue-collar women wore pants to work. Now executive women are also wearing trousers in even the most conservative offices. More female lawyers are wearing pants to court, for example.

Nobody has to tell you that women are wearing pants now because company dress codes have been crumbing. As a result, women have become more relaxed about their business attire. For many, that means pants.

But some image consultants believe pantsuits are okay only in a creative environment. Otherwise, a skirt is more appropriate, especially when you're interviewing for a position.

While it's acceptable for women to wear slacks and pantsuits in most professions, many feel dressier, and that they make a better impression, when wearing a skirt.

Before you wear pants to a new job, observe what the other women are wearing. Pants might have been okay in your previous workplace. But at your new office, women may not be wearing the pants.

❖ ❖ ❖

How to Make a Good First Impression

Knock 'Em Dead in the First Thirty Seconds and Win the Interview

Your interviewer has already made up her mind about you by the time you walk through the door and shake her hand. That's why making a good first impression is the most important part of the interview. And it only takes thirty seconds.

A survey showed that buyers for large corporations make over 80 percent of their major purchase decisions within a half of a minute of meeting a salesperson. You'll notice decisions are not made because of price or service or guarantee, but solely because of the personal marketing of the salesperson. We're talking seconds here—not a half hour.

Making that instant connection is even more important than the benefits you offer. Hiring managers already know you have what it takes. They've read your résumé. Why do you think you were invited to interview?

As interviewers size you up, they also need to determine if you'll fit the corporate culture. They'll make that judgment by looking at your overall appearance, which includes your hairstyle and how you dress and look. This is the time to flash your nicest smile. You have only thirty seconds to make a good first impression.

❖ ❖ ❖

The most important segment of your interview is the first half of a minute. That's all the time it takes to make a good first impression, and your interviewer's initial perception about you will stick with him throughout the interview.

If your first impression is good one, you could not botch the rest of the interview, even if you tried. The reason? Having made an excellent first impression, you have created a halo effect. That's when your interviewer makes an overall rosy evaluation of you.

It's based on your smile, the way you shake hands, how you introduce yourself, and how your hair is styled or cut. Other factors include how you dress and carry yourself, your attitude, your posture, and your facial expression—all of which should convey you are glad to be there.

You'll find it easier to establish an overall first impression when you arrive twenty minutes early to an interview site. Then you can be yourself because you won't show up in a state of panic.

The first message you communicate is always about you. And it takes only thirty seconds or so to do it.

❖ ❖ ❖

An interviewer first notices your hair. To make a good first impression, get a haircut. Personal marketing consultant Camille Lavington advises men and women to keep their hair short. "You may have been the prom queen or a football hero," says Lavington, "but if there's a new style in hair length or styling and you don't keep up, you've dated yourself."

When you were a young woman, long and flowing locks were cool. But women in almost every field who are moving ahead with their careers are well groomed. "Take a good look at Katie Couric," advises Lavington. "If you want interviewers to take you seriously, cut your hair. You need to show your jawline. And that means getting your hair up off your face." Men's hairstyles also need to expose their strong jawlines.

Women who want to play on the same field need to present the female version of professionalism by matching men's clean-cut looks. Your hair is your crowning glory. The personal marketing consultant says you'll make a good first impression when you keep it short.

❖ ❖ ❖

Men need to pay as much attention to their hairstyles as women do. This is especially true for those older men who attempt to look younger by letting their hair get longer around the sides.

When there isn't much left on top, don't try turning back the clock by attempting to keep every remaining hair in place; don't try to hide your baldness by sweeping your thicker hair from the far right across your dome and over to the far left of your head. Everybody knows what you're trying to hide. Besides, it gives you a weird look.

Men who sport such bizarre hairstyles would look better if they went to a hair stylist instead of to an inexpensive barber. You can choose how you want your hair to look by studying magazine ads for male models your age with the kind of hair you have.

When it comes to making that all-important first impression, the first thing someone notices about you is your head. So be sure to have what covers it cut and styled sensibly.

Even if your stylist agrees there's not enough hair to be styled, you can always do a Michael Jordan. Shave it off. It's trendy to be bald.

❖ ❖ ❖

A study conducted by Germany's Emnid Institute indicates balding men have less of a chance of getting the jobs they want than those with full heads of hair.

Researchers sent phony résumés with photos of three bald men and three guys with full heads of hair to one hundred leading international firms.

The photos were actually of the same three men, but half of the pictures had been altered to show them with balding heads. Almost 15 percent fewer baldies were called for interviews than men with full heads of hair.

A spokesman for the Emnid Institute was quoted in the *New York Post* and said the results showed that bald job hunters were at a clear disadvantage over men with full heads of hair. While the survey indicates society's belief that hair is sexy and bald is old, remember the old saying "beauty is only skin deep."

But when the skin is on the top of your head, you might need to try a little harder to convince prospects to look deeper to where your talents reside.

❖ ❖ ❖

Gentlemen, shave you beards. Facial hair will not enhance the first impression you make. Interviewers will think you're either trying to get attention or to show you're intellectually superior, or you are a nonconformist, artistic, or too lazy and undisciplined to shave every morning.

Older men often think growing a beard makes them look younger. But instead of looking cool, aging men with beards are often the butts of their fellow employees' jokes. "They're saying, 'Look, I'm still virile enough to grow hair on my chin,'" says personal marketing consultant Camille Lavington.

A beard covers much of your face, so you give the impression you're trying to hide something. Even if you're only hiding a weak chin, you've already made a negative first impression. Interviewers might consider you lower class because you groom yourself less often.

In today's business world, beards are out. The clean-shaven look is in. If you're entering the job market wearing a beard, shave it off. If you insist on harvesting facial hair, you can always grow it back after you land.

❖ ❖ ❖

Your handshake is a part of the first impression you make, yet job candidates are often confused about how to shake hands. Men sometimes ask if they should extend a hand first to a woman interviewer or wait until she goes first, and some women ask if it's good form to shake another woman's hand.

When it comes to who goes first—the man or the woman—there are no rules. Most of you will extend a hand automatically when you are being introduced. That's correct. And it has always been correct for women to shake hands with each other. However, it used to be considered improper for a younger person—either a man or woman—to extend a hand before an older person did.

The only error you can make is to ignore a hand that has been extended. You will embarrass somebody whose hand is left dangling in midair.

And when you shake hands outdoors on a cold day, it's a mistake to say, "Pardon my glove." Although men need to remove their glove when shaking hands, women don't have to.

❖ ❖ ❖

Men also need to be careful when greeting a woman interviewer. Many women wear rings set with stones on their right hands. Etiquette expert Judith Martin writes, "On a scale between seeming wishy-washy and slicing off a woman's finger at the knuckle with her own diamond, a man should err toward the wishy-washy side."

The writer of the nationally syndicated "Miss Manners" column also suggests you adjust your pressure in response to the strength of the other person. So your squeeze can be in proportion to your partner's.

And when shaking hands with somebody who is handicapped, take the lead from that person. If you are offered an artificial limb or a left hand, remember to shake with your right hand. That's all you need to know. Shake whatever is offered to you.

But you don't always have to shake with your right hand. If someone is unable to shake with his right hand, offering your left hand is a thoughtful gesture.

❖ ❖ ❖

An interviewer's first impression about you is the one that sticks. When you make a good first impression, you create a halo effect. That's the term for when your interviewer makes an overall rosy evaluation of you based on a single outstanding personality trait observed during the first half of a minute of your meeting. When you achieve this halo effect, the good impression you've made will last throughout the interview, even if you botch it.

There are three things that will help you make a nice first impression. First, when you decide to get your hair cut or styled. Second, when your attitude, posture, and facial expression conveys you're pleased to be there. That is achieved by smiling as you meet and greet. And third, how you dress and carry yourself.

Appearance counts for over 50 percent of that initial impression. An interviewer is most comfortable when you match his idea of what a candidate should look like.

Remember, the first message you communicate is always about you. After you sit down to interview, it's about what you can do.

❖ ❖ ❖

CHAPTER 11

How to Turn Interviews into Job Offers

SIXTY-FOUR VALUABLE COACHING TIPS TO HELP YOU ACE ANY
INTERVIEW

1. How to Make Interviewing the Centerpiece of Your Search

Many of you show up for interviews feeling hopeless about the result. You think you'll automatically be disqualified for various reasons. Perhaps it's your age, lack of credentials, or gender.

You had better snap out of it. While you might feel hopeless in a given situation, you're certainly not helpless. No matter what your situation is, there is a job for you out there. It's the interviewing process that inevitably leads to a job.

In order to get it soon, you need to learn how to give good interviews. After all, a job interview is the centerpiece of a search. You're on center stage with an opportunity to strut your stuff. You'll give a virtuoso performance when you're well prepared.

The way to get ready is to do your homework. Preparation is a two-step process. First, learn what you can about the position in question. Second, decide how to link your skills to the requirements of the job. When you can do this preparation two-step, there's no need to fear being put on the spot while you're on stage.

This coaching vignette mentioned age as a possible concern. You'll feel more confident about the outcome of an interview when you realize that age can be can be a tremendous asset.

Studies show that older workers are more experienced, produce higher quality work, are more punctual, set an example for other employees, and love to be challenged.

2. Gain Self-Confidence with Two-Way Street Interviewing

Well don't just sit there, say something! Some interviewees think they just have to sit there and answer questions. Not so. Interviewing is a two-way street. It's a legitimate exchange of information between you and a prospective employer. You're expected to ask questions. That is why an interview is almost like a regular conversation.

While a social gabfest can amble across various topics that are unrelated, successful interview conversations do not. Both you and the interviewer need to stay on point. She wants to know how your background can benefit her department, and you want to show how your skills can do just that. You'll be more self-confident when you understand the interview is really a two-way exchange of information.

Let's say a fear of being turned down gives you some doubts. Then welcome to the club. Rejection is an inevitable part of the interviewing process.

Yet with each turndown, you become a better candidate because you learn more about the job marketplace and about yourself as a contender. When you understand that, you'll be more self-confident.

3. The Magic Power of Listening

You'll give great interviews when you think of them as regular conversations. Following the old safety advice to stop, look, and listen can help you remember that an interview is a give-and-take conversation.

You need to stop thinking about what you're going to say next. What you need to say will come to mind as it's needed. That will happen when you've rehearsed your interview lines and anecdotes beforehand.

You need to look at the interviewer, especially as you meet and greet. However, making eye contact with someone doesn't mean staring at her. You don't want to freak out a good job prospect. What you want to look for is the your interviewer's expression. Body language indicates how the interview is going. It's going well when your interviewer smiles, nods her head in agreement, or is taking notes.

Listening is the most important part of stop, look, and listen. Because you were born with two ears and only one mouth, you should listen twice as much as you talk.

Interviewers will like you more when you pay attention to what they're saying. That's because you're paying them the supreme compliment that their words are worth listening to.

4. It is better to know some of the questions than all of the answers.
—James Thurber

You must ask questions while interviewing for a job. Not doing so means you have the wrong idea about how to conduct an interview. You think an interview is a one-sided exchange. And that all you have to do is sit there like a dummy and avoid asking the prospective employer any questions.

An interview is a two-way street. While the interviewer is evaluating you, you should be evaluating the interviewer, along with the organization you're applying to. That's a valid reason for attending an interview—to evaluate the interviewer, the company, and the job. You need to determine if you want to work there even if the company makes an offer.

When you fail to ask questions, the interviewer will evaluate you as either unprepared or stupid. So you must ask them questions. Write down a list of questions in advance:

* "What are the duties and responsibilities of the job?"
* "To whom would I report?"
* "What do you expect me to accomplish during the first year?"
* "How will my performance be evaluated?"

Remember that the best way to make interviews an equal exchange of information is to ask questions.

5. You'll Impress Interviewers by Asking Questions.

When you think about your next interview as a legitimate exchange of information, you'll turn it into the two-way street an interview is supposed to be. So there's no need to be shy about questioning interviewers. They expect you to ask questions.

That is how to learn more about the job and what a prospective employer is looking for. Answers inform you about how to match your skills and accomplishments to an interviewer's needs. Bring a list of prepared questions to the interview. You'll find some examples in the previous coaching vignette.

There are two ways to get your questions across: asking them as the interview progresses, or waiting for the interviewer to throw you a cue. That usually happens when the interview is almost finished and you're asked if you have any questions. That's your cue to take out your list and fire away.

Interviewers will be impressed when you ask questions. You will demonstrate your interest in the job and company and show that you cared enough to do some homework.

By the way, when an interviewer asks a question, don't say, "That's a good question." It implies other questions asked by the prospect were not so hot.

6. Why Focusing on your Interviewer Gets Remarkable Results

When you're interviewing for a job, forget about the interview techniques you've learned. You need to focus on the two-way conversation an interview is. Trying to remember the right technique to use will prevent you from listening to the interviewer.

Attempting to carry techniques to an interview is akin to carrying a canoe on your back once you've paddled it to your campsite. The craft has served its purpose, so leave it on the riverbank.

Interviewing techniques are the scaffolding of interviews. When you go to them, it's time to remove the platform. The building is complete.

After you've learned a technique, you've gotten the message. Now hang up the phone.

Devices like telephones are aids. The biologist doesn't continually keep his eye glued to the microscope's eyepiece. He walks away and works on what he's seen.

When you've seen and memorized an interview technique that feels comfortable, it will come to your mind when you need it. But while you're interviewing for a job, forget about the tactics you've learned.

As psychologist B.F. Skinner said, "At this very moment we have the necessary techniques...to create a full and satisfying life."

7. Think of Interviews as Business Meetings

Interviews weren't invented so hiring managers could watch you squirm. Really. So why not just fill out an application instead? Knowing the answer to this question demystifies the interviewing process, leaving you feeling more relaxed about it.

Face-to-face meetings enable interviewers to decide whether to introduce you to hiring managers. To make this decision, they need to determine three things: if they like you, if you have what it takes to do the job, and if you'll fit in with the rest of the staff.

They can't learn those things from reading an application. You'll notice the first thing on an interviewer's mind is if she likes you. When you want to be hired, you must be liked. And to be liked, you must be seen.

We've already compared interviewing to a two-way street. While a company takes a look at you for the three reasons just mentioned, you get to take a look at them and also get to decide three things: if the job is a good fit, if you want to work with those people, and if the price is right. However, you might not learn about a salary range during the first interview.

When you think of interviewing as a business meeting where you and a company have the chance to size each other up, you might even get to enjoy the experience.

8. The Amazing Magic Formula for Interviewing

Where is it written that you must tolerate a hiring manager's obnoxious behavior during an interview? Nowhere! Interrogations can be tough enough without your having to sit there and take it from some corporate sleazebag.

On the slim chance that an interview turns that negative, there's a magic formula you can use as a defense. The formula will be introduced in a moment.

But first, keep in mind that an interview is a reciprocal situation. The hiring person gets to decide if he likes you, and you get to decide if you like him. When you don't, it's time to think about whether you want to work there, even if an offer is forthcoming.

So let's invent a situation where you're having a run-in with a repugnant hiring manager. You have several choices: you can ask the interviewer what the problem is, present your credentials again, or bolt for the door.

Bolting is a rational response to the irrational behavior of Mr. or Ms. Obnoxious. In that case, it's okay to assume you weren't liked. But sometimes it's hard to tell whether interviewers like or loathe you.

How likeable you are needn't be an issue. Your energies must be invested in doing your best each time, to match your credentials to the needs of an interviewer each time. Here's how to let not being liked roll off your back—apply the magic formula:

SW, SW, SW— – NEXT!

Translation: *Some will, some won't, so what— next!*'

On the slim chance that you run into a corporate thug or thugess who turns your interview into a nightmare, just go on to the next interview.

After all, job finding is a process of getting next interviews until you land.

9. Networking Is the Quick and Easy Way to Generate Interviews

There's only one way to be hired. You need to be interviewed. There's no way around it.

Methods used by most job hunters to get interviews include hopping on the Internet to check out job postings, answering classified ads in the papers, and applying to employment agencies and to executive recruiters. Although those are proven methods for being invited to interviews, they're the least effective.

Advertised jobs are like the tip of a titanic iceberg. Most job hunters aren't aware that, according to a Harvard University study, the vast majority of jobs—around 80 percent of them—lie below the surface. You cannot see those unadvertised jobs.

But you can tap into them by using networking techniques. Interact with people you know who can recommend you to their contacts. Networking has always been the most productive method of generating interviews for blue- and white-collar positions.

By all means, use all of the tactics at your disposal to obtain interviews. But spend at least 80 percent of your time networking in the hidden job market. That's where most of the action is.

By the way, there's a reason why networking is the quickest way to generate interviews: you often learn about job openings before they're advertised or posted.

10. The Value of Listening First, Talking Later

When an interviewer says, "Tell me about yourself," it's a mistake to make a blind presentation. Some of you talk incessantly about what you've done without knowing what the interviewer is looking for or what will get her excited about what you have to offer.

You'll arouse an interviewer's interest when you first discover what he wants. Then you can tell him how your skills fit the requirements of the job in question.

A nice way to uncover the needs of a prospective employer is to ask the interviewer, "What does this job require?" or "Would you please describe the ideal candidate?"

Let's imagine the interviewer responds by saying that customer service is a major requirement. Then you can focus on how you've interacted with customers.

After you've asked a prospect what she's looking for, be an active listener. That means giving 100 percent of your concentration to your interviewer as she speaks.

You make a horrible mistake when you talk incessantly about yourself or recite a memorized pitch about yourself. That is an inferior tactic—it's making a presentation without first learning the needs of a prospective employer.

11. Why You Shouldn't Leave Home without Job Specs

You'll be more relaxed at your next interview if you consider it just another business meeting. But there is a difference. Unlike a social conversation, an interview meeting takes planning.

You need to know what the job requires beforehand. Then you can demonstrate to the interviewer how you can deliver.

There are four easy ways to find out what an interviewer is looking for:

1. Check the classified ad or Internet posting you responded to. Job specifications are often listed there.
2. Check a company's Internet home page for job specs.
3. Ask the corporate or agency recruiter with whom you're setting up an interview for the job specifications.
4. Ask the interviewer to tell you what she's looking for.

When you know a job's requirements ahead of time, you'll be able to tell an interviewer what you think he wants to hear. That kind of preparation results in winning interviews.

You'll be more self-confident because you'll be able to show a prospective employer how you can help to fill a specific need. That will make you enthusiastic during your presentation.

It's your enthusiasm and presentation that results in job offers.

❖ ❖ ❖

12. A Proven Way to Improve Your Chances of Being Hired

Never be late for your interview date. You'll create the wrong impression when you're late. A prospective employer will become upset because you will have not only wasted his time, but you'll also be viewed as a candidate who is unreliable, not at all considerate, and disorganized.

To insure you get to an interview on time, arrive twenty minutes early. That will help you plan for the unexpected traffic jam or the train or bus delay. Arriving early with time to spare will let you collect yourself and relax a bit.

When you're not sure where the company is located or how long it'll take to get you there, make a dry run the weekend before. Then you'll know the location, the amount of time it takes to get there, and where to park. Circling around to find a parking space can make you late and can also give you an extra dose of stress you won't need before interviewing.

Also, bring along your contact's phone number. Then you can call ahead if you're delayed to explain the circumstances and, if necessary, to reschedule the interview.

Don't just fail to show up. It's a small world.

❖ ❖ ❖

Some job candidates have balked at the idea of arriving at an interview twenty minutes early. However, after I explained the tactic to them, it made sense to them for several reasons.

First, what if you experience heavy traffic? Or what if your train, subway, or bus has been delayed? The twenty-minute cover is your insurance for arriving on time.

Second, arriving early with twenty minutes to spare gives you the chance to calm down by doing a few things that'll help you make a better impression.

For example, when you're wearing an overcoat or a jacket, ask where a closet is located, and then hang your coat or jacket up. You want to look and feel like you're part of the company. That's hard to do while you're lugging part of your wardrobe into the interviewer's office.

Then ask for directions to the restroom. On the way, look around you to observe the surroundings and how employees dress and act.

And third, arriving early gives you another chance to research. Many corporations place brochures and portfolios in reception areas. They're chock-full of goodies like articles and publicity releases that can give you more ammunition for the interview.

Those are just three reasons why showing up twenty minutes early gives you both a head start and a leg up.

❖ ❖ ❖

13. You'll Make a Good First Impression When You Smile

The ancient Chinese said it: "A person without a smile should not open a shop." This is also special advice for job hunters and salespeople. Your smile tells prospects that you're happy to be there. There are various styles of smiles.

Take the polite smile. It's the one you give when your boss tries to make a joke. It involves only your lips, and they're usually tilted up on one side of your face.

There's the miserable grin-and-bear-it smile. That's the one you make when the interviewer says, "You're overqualified." Then your lips are pressed together with the lower lip pushed up.

And the unbecoming smile. It's called a smirk. It's when your lips are curled into a hostile smile.

Finally, there's the smile of joy. It involves your lips and the muscles around your eyes. Crinkling your eye muscles is a sign of joy. That's the smile that shows interviewers you're happy to be there.

To develop your interview smile, stand in front of a mirror and say, "cheese." Practice that smile all day. Then you'll automatically remember to bring your cheese to interviews.

❖ ❖ ❖

People will like you more when you put a smile on your face. Hiring managers want to recruit the candidate with whom they feel the most comfortable. Whenever you wear a smile, you're telling an interviewer that you're happy to be with her and that you like her.

Perhaps you're one of those job hunters who disagree. You think looking serious and nodding is more suitable to business than smiling. Not so. Nobody wants to hire a nodding bobblehead.

A smile is the simplest way to make a good first impression. That isn't to say that you must grin like an idiot throughout the interview. That, along with flashing a smile every once in a while, does look phony. So you need to develop a natural smile and make it a part of your life.

You'll cultivate the smile that's natural for you by remembering to smile all day. Then the corners of your mouth will automatically be turned upward at interviews. Smile at everyone you see—just for today. Most people will return your smiles. Sure, others might turn away. But hey, that's their problem.

Practice smiling on the telephone too. You'll sound a whole lot friendlier when you smile while you dial. That old song, "When You're Smiling," makes the point: "Keep on smiling, 'cause when you're smiling, the whole world smiles with you."

14. It's Not What You Say but How You Listen

There are times in your life when you don't want to miss the opportunity to shut up! Interview situations are one of those times.

After you make a point or answer a question, stop talking. Statements and answers to questions need to be short—no longer than sixty seconds, but shorter than that is better. Brevity is one of the keys when talking to a prospective employer or to a new business prospect.

The other key is listening. You need to spend at least 50 percent of your time listening at interviews. The benefits you get from listening are twofold:

You'll receive more information about a prospect's needs and will be able to present yourself accordingly. And when you listen more than you talk, you'll come across as a thoughtful and intelligent job candidate.

When you rehearse what to say along with how to respond to questions, the words you need to convey will automatically come to your mind when you're interviewing.

Here's how to acquire the skills of brevity—making a point in a minute or less—and listening: Practice them in everyday conversation. They will carry over during interviews.

You might not get the job just because you have experience, but experience gives you an advantage when you learn how to apply the two key tactics in communication: brevity and listening.

❖ ❖ ❖

You need to listen more than you talk because you were born with two ears and only one mouth. That means that God intended you to listen twice as much as you talk.

You'll make the best use of your two ears and one mouth by allowing the prospective employer to talk at least half of the time.

You can get the interviewer to talk by asking a few questions when the interview begins. You might lead off with by saying, "Would you mind describing the ideal candidate for this job?"

After you ask a question, stop and listen for the answer. That's how to catch the drift of what your prospective employer is looking for. Then you can talk about how your skills are a good fit for the job under discussion.

Whenever it's your turn to talk, keep your comment to a minute or less. Rehearse what you'll say, especially in response to questions you know you'll be asked. For example, you know the interviewer will ask why you want to work there and what you're strengths and weaknesses are, and she'll ask you to "Tell me about yourself?"

Because an interview is more of a listening than a talking session, a good way to give a good interview is to be a good listener.

❖ ❖ ❖

It's not what you say, but how you listen. Active listening is the first aid of interviewing. It helps you determine the needs of a prospective employer so you can help to fill them.

Active listening is when you concentrate on the speaker with your ears and eyes and your heart and soul. Its formula consists of four simple steps: **intention, listening, pausing**, and **reflecting**.

Before an interview conversation begins, confirm your **intention** to truly listen to what the interviewer has to say. Then act on that intention. It's not your job to solve their problem right away. You can do that later.

After listening to the speaker, **pause** before responding. You should remain silent a little longer than what you feel comfortable with. That shows interviewers that you've heard and understood what was said, and they'll like you more because you listened. After all, people want to be heard. As you listen actively, interviewers will feel they can open up to you. Consequently, they'll feel more connected to you.

After pausing, **reflect** back on what was said to you. You can repeat, "Oh, you're looking for TV news reporting skills." Then identify the speaker's needs by saying, "Then it must be important for the candidate to also offer street reporting along with the anchoring experience you advertised for. Would you tell me more about that?" Then listen some more. You'll pick up additional clues about what else the interviewer wants.

Now you can understand why God gave you two ears and only one mouth. It's so you'll listen twice as much as you speak. You can make this listening formula your own expression of interest by remembering it's not just what you say that gets you hired. It's how you listen.

❖ ❖ ❖

Many of you blow job offers because you're focused only on your needs. You think about getting only what you want. As a result, you talk only about you all of the time. When you do that, you become like one of those kids in class who compulsively keeps raising his hand.

You think you're giving a good interview by parading all of your knowledge at once. That's a brain dump. It's guaranteed to turn off your listener.

The way to arouse an interviewer's interest is to understand that any conversation, especially interviews, is give and take. Someone is always giving while the other is taking. You want to be the taker—the someone whose takes it all in. That's the trick to getting what you want—listening.

And you want to listen twice as much as you talk. Only then will you be able discover the speaker's needs. That enables you to target your responses to what a prospective employer is looking for.

So base your search on careful listening. When the interviewer talks, you listen. And listen with all of your heart and mind. That will give you time to figure out common interests, what the interviewer expects, and how to match your experience to those needs.

15. You Need to Know What's Required before You're Hired

Before you step inside an interviewer's office, you need to do two things. You need to discover what the job requires in order to match your skills to its specifications and uncover enough information about a company and its industry to demonstrate your interest not only in the job, but also in the company.

Where can you dig up this information? On the Internet and in a public library. A library is a cornucopia of corporate intelligence, and there are many ways to conduct your research in a library:

- Read back issues of your interviewer's trade journal. There, you'll get insights into hot issues and learn industry buzzwords. Then you can talk their language while interviewing.
- Research background information about a company in magazines and newspapers.
- Check out *Who's Who* to see if your interviewer is in it.
- Study annual reports to learn about a company's financial situation, a summary of the year's corporate events, and the introduction of

new products and services. The information you glean can help you answer the question, why do you want to work here?

Furthermore, when you know someone who works at the company you're researching, take that someone to lunch. Ask what's going on there, and request a copy of the company newsletter in order to learn what's new in the workplace.

Although you might not feel like doing so, it makes sense to spend time and effort to gather corporate intelligence. You'll impress interviewers with your knowledge about their companies. You'll boost your self-confidence. And doing homework can mean the difference between getting an offer or not.

16. How to Know When You're a Good Fit

Interviews are not about convincing hiring managers to hire you when they don't want to. Your prospects will feel manipulated. Interviews are about matching your skills to the requirements of a job. When you know what interviewers want, you can tell them what they want to hear. Then you'll be hired.

When an interview begins, feel free to ask these questions: "What are you looking for?" or "What's important to you about this job?" The answer will inform you about the criteria a prospective employer will use to make a hiring decision.

At that point, ask yourself whether you're a good fit for the job as it's been described. If you are, go for it. You have the information from the interviewer to demonstrate how you're the candidate she's been looking for. To quote an old advertising slogan, "When you got it, flaunt it."

What happens when you believe you don't have it—when your skills aren't a good fit for the job? Be the first to break off the conversation. You can say, "I don't think my background can help you at this time," or, "Is there anyone else at this company with whom you think I should be talking?"

To repeat the point we began with, prospective employers will feel manipulated when you try to convince them to hire you when they don't want to. That is why it's so important to get information upfront. In fact, it's the most important part of an interview.

When you believe your skills are a good match, flaunt them. And interviewers will want to hire you.

17. How Debriefing Will Improve Your Interview Performance

You need to debrief yourself after an interview. Then if your interview bombed, you can ask yourself what went wrong and how you might execute it differently the next time at bat.

A post-interview debrief enables you to snatch some victory from the jaws of defeat. That's because it will keep you from repeating the same interview boo-boo over and over again.

You can even rectify some interview mistakes after the interview has ended. Let's say you forgot to present an important selling point. You have a second chance to do so in a follow-up letter or e-mail.

Although interviews aren't dress rehearsals, you'll blunder less by interviewing for some jobs you don't want. Then you can make your mistakes and fix them before interviewing for the jobs you'd die for.

You needn't worry about sabotaging yourself by making mistakes. Blunders give you the experience you need to give better performances.

Oscar Wild said it well: "Experience is the name everyone gives to mistakes."

18. The Fantastic Results of Writing Follow-Up Letters and E-Mails

Just because you forgot to say some of the things you rehearsed, don't whack yourself on the side of the head. You gave it your best shot. So chill out. Besides, leaving something that you had rehearsed out of an interview is par for the course.

You always give three interviews: the interview you rehearsed, the presentation you gave, and—oh my gosh—the interview you wish you'd given. Instead of replaying your mistakes, make some notes.

After leaving the interview, write down who said what, what was hot and what was not, and your plans for following up. Plans should always include writing a thank-you letter within three days after an interview. The notes you've made contain all of the material you'll need for writing that letter or e-mail.

Following through in writing gives you a second chance to present new material. That's the stuff you inadvertently forgot to say. Your letter can be based on this five-point list:

1. Thank the interviewer for his time and interest.
2. State your interest in the job and give reasons why you're interested.
3. Emphasize and repeat your strong points.
4. Clear up muddy areas of the interview.
5. Ask for the job.

Writing a post-interview letter or e-mail is part of interviewing protocol. Besides that, it gives you a leg up over competitors who fail to follow up. That will include practically all of the contenders for the job you want.

A written follow-up also keeps your name in front of prospects when they're deciding who will get the offer.

❖ ❖ ❖

You might think an interviewer is holding on to your every word. That's not always the case. When two people are conversing, it's perfectly normal for both minds to wander from time to time.

Because we're more focused while reading, the best way to get an interviewer's full attention is in writing. An effective interview follow-up letter can be created in about five paragraphs.

You should begin your letter by thanking the prospect for her time and interest and by expressing appreciation for the opportunity of meeting her to discuss the job you're pitching for.

Based on post-interview notes you've taken (which are discussed in the previous coaching vignette), repeat the interview's positive points in the second paragraph. Those facts will explain how your skills match the job specifications. Your positives might fill two paragraphs.

Anything you forgot to mention can be stated in the third graph. That is also the time to clear up a misunderstanding or negative impression you might have left.

In the final paragraph, be sure to tell your reader how much you want the job and why you want it.

Mail your letter or send an e-mail within several days after the meeting. Nobody gives a perfect interview. But writing a follow-up letter gives you a chance to improve the one you gave.

19. A Tested Method of Preparing for Your Next Interview

You'll go bonkers at interviews if you try to remember everything you've learned about the subject. A terrific way to keep your cool while preparing for interviews is to work with the acronym "KEEP." It's a method Bob Cuddy, an executive coach, has used for years while training executives on how to interview.

As Cuddy explains it, *K* stands for knowledge, *E* means experience, the second *E* signifies enthusiasm, and the *P* is for presentation. "Most people applying for the same job have the same background," says the Connecticut-based executive coach. "So what separates you from other applicants is the second *E* and the *P*—enthusiasm and presentation."

The acronym KEEP is all you need to know to prevent yourself from going bonkers during interview preparation. Let's take a moment to examine it.

When you have **k**nowledge about the company and the job it's offering and can match the position's requirements with your **e**xperience, you'll automatically be **e**nthusiastic about what you have to offer. As a result, your enthusiasm will come across at interviews.

"Enthusiasm is a gift you can develop by practicing KEEP," Cuddy says. "It's the way to come alive at interviews."

20. Enthusiasm Is Contagious

"You can do anything if you have enthusiasm," wrote American industrialist Henry Ford. "Anything" includes your ability to give winning interviews when you're blessed with enthusiasm.

You might think being enthusiastic is just about being animated. Not so. You can turn off animation in an instant. Well, if enthusiasm isn't animation, what is it? The dictionary defines enthusiasm as "intense and eager enjoyment." So "enthusiasm" is based on a reaction that comes from within because it springs from a belief you hold about something.

You'd better believe in your skills and accomplishments, because interviewers are not impressed when the mind of a candidate is full of self-doubt. You need to impress yourself first by learning how to talk about your skills and accomplishments. The more enthusiasm you can discuss them with, the more enthusiastic the interviewer will become about hiring you.

The anonymous quote "enthusiasm is contagious" applies here. Why not start an epidemic as you progress through the interviewing process?

21. How to Make an Awesome First Impression

The most important part of the interview is the first impression you make. That happens during the first twenty seconds of meeting your prospect.

When you make a good first impression, a halo effect is created. That means the good impression you've made will last throughout the interview—even if you botch it. You can imagine that invisible ring of light hovering over your head and staying with you all through the interview.

It's important that you dress properly. Studies show that appearance counts for over 50 percent of that initial impression. An interviewer will be most comfortable when you match her idea of what a candidate should look like.

After all, how would you feel if a job seeker you were interviewing for a customer service job showed up in a T-shirt and jeans? What if he showed up in an acceptable interview outfit—like a blue suit—with wrinkles? Or wearing a white shirt with a ring around the collar?

You need to wear the proper interview outfit in order to create an excellent first impression. If your specialty doesn't require a suit, dress your best for the environment.

If you can't be bothered to show up at interviews dressed for success, employers will conclude you're lazy—and sloppy. If that's the case, someone else will be hired.

❖ ❖ ❖

There's a reason the most important part of your interview is the first thirty seconds: that's all the time it takes to make a good first impression.

The first perception an interviewer has about you is the one that sticks. If it's a good one, you couldn't botch the rest of the interview, even if you tried. The reason? You've created the halo effect.

A halo effect is when your interviewer makes an overall rosy evaluation of you—and it's based on a single outstanding personality trait your prospect observed during the first half of a minute of your meeting.

Making a nice first impression starts before you shake hands and introduce yourself. You start producing it well ahead of an interview when you decide to get your hair cut or styled and how you will dress and carry yourself. Also, your attitude, posture, and facial expression need to convey you're pleased to be there.

Getting to your interview twenty minutes early can also help you make a good first impression. You won't arrive in a state of panic, and you can be yourself.

Remember that the first message you communicate is always about you.

22. How to Stand Apart from the Job-Hunting Robots

Job candidates who are professionally coached and well rehearsed all sound alike. So how do you compete with them? Instead of trying to outdo those interviewing robots, let your real self shine.

Your inner light will glow when you show prospective employers that you love your work and are well suited to it. Hiring managers want results. They know the value of employees who are matched to their jobs. Studies show that workers who fit the bill offer supervisors three huge benefits: they produce better results, are motivated by the work, and need less supervision.

Hiring managers also need to predict the future. Your task is to help them do that by clarifying the work they really want you to do and then demonstrating how you'll provide the best return for a prospect's investment.

Here's how to stand apart from the job-hunting robots: reassure an interviewer you are the best possible choice for the position because you like it and are a perfect fit.

23. Perfect Your Interviewing Technique with This Powerful Method

A good job is hard to find even when the economy is booming. So in any job market, you must convince prospective employers that you fit the given job well.

You can't do that by walking in cold and hoping for the best. You need to sharpen your interviewing skills. One way to do so is to select examples of what you've done and practice talking about them.

Where will you find some cases in point? Your wonderful accomplishments are listed in bullet points on your résumé. They can tell you what you've done and the results. Have you initiated a project, generated new clients, or handled a conflict? Talk about that at interviews.

But first, you must rehearse. The way to practice talking about each accomplishment is to describe what you did and the result. Then use the video camera in your cell phone to analyze your performance.

This process of perfecting your interviewing technique will also help you overcome self-doubt. Your self-esteem is linked to the work you do, so when that work goes down the drain, your self-worth often flows along with it.

Reinforcing how good you are is vital to the success of upcoming interviews. When you can talk with enthusiasm about the contributions you've made in past jobs and their results, hiring managers will be convinced you're a good fit and be motivated to hire you.

24. Use This Icebreaker at Interviews and Networking Meetings

No wonder your knees tremble when you interview and your heart thumps during business meetings and conventions. Those are the scariest ways to meet people. Surrounded by strangers, you're armed only with a résumé or a pocketful of business cards. But when you know how to break the ice, meeting new people will be a piece of cake.

An icebreaker is a brief introduction that tells who you are and what you do. For example, "Hi, I'm Deloris Dooley, a copywriter who convinces target audiences to buy products." That icebreaker told who Deloris is and what she does in about six seconds.

Before the next meeting that's related to your search, prepare a single-sentence introduction. Then time how long it takes you to deliver it. You risk losing a listener's attention if your introduction runs over ten seconds.

When you intend to use an icebreaker at networking meetings, don't cling to people you already know for security. They won't give you business. You're there to meet new contacts who will.

Whether you're attending a network meeting or an interview, walk over to your prospect, extend your hand, and deliver your icebreaker. Then show interest in the person and his businesses—or in the job you're being interviewed for.

And don't be a toucher. To reach out and touch someone after shaking hands is unprofessional. It can also be a sensitive issue for women and men. Besides, who wants to be squeezed on the shoulder or slapped on the back?

25. Make a Winning Impression by Creating a New You for the Interview

Maybe you're not getting job offers because you insist on just being yourself at interviews. Get real. You need to sell. But instead of thinking about making a sale, you rely on just being you—and then wonder why you're not getting hired.

You think "selling" means "faking it." And that's not what you're all about. But the real you is the person who sometimes gets angry at the wrong moment, makes inappropriate statements, and puts your foot in your mouth. This is just one of the reasons why you need to create a new you for the interview.

Recreating yourself is no big deal when you understand what self-marketing is all about. Figure out what you want prospective employers to think after they've met you, and then communicate it. Now you've created the new character you want others to see all of the time.

Actors make careers out of recreating themselves while taking on new roles for TV, movies, and the theater. You've done it, too. Haven't you created a new you in order to make a winning impression on a first date? That's selling! If you created yourself that well at interviews, you'd be working already.

Create the new you right now. Write down what you want an interviewer to think after having met you, and then act it every moment. The role you've taken on will become a habit in the twinkling of an eye.

What's more, you won't need to turn it on just for interviews. You'll already be the new you who is about to get hired.

❖ ❖ ❖

There's another reason you need to create a new you for the interview. You'll no longer be hired just because you've been there and done that. The old premise that supported most hiring in the past is no longer a factor. It was the skills to fill illusion that your prior experience qualifies you for a similar position.

In today's fast-changing business world, you'll be offered a job because of what you're capable of learning and willing to try. That kind of information doesn't leap out from the pages of your résumé. Nor does it fit into a little box on an application form. You need to sell these personality factors at interviews.

All candidates competing for the same job are qualified to do it, yet no two applicants are alike because of their personal qualities. There are four personal traits that can make you stand apart from others:

1. Empathy for others
2. Taking initiative
3. Respect for deadlines
4. Emotional stability

Many hiring managers consider this tetrad of personal traits to be 85 percent of a prospective employee's success equation.

You need to express these qualities at interviews because you're résumé won't express them.

26. Why Knowing the Three Legs of an Interview Tells You Where You Stand

You'll seldom be hired after a single interview with a corporation. If the first interviewer likes you, there's a good chance you'll be invited to interact with as many as a half of a dozen other decision makers.

The way to ace those interviews is to think of the series as a tripod firmly supported by three legs and to know which leg you're standing on.

The first leg is usually, but not always, with human resources (HR). They're the top dog, and you're the underdog. The HR recruiter will try to screen you out in order to submit a small number of potential candidates to a hiring manager. Consequently, she's not your friend. Your objective is to be one of the candidates who are referred.

Now you're standing on the second leg. You can expect to have one or more interviews with potential bosses and colleagues. Although they're still the top dog and you're the underdog, you can begin to take control.

Most hiring managers haven't been trained in how to interview candidates. For that reason, they would rather be doing their own jobs than talking to you. Some might feel as nervous as you do. You can put them at ease by guiding the conversation when necessary. They'll like you for that.

Employers hire people they like. So when you're liked, you'll have a good shot of being invited to the third leg—the offer interview. That's when a company, having decided it wants you, makes you an offer. You're expected to negotiate.

While you're working on first two legs, go for the job. Talk about how much you want the position while trying to avoid conversations about salary, vacation, and benefits. The time to go for them is when you're on the third leg.

27. Create a Cover Story to Explain Why You're Looking for Work

When you're asked why you left your last job, you'd better have a cover story prepared. Prospective employers tend to be suspicious about why you're out looking, so they want to screen out problem employees.

When you're unprepared to answer why you're looking for work, a red flag is raised in the interviewer's mind. This coaching vignette and the one that follows it will show you how to create a cover story.

When your exit was through no fault of your own, tell the truth. You can explain how you were one of many employees who lost their jobs when the company downsized. Similarly, you can tell interviewers if your job was outsourced to Indiana and you chose not to move there.

On the other hand, if you needed to get out of a bad situation at work, put a positive spin on your move. Say you went as far as you could at your company and are looking for a position that provides new challenges with room for growth.

But you must perform damage control if you were fired. Ask your firing manager to support a cover story that you mutually agree on. If the creep refuses to help, simply remind your interviewer that you left to find a job that makes better use of your talents. That positions your ex-boss, not you, as the problem. You can further support your position by supplying references from friendly supervisors.

A well-crafted cover story designed to assure interviewers that you left a job for valid reasons will move your interview smoothly over this impediment.

❖ ❖ ❖

Prospective employers want to know why you're in the job market. Because they need to screen out problematic candidates, you need to assure them that you left, or are leaving, for valid reasons.

You'll be prompted to give an accounting of yourself when interviewers pop one of the following questions:

- Are you still working for the Awesome Agency?
- What happened to your job at Awesome?
- What brings you here?
- Why are you out looking?

The answer to any one of those questions is your cover story. Because a cover story needs to sound positive—even when it isn't—you don't want to say that you're out looking because you cannot stand your boss.

Answers need to explain plausible reasons that you're looking for work. A cover story should be based on the facts about why you're searching.

For example, have you gone as far as you can in the current job? Then make that your cover story by explaining that you want to move to a larger company that will provide more challenges with room for growth.

Was your job outsourced? Then make it clear that the position was moved to Bangalore and that you need to find another job.

Was your entire department downsized due to a redundancy caused by a merger? Then spell out your cover story: "Due to Awesome's recent merger with the Unimpressive Company and its subsequent downsizing, mine was one of the hundreds of jobs eliminated. So I'm looking for another opportunity where I can continue doing what I love."

While you might need to embellish its details, remember to base your cover story on the facts about why you're in the job market.

28. Four Showstoppers Guaranteed to Break an Interview Deal

Some of the comments job hunters make are guaranteed to turn off prospective employers. A typical showstopper is beginning your sentence with the expression, "I'll be honest with you." That gives your listener the impression that everything else you've said has been dishonest.

For the same reason, don't lead off with the word "frankly," or your listener might think everything else you said was not so candid. And when you're talking to a prospect on the telephone, don't ever ask, "Would you mind spelling your name?" The person on the other end might take that as an insult.

Dale Carnegie wrote, "A man's name is to him the sweetest and most important sound in any language." So if you don't know how John Caddiccilpo spells his last name, don't ask him. You should call back and ask someone in HR, the receptionist, or the company operator.

Then there's this telephone showstopper: "Hold on while I get something to write with." Oy vey! Besides being uncool, that statement can cause a listener to lose interest or even hang up. Prospective employers know that a good candidate is a prepared candidate. You should always have a pen and paper or a live computing device at the ready.

Look, I'll be honest with you. Frankly, asking how to spell someone's name or saying "hold on while I get a pencil" are just a few things job candidates say that are really pea brained.

29. Why Keeping It Simple Is the Approved Way to Interview

You've heard the acronym "KISS." The letters stand for **k**eep **i**t **s**imple, **s**tupid or **k**eep **i**t **s**imple, **s**weetheart. However you prefer to say it, keep your responses to interview questions simple.

Too many job hunters are like big pitchers of water. They're so eager to say everything they know that they pour out all of their information on the poor listener. That's known as a "brain dump."

Your listener's mind can retain only so much. You need to think of an interviewer as a six-ounce cup. When you answer questions or give examples of your achievements, respond briefly. A half of a minute to a minute will do nicely.

You'll be able to keep your responses to interview questions simple by giving just the facts that apply to what your interviewer wants to know. Then stop talking.

Your listener will usually jump in to resume the conversation. But if your pause is met by silence, say, "Does that answer your question?" or, "Shall I move on to the next point?" When you're talking to a job prospect or even writing a letter, remember the word KISS. The acronym can also stand for **k**eep **i**nterview **s**tatements **s**hort.

30. How Using Positive Words Achieves Remarkable Results

You'll conduct a more successful search when you communicate with positive words. "I want the job" is a positive statement. It makes a much better impression on interviewers than saying, "It seems like yours is the kind of position I might consider." Yet that's what most job candidates say.

Studies show that listeners and readers react more favorably to affirmative language. So when you use positive words in cover letters and during phone conversations and interviews, you come across as a confident person with a can-do attitude—exactly the kind of candidate companies love to hire.

Some Eastern philosophies say our minds are like batteries with positive and negative charges. Positive thoughts attract people, while negative ones repel them. Well, it's hard to think positively if you're out of work and worried about paying the mortgage. Despite that, you can choose to use positive words in order to attract positive thoughts and results.

Let's say that you accept what those ancient sages tell us about our minds being able to attract and repel depending on our thoughts and the words we use. If you do, then choosing positive words during your search can attract and impress the right people and situations.

31. Beginners Can Use This Handy Device to Get Interviewing Experience

The more you interview, the easier it gets. "It takes about six interviews to reach your peak," says Bob Cuddy, the Connecticut-based career coach we met earlier in this chapter. "Only then do you have your story down well enough to sound enthusiastic and knowledgeable."

But you needn't feel inadequate if you're a beginner or haven't interviewed for a while. "There is a shortcut," Cuddy says. "And that's recording yourself answering typical interview questions."

What kinds of questions should you rehearse into a recording device? "They can run the gamut from what type of job are you interested in, what have you done in the past that you enjoyed the most, and what type of things did you perform in your last job; to tell me about yourself, what are your strengths and weaknesses, and what do you want to be doing five years from now?" Cuddy says. He also suggests that if you listen to the recording about two days later "you'll hear yourself just as an interviewer would."

Remember that the more you interview, the easier it gets, and the better you get. Beginners can get that experience right now by recording their answers. "Then you'll have the background necessary to go out on interviews."

32. Yes, It's Okay to Use First Names Much of the Time

The days are long gone when it was considered taking a liberty to call somebody you've just met by his first name. While it has become conventional to use first names, it's still considered rude in some business and social circles.

Socially, using a first name can make a sham out of friendship and equality. You shouldn't use a first name with your parents, when you haven't been introduced to a person, or with someone holding a title like senator, representative, governor, or judge.

In business, you'll feel comfortable using "Mr." in a formal office setting. When the meeting becomes more informal, it's fine to begin using first names. This is true especially after a person suggests it. If you're not sure, use "Mr." or "Ms." When a woman is wearing a wedding band, use "Mrs."

While it's true that you need to create instant rapport when you introduce yourself on the phone and at interviews, there's no such thing as instant intimacy. For that reason, you need to use good judgment when contemplating the use of a first name.

It's always nice to be on a first-name basis whenever possible. By doing so, you create intimacy along with friendship and a quicker bond. Also, using a first name puts you on the same level, not beneath, the person you greet.

33. How to Turn Long-Term Employment into a Benefit

If your interview skills have rusted because you've been on the same job for the past twenty years, don't worry about it. Congratulate yourself instead. Your longevity shows prospective employers you are a loyal and committed worker. That's what they're looking for these days.

Until chopping heads became the name of the game, having many jobs was considered a plus. Not so today. Companies have second thoughts about losing employees with valuable experience, and interviewers want to hire applicants who they think will stick around awhile.

That's the reason a job candidate who has been with the same outfit for a long time often has a better chance of landing than someone with just more interviewing experience. That person has not been working as steadily as you have. Besides, they'll be just as anxious as you are while they're giving their interview performance.

The only way to eliminate interview anxiety is to go out and do it a half dozen times. Sure, you'll be uncomfortable at first. But just knowing you survived many years on the same job will mean less interview stress. You'll have the self-confidence that comes from knowing this.

Then you'll be able to tell prospective employers about your old-fashioned record of commitment and loyalty to just one company. That's exactly what they want to hear.

34. You'll Nail Down Interviews by Showing Samples of Your Work

You might be able to talk the talk. But you won't nail down interviews unless you can prove you can walk the walk. That's easy to do. Just bring samples of your work—things you accomplished at previous jobs—to the next interview.

Managers can bring memos and printouts of e-mails that show leadership skills. Engineers might show pictures and plans of their projects. When a job requires writing skills, bring samples of letters and presentations you've written. And for a sales position, come with a copy of that winning proposal you wrote, along with letters of commendation and testimonials. This is how lawyers win cases. They gather objects as evidence to prove a fact is true.

Your evidence may be composed of samples that prove you've already done what you talked about doing. Put your evidence in an inexpensive presentation folder. You can buy one at any office supply store.

At the interview, do a show and tell, but in reverse order. Tell first, and then show. The showing is evidence that you not only talk the talk, but can also walk the walk.

35. A Good Way to Handle the Issue of Being Overqualified

When an interviewer says, "You are overqualified," bells and whistles should erupt in your head. "Overqualified" is often a code word that indicates some kind of prejudice. There could be a bias against your age, size, gender, or the color of your skin.

When a deceitful interviewer sticks the overqualified label on you, it's only an objection, so try not to take the comment at face value. As a matter of fact, you should learn to welcome objections. Your job is to help the interviewer feel less worried about making a hiring decision.

A fitting response is to ask, "What do you mean by 'overqualified'?" That invites conversation. Overqualified might simply mean your interviewer thinks you have so much experience that you might become bored and quit.

In that case, you can say to the prospective employer, "If you're worried about my being challenged in this job, in all of the positions I've held, I always stayed and made my own challenges by seeking extra projects and responsibilities."

You can also expand on that theme by explaining how much you love challenges. Then give an example of how well you performed when challenged.

36. You Can Put a Positive Spin on Having Been Fired

It's painful to admit you've been fired. So never use the *f* word unless you have been. "Fired" means you were given the boot because of a shabby performance.

Because most of you were victims of a downsizing, there's no need to say you were fired. Your job was eliminated. If you were asked to resign, you resigned. And that's all there is to it.

But some interviewers—the kind who love to watch you squirm— might throw in a zinger by asking if you've ever been fired. Let's say you were dismissed for a cause at some point in your career. Take responsibility for it. You can explain how you've grown from the experience and how happy you are that the difficult times are behind you. Be sure to talk about your victories since the firing.

If you were just fired, try putting a positive spin on it. You can talk about contributions you made to that job. Remember to keep your answer brief. A minute or less will do nicely.

And do not bad-mouth your boss or your coworkers. Even if you have good reasons to talk against some sleaze ball you worked for or with, remember that no matter how true, dissing others reflects poorly on you.

37. Why You Should Welcome Objections to Your Candidacy

You'll find it easier to close an interview deal after discovering how you measure up to other candidates being considered for the same spot—and how the interviewer feels about your candidacy.

A good time to get this competitive information is toward the end of each interview. That's when you're usually asked if you have any questions.

After you ask about the job itself—its duties and responsibilities, what you'd be expected to accomplish, and to whom you'd report—you'll also want to know how you compare to other candidates. You can ask, "Am I a candidate?" and even, "How do I compare to the candidates you've interviewed so far?"

You'll get answers that can help you close the sale. Let's face it. Whenever you buy something that costs a lot of money, you think of reasons for not buying it. So why shouldn't interviewers have some concerns about buying your services, which also cost a lot of money?

That is why it makes good selling sense to get the objections on the table. That way, you can address any concerns then and there or in the obligatory follow-up letter. Either way, objections are really requests for more information. They're not invitations to argue.

Interviews are the beginning, not the end, of the hiring process. Prodding for objections and competitive information informs you about your competitive standing—and about what kind of additional evidence you need to present to convince the interviewer you should be the company's first choice.

38. The Value of Telling Stories at Interviews

You risk putting interviewers to sleep by reciting dull facts about yourself. The way to keep them awake and interested is to give examples of your achievements.

"Telling stories is one of the ways we connect with people who buy products or services," says Marcia Reynolds, a Phoenix, Arizona–based motivational speaker and career coach. "Most interviewers just want you to get to the point right away," Reynolds continues. "When you tell a long story to someone who wants brevity, their eyes will glaze over, and they won't hear you."

How long should anecdotes be? "Distill what you're saying to the essence and get to the point right away." In today's world of television sound bites, less is best when telling stories and answering questions.

An anecdote can be about a successful work experience and the result you achieve. For example, you could talk about how you saved your department money by streamlining a procedure or designed a new website that increased the number of hits by 70 percent.

Marcia Reynolds advises never belittling yourself for not having enough experience to come up with anecdotes. "Even if you're only twenty, there are always some successful experiences you can relate."

❖ ❖ ❖

Job candidates with the best communications skills win. That's true even when you're up against someone who is somewhat better qualified.

Just think back to when you applied to colleges. Applicants who list extracurricular high school activities have the edge over strictly academic students. Activities show you have a personality that lets you communicate and get along with all kinds of people.

To communicate in the job marketplace, learn how to talk about your activities in past jobs. You've already listed them as achievements on your résumé. Select the activities that apply to the job in question, and then discuss them as anecdotes.

Give each story a beginning, a middle, and an end. The beginning is when you introduce the situation. The middle of your story is about what you contributed to the company. The end is the result of your contribution—like how much money you saved the company, the percentage of user increase, or the reward you received for leading a project. Your anecdotes should be presented in a minute or less. Learn them well.

There is no substitute for a good performance at interviews. It's the trademark of a successful job candidate.

39. Helpful Hints on Answering "Are You a Team Player?"

You have been hoodwinked about having to be a team player. That's why you shy away from talking about yourself at interviews. Instead of saying, "I wrote a report," you say, "We wrote a report." What's this "we" business? Do you plan to bring former colleagues to your interviews?

Although the words "team player" have been trendy for a long time, they've also been overdone. "Are you a team player?" is a lame-brained question. You're certainly not going to answer "no."

It's true that you're often part of a team. However, you've been brainwashed into thinking that taking any credit is a no-no. And that's nonsense. A team is a group of people who play on the same side. Teams need stars—slam dunkers who score. And teams also need followers—members who pass the ball around and let someone else take the shot.

So whenever you interview, take credit for your accomplishments in the team effort. Then describe the activity's result. You can say, "I designed a program for a new system that saved the company a million dollars." If you didn't design the entire program, talk about the part you did design.

Either way, it's not "we designed." Employers are hiring you.

40. Selling Is about Telling

Until you sell yourself to a prospect, you are going to stay unemployed. But many job hunters who lack sales backgrounds are turned off by the very thought of having to sell. What a predicament. You gotta sell yourself, but selling repels you,

The way out of this dilemma is to think not in terms of selling, but of telling. You need to tell your story. However, it's best to avoid talking only in terms of your background. Monotonous monologues put listeners to sleep.

Interviewers want to hear how you can help them. You must discover their needs before doing so. Then you'll have earned the right to tell about applicable accomplishments and their related benefits.

By way of a hypothetical example, let's say a major television network is looking for a sales trainer with experience in broadcast sales to boost lagging advertising revenue. One of the applicants, Betty, is a sales training professional. Betty talks about how she designed and presented a sales training program to the twelve-member sales staff of a major TV station in Chicago. The program increased its sales by 27 percent.

In a nutshell, selling yourself is telling about yourself in ways that show how you can help solve the needs of an employer.

41. Why You Should Never Bad-Mouth Your Boss

Do not bad-mouth your former boss. Not ever. Especially during interviews when you're asked this sneaky question: "So, you worked for John Sullivan at Acme. What do you think of him?"

A new business prospect asked this writer that very question about the manager of a broadcast organization where we had both worked. I answered affirmatively in a positive way because the manager was a wonderful person with whom I got along. "Had you not liked him," the interviewer responded, "I wouldn't have hired you, because [the manager] is one of my best friends."

But what if your boss was a creep? If you tell the truth about the weasel, you will have shot yourself in the foot. The interviewer might think you have a problem with authority. So when asked to rate a previous employer, make nice. Talk only about someone's strengths. Everyone has something good you can say about him.

And what if your interviewer knows that you and the old boss didn't get along? Stay away from using the term "personality conflict," or you'll become known as the personality-conflict kid and never get an offer.

Instead, use this three-step process for successfully handling the question:

1. Explain that because you and your boss had different work styles, you're now looking for an opportunity where your values will be more appreciated.

2. Then add, "I'm sure I'll never have to be in that same situation again."

3. Finally, explain what you learned by saying, "I grew from that experience as I acquired a knowledge of --"

Prospective employers will appreciate this answer because if you're hired, they'll know you won't bad-mouth them either.

42. How You Can Use Evidence to Enhance Interviews

You'll ace the interview by demonstrating some of your achievements visually. To "demonstrate" means to make clear by showing evidence of what you've done.

Let's say your interviewer is looking for excellent written communications skills. You can talk about how well you match that requirement and then show your interviewer a sample of your writing.

Be creative with what you include in your interviewing portfolio. Have you written a letter that got results? Slip it into your portfolio. How about that inspiring memo you wrote? Show that to your interviewer, too.

Bring along anything else that visually demonstrates your value. That could be letters of commendation and awards you received. If an award happens to be a plaque, take a picture of it and include it in your bag of tricks.

As a job hunter or career changer, you are a product that needs to be marketed. All products can demonstrate visually at least one customer benefit. When you're armed with visual evidence that proves your value, you're more likely to be remembered and hired.

Studies show people remember what they see 60 percent more completely than what they just hear. That explains why visual aids are such a powerful tool for communicating ideas more effectively.

❖ ❖ ❖

A job candidate was asked, "If your boss were here, what would he say about you?" The candidate showed the interviewer a letter from his boss. It praised the job applicant's work.

That visual demonstration impressed the interviewer a lot more than anything the job hunter could have said. Recent research shows that visual communication is more powerful than verbal communication. People retain information presented to them visually better than they retain information presented just verbally.

That is why you need to bring some visual material to your next interview. You can buy an inexpensive presentation binder at an office supply store. Then when the interviewer says, "Tell me about yourself," you can talk about how you designed a new reporting system that saved your company money. Remember to support your point by showing the questioner samples of your work.

What kind of evidence can you show? The proposal you wrote for creating the reporting system. The form you designed for it. And the e-mail from your boss, thanking you for a job well done.

You will stand out from competitors when you demonstrate your achievements with visual materials.

43. To Brag or Not to Brag—That Is the Question

Job-hunting advice from an expert in mathematics? Get outta here! On second thought, why not? Mathematician G.H. Hardy wrote, "Good work is not done by humble men."

You'd be well advised to apply Hardy's words to your next interview. Winning interviews are not achieved by being humble. To sell yourself for a job, you have to brag—but not at first. Like a musician, you need to build to a crescendo.

Your interview should start on a conservative note. That can be accomplished during the first half of a minute. That's all the time it takes to make a good first impression. Then build rapport with your interviewer during the small talk that follows the introductions.

And when you begin talking about yourself—what you've accomplished at work and the results—brag about it. When you don't think you are the greatest thing since sliced bread, your interview won't be worth even half a loaf.

Finding a new job or career is all about tooting your own horn. Because if you don't toot it, no one else will.

❖ ❖ ❖

You are perplexed about boasting at interviews because you were taught it's a virtue to be humble. What a paradox. When you're proud to be humble, you've lost it.

The question about boasting at interviews versus acting humbly is not just a cultural issue. English poet Thomas Stearns Elliot wrote, "Humility is the most difficult of all the virtues to achieve; nothing dies harder than the desire to think well of oneself."

Well, if you don't think well of yourself, who will? People of great achievement are expected to be humble. Mac Davis addressed this conflict when he sang

> Oh, Lord, it's hard to be humble
> When you're perfect in every way
> I can't wait to look in the mirror
> 'Cause I get better lookin' each day.

You'll strike the right balance between humility and boasting by strutting your stuff in an unpretentious way. The rule of the game is to talk about an accomplishment with pride and enthusiasm, and then to end by explaining what you learned.

It all comes down to what Walt Whitman wrote about boasting: "If you done it, it ain't bragging."

❖ ❖ ❖

The ideal solution to the problem of bragging is getting others to broadcast your achievements. Then all you have to do is handle the humility part. That's easy to do if you're a big shot CEO or a famous actor. Then you can get the media to boast for you.

But how can a humble and unknown job hunter can get others to do her boasting? It's easy. You can do it with visuals. Collect letters of reference, commendation, and recommendation from satisfied customers and former employers. Present those letters, along with samples of your work, at interviews. Visuals are part of the interview portfolio.

Remember that a useful approach is to talk about an accomplishment with enthusiasm and pride, to show a visual that supports the achievement, and to act humbly by explaining what you learned.

But don't act too proud. English poet and philosopher Samuel Taylor Coleridge expressed it very well in his poem "The Devil's Thoughts":

"And the Devil did grin, for his darling sin
Is pride that apes humility."

❖ ❖ ❖

"Oh, Lord, it's so hard to be humble" while selling at interviews. That's because self-marketing is boasting. You can't get away from that. But another technique called "Artful Boasting" can help you solve the problem.

Artful boasting combines selling yourself with acting humble. The usual variety of false humility disgusts potential employers and bosses. That's where you claim to feel astonished that something happened to you.

Artful Boasting contains two parts. First, you gracefully establish that you have reason to be proud of an accomplishment. And second, you become contrastively humble. You blend the two parts by giving all of the information necessary to make your argument about an achievement while keeping the facts decently attired in the language of humility.

False humility says, "Gee, I don't know why they picked me to design the new system." Artful Boasting says, "I was honored to be given the responsibility of designing a new system that saved the company millions of dollars. I was proud of that achievement."

You won't struggle with bragging when you showcase your accomplishments at interviews with Artful Boasting.

44. How a Little Research Can Yield Big Wins at Interviews

Knowledge is the power you need to give a winning interview.

And you don't always have to drag yourself to a library or do computer research.

The most direct way to get information is to ask for it. So pick up the phone before each interview and talk to people you know who are in the know. They would be your friends and business contacts who are doing the same work you're trying to get. Ask them to tell you what they do, what they like and dislike about their work, and the pay range for the position.

You should also try to get information from two more sources: people who work at the company you're planning to visit and someone who does business with that company. Ask them what it's slike to work there, and try to get the scoop on your interviewer.

Look at the power this knowledge gives you. You'll be able to match your skills with the qualifications for the job. And when you're asked, "What kind of money are you looking for?" you'll be able to give the interviewer a figure.

❖ ❖ ❖

Interview butterflies flutter across your nervous system before interviews because you're playing by the rules of your interviewer's game. The problem is that you don't know what the rules are until you sit face-to-face with a prospect. You'll clear this hurdle by empowering yourself with research before interviewing. Then you'll be playing by your rules.

Research can be done at a library, on the Internet, and, as mentioned earlier, by talking to people you know who are in the know about the kind of job you're after.

You might think research is an extra step to take only if you have time. That assumption is incorrect. It's vital that you go to an interview with solid knowledge of the company and job.

What do you say when you're asked why you want to work for a company? Answers like, " Gee, I don't know," or, "Because your offices are close to home," or, "Because I need a job," won't hack it.

So go to a library and ask a research librarian to help you locate publications you need in order to find the information you want.

A considerable amount of information available in print can be found on the Internet, but a few small and privately owned outfits might not have an Internet presence.

Empowering yourself with knowledge gained through research boosts your self-confidence while chasing away those interview butterflies.

❖ ❖ ❖

The first step in making a sale is to get information about your prospect. When it comes to selling yourself, you need to get the skinny on both the company and the job you're interviewing for. Then you'll know how to tell employers how you can help and give reasons why.

Until this fact-finding mission is accomplished, you haven't earned the right to open your mouth in the presence of an interviewer. With competitive facts in hand, however, you'll be able to ace the interview by matching your abilities to the needs of the job you're interviewing for.

This coaching vignette will focus on obtaining information about the job itself. You can learn about job specifications from the agency or recruiter who is sending you to the interview, or you can ask the company contact to give you those details beforehand.

You can also obtain job information during interviews. When introductions and small talk have ended and you're offered a seat, be the first to speak and say, "Before we get down to business, Judy, would you please describe the ideal candidate?"

If Judy tells you what she's looking for, she's given you the ammunition necessary to target what you offer to the requirements of the job. That will show what a good fit you are.

Now you can understand the reasoning behind the idea of not making a personal presentation until you've earned the right to do so. That right is earned after you've acquired information about the job that will empower you to match your skills to an employer's needs.

❖ ❖ ❖

You are responsible for learning as much as you can about a company before the first interview. The only way you can determine how much ability or background a company is looking for is by researching. You might be pleasantly surprised to discover the job requires less experience than you had thought.

The quickest way to do your homework before being evaluated is to talk to someone who is already employed at the company. Explain that you're being considered for a job and want to know about the company's climate from an employee's perspective.

When you don't know anyone who works there, identify people on your network list who can tell you about the company or introduce you to people who work for it.

Should you come up empty-handed on both counts, you'll need to perform standard research techniques, including reading business magazines along with a company's 10-K and annual reports.

There's an important reason why it's necessary to do your homework before interviewing. After reading about what a company says about itself, you can turn its words to your advantage.

Then when an interviewer asks, "Why do you want to work here?" instead of just replying, "Well, I like this company," you can spell out exactly why you like the company and how you can help.

45. You Can Research during Interviews, Too

It's important to stop letting "shoulds" get in the way of your job search. For instance, you've been told you should do library research before each interview. Nice idea. But what if you don't have time for homework?

What you need to know about the job can be learned during the interview. After the introductions and the small talk that follows it, ask your interviewer this question: "Before we get down to business, George, would you describe the ideal candidate?" If George responds, you've let him load your quiver. Now you can target your responses to what the interviewer is looking for.

But suppose George doesn't bite and responds with, "I'll tell you about the job later, but first, tell me about yourself." Don't go into a long pitch. Instead, talk briefly about a strength or a skill you think the interviewer is looking for, and then ask if that part of your background applies to the job.

There are two more benefits to doing this instant research as an interview progresses: you'll develop a two-way conversation, and you'll feel as though you're participating in just another business meeting instead of a sticky interview session.

So remember to remove the "shoulds" from your search and life. A perfect research model is only that—a model. When you're preparing for an interview, just do the best you can. That often means doing some investigation by asking strategic questions as the interview unfolds.

46. Body Language Speaks Louder than Words

Your body language speaks louder than words. So when interviewing, you need to appear to be relaxed even when you're not. The right body posture will do the trick

When you're invited to take a seat, do not sit back, slouch, and cross your arms and legs. That posture makes you look like a pretzel. That's okay while talking to a friend, but when you assume the pretzel pose while you're interviewing, your energy becomes locked inside you. That causes even more anxiety.

You can learn to sit properly with this two-step process. When you take a seat, sit toward the edge of a chair, and then assume a position where you're leaning slightly forward and up. You'll feel more at ease in this position because your energy will be able move forward, and you'll be free to use your natural gestures while speaking.

When you sit ramrod straight like a statue, your body language bespeaks nervousness and defensiveness. And instead of clasping your hands, hold them open while moving your body and gesturing as you would if you were talking to a friend.

With positive body language, you'll come across as an alert and attentive candidate who is interested in landing the job.

47. How to Know When It's Time to Go: Signals that Tell You the Interview Is Over

Because you can overstay your welcome at interviews, you gotta know when it's time to go. It's true that your job at interviews is to keep the conversation going. The same holds true for network meetings and sales calls. But enough is enough. A good way to make a bad impression is to overstay your welcome.

So after you've done your best, it's time to shut up and go home. You'll know when it's time to go by observing the interviewer's verbal and body language, which will inform you the meeting is coming to a close.

Verbal language could include phrases beginning with "Well, it's been nice," or, "I want to thank you for coming," or, "Is there anything else you want to tell me?" Some interviewers might just bluntly say, "Our time is up."

Body language is when an interviewer sighs, keeps looking at his watch, yawns in your face, and pushes back her chair from the desk.

Then you'll know the listener has heard enough and it's time for you to say, "I'm outta here."

48. Why Successful Candidates Display Their Unique Attitudes at Interviews

Interviews are conversations with an attitude. The "attitude" is your conviction that you can present yourself in a way that matches your interviewer's needs and your confidence that you can handle the toughest, most embarrassing question you could be asked.

It's okay to interview with this attitude. Just as conversations are two-way streets, so are interviews. And copping the attitude of a can-do candidate who is certain about his ability to do a job will help you ace the interview.

But you must first decide what kind of information you need from an interviewer in order to show how you can fit the bill. It's cool to gather information about the company and job while your interview is underway.

In order to assemble this data, you'll need to prepare questions beforehand about what you need to know. It's perfectly all right to refer to your list during the discussion. Preparation makes you look organized and professional.

When you make each interview a two-way conversation with an attitude—the attitude of a winner—you'll be more relaxed and self-assured. That will put you head and shoulders above the competition.

49. So, You're Thinking about Using Humor at Interviews

Take my job—please. So you have a sense of humor and want to be funny at interviews. A deadly serious interview is a drag. But a good way to be remembered is by tickling somebody's funny bone.

You should only use humor at interviews if you think you can pull it off—and recognize the right time to use it. That would not be at the beginning of an interview. If a prospective employer gets to know you first, your humor can come across in a charming way.

What is a sense of humor, anyway? It's not trying to be funny by using a serious question as a straight line for a comedy routine or poking fun at your interviewer. That would be in bad taste. If you're going to poke fun at someone, make yourself the butt of the joke.

A sense of humor can help you get through the day. You can develop the ability to perceive humor just by observing what's amusing. After a while, you'll develop the ability to catch sight of humor naturally without trying to be funny.

Humor needs to appear to be spontaneous. If you crack a joke, it could look like you rehearsed it. While your sense of humor software is always running in the background, keep a businesslike approach in the foreground while answering questions.

Although well-placed humor can help to lighten the mood and put an interviewer at ease, use it sparingly. A job interview is no laughing matter.

50. Practice Is the Best of All Instructors
   —Publilius Syrus

You learn how to give a terrific interview the same way you get good at playing a sport. You practice a lot. Tiger Woods didn't learn how to putt by playing in the Masters Tournament. He practiced alone. When the golfer mastered the use of his putter, he entered competition.

You haven't earned the right to compete at interviews until you've practiced alone awhile. A cover story needs to be practiced. That's the story that explains why you're out looking. You also need to practice answering the question, "Tell me about yourself." You answer it by presenting short success stories about how you used certain skills to benefit a previous employer.

An easy way to practice is by using the nickel-and-dime technique, which refers to practicing during that five-minute drive to the store or during the ten-minute walk to the bus.

Preparation is so important that Aesop explained it to children. In his story "The Ant and the Grasshopper," the legendary composer of fables wrote, "It is thrifty to prepare today for the wants of tomorrow."

51. Why Using a Preinterview Checklist Can Save Your Interview Day

If anything can go wrong before an interview, it usually will. While getting dressed, for example, you could discover the top button on your lucky interview shirt or blouse is missing. What's a candidate to do? Prepare!

Getting ready for your interview is like taking care of logistics before a battle. Here are five items for your interview checklist:

1. Coordinate your interview outfit ahead of time.
2. Take the guesswork out of how long it takes to get there and remove your worry about running late by making a dry run from your home to the interview site before the big day. Your chances of getting a job offer are at risk when you walk in late.
3. Bring lots of cash for parking, tolls, or train fare.
4. Carry your contact's phone number so you can call ahead if you face unavoidable delays.
5. Check your gas tank the night before. Then you won't have to stop to fill 'er up. Even worse than a missing button is spilling gas on your suit.

52. Organization and Planning Are Keys to Getting Hired

You always have a couple of choices before interviewing: you can become stressed out or organize yourself. The key to getting hired is getting ready for interviews.

It's a buyer's job market. Companies expect you to be ready to answer and ask some tough questions. If you just sit there—duh—nobody's going to hire you.

Preparation starts when your job hunt begins. Then you'll have lots of time to practice talking about yourself. How? Your skills and accomplishments are right there on your résumé. Drill on them. Getting ready includes researching each company. When you know about an organization, you'll leave a good impression.

From your research, you can prepare a list of questions to ask about the company and the job. Most interviews have a question-and-answer period. You need to be just as engaged as your interviewer is when you're asking and answering queries.

And dress for your part. Hiring decisions are based mostly on the first impression you make. That's the image your present when you walk through an office door.

❖ ❖ ❖

Gone are the good old days when all you had to do was just show up for an interview and answer some questions. Interviewing is a proactive sport these days. As lyricist Daniel Quine Auerbach put it, "And it's about time you see things ain't like they used to be."

Today, you need to make personal presentations to prospective employers. An interview is a performance that shows how you would do the job if you worked there. To perform, you need to know—before each interview—what you can do for an employer.

Planning for interviews entails researching and asking yourself questions. Research is like a double-edged sword. You need to uncover details about the job and information about the company that's offering it.

Then create two sets of questions. The first set should be questions you would ask if you were hiring yourself for the job. Write them down. The bulk of your sales presentation will be based on the answers to those hypothetical questions.

Next decide what information you need from an interviewer in order to determine if you want to work there. Create a second set of questions designed to get those facts. You'll blend them into the interview.

With this fistful of facts, you'll put yourself on the same page as the interviewer. You'll be able to discuss the job from the interviewer's viewpoint instead of just being concerned about how you'll come across. That's how to get a leg up on your competitors.

Yes, things ain't like they used to be. To get offers, you need to be proactive and communicate the reasons why you're the best candidate for the job.

❖ ❖ ❖

You want to excite interviewers, not chill them. Exciting job candidates give their prospects what they want during an interview. What they want is to see how your skills and achievements link up to the job's requirements. Unless you know the needs of the prospective employers to whom you're presenting, you will chill them.

So before interviewing, take the time to do some homework: learn about the company and the job's requirements, rehearse parts of your presentation out loud or into a recorder, and decide how you're going to answer questions.

What you need to do is give a custom-tailored presentation each time. Because employers have different needs, your job is to find those needs and to talk about how you can fill them.

For that reason, you'll screw up if you give interview presentations exactly the same way to everybody.

I'll offer a last bit of coaching on this topic: Don't talk too much. The material you present needs to be short. Nobody wants to hear a long speech unless it's absolutely riveting. Answers to "tell me about yourself" certainly are not.

❖ ❖ ❖

Many hiring managers dislike interviewing candidates. Don't take it personally. They don't know how to interview. Consequently, some managers would rather be doing their own jobs than talking to you. When you face a reticent manager, you need to take the lead and guide the interview.

That is one of the reasons you need to prepare. In this situation, "preparing" means doing your homework of learning about the company and the job being offered, and practicing at home. Practice entails rehearsing the presentation of your skills and achievements. That's how you prove you're a great fit for the job in question.

You can learn even more about the position's requirements during the interview itself. Ask your interviewer what criteria he'll use to select the person for the job. If she chooses to respond, your task will become easier. Just show how your skills and past successes match what your prospect said she's looking for.

So condition yourself for interviews by researching, practicing, and asking interviewers to describe the ideal candidate. That will give you some control. You'll be able to keep the discussion on target while making your interviewer's job much easier.

53. When You Don't Fit In, You're Out: Culture Clash

Sometimes when you're offered a job, you need to say, "Thanks, but no thanks." Some companies are lousy places to work. You don't read about them in published reports about the best companies to work for.

The only way to avoid the bad places is to critique each interview you attend. You'll notice some signals that indicate whether a company is a good place to work or a horrible work environment.

You should be on the lookout for two signals that warn of a culture clash: The first is when everyone who interviews you at a company asks the same questions. That informs you of a rigid corporate culture that smothers individuality. The second warning signal is when the people with whom you interview seem impatient, overworked, or tired. That informs you that they're probably overworked and have no time for their families—and neither would you.

Signals that indicate a good cultural fit include when your interviewer gives you the personal touch and when workers seem happy in their environment. A good workplace shows respect and concern for employees both as workers and as people with lives outside of work.

You'll find a good boss and a decent work environment only by evaluating the content of each interview. And when you're coming from a bad work place, take heart. It's a picture of what to avoid.

53. Why You Should Avoid Culture Clash and How to Do It

It's called a "culture clash." That's when you don't fit in with the customs of an organization. When employees are given the old heave-ho, they're often told there was a poor cultural fit.

Companies have unique personalities and cultures just like countries do. To get along anywhere, you must know what the community is like. Then you can try to fit in.

Just because you succeed in one kind of work setting doesn't mean you'll do well in another. You know what I mean. After a merger, you're flabbergasted to discover how differently workers from the other company do things.

Whenever there's a shake-up, get information about the style of the new leader. His managers will try to emulate him, and they'll want to hire and work with a person they're comfortable with. That's why new bosses are inclined to replace employees with someone they've worked with from other companies.

The sum and substance of it all is that you need information about a company's culture to determine if you can adjust. You'll learn how to come by that information in the coaching vignette that follows.

❖ ❖ ❖

When you don't fit in, you're out! Getting the boot seldom has to do with poor job performance. It could be that you simply clashed with your company's culture. That is why a critical part of an interview is learning about the company's atmosphere along with the important objectives of the job.

Because interviewers can pay more attention to your cultural fit than to your skills, you need to learn if you fit in. And you can do it while interviewing by asking questions and using your eyes and ears.

The answers to the following seven questions will help you determine if a corporate culture is or isn't a good fit:

1. What is the company's dress code?
2. What are typical work schedules like?
3. How are executives addressed?
4. How do employees get feedback on their performance?
5. How are raises and promotions decided?
6. Who are the stars, and how did they get to the top?
7. What qualities would I need to succeed here?

You can also take your research beyond the interview by asking your interviewer to introduce you to some of the people who work there. Check out the company's atmosphere with them, and observe how people greet and treat each other.

Job finding is similar to life. Everything you need to know is in front of you. Just use your eyes and ears.

54. Doing Lunch: Why Lunchtime Booze Is Bad News

What if your interviewer invites you to lunch? Accept the invitation graciously, but understand you're not being taken to lunch because of your dazzling personality. A prospective employer decided to invite you to lunch because she's interested in hiring you and wants to see how you handle yourself in a social situation.

When you find yourself out to lunch as part of the interviewing process, don't order a drink. Not even if others do. Just one cocktail might cause you to loosen up a bit too much.

Even when you have a job, drinking is a bad idea. With leaner and meaner staffs, employees are meant to be more productive. That's not possible with an after-lunch buzz from booze. Even if drinks don't affect you all that much, your boss might smell it on your breath.

In short, don't drink at a business lunch. Booze has ruined many a business career. Besides, if you feel the need for alcohol at lunch, you might have a drinking problem.

So if you're over inclined to raise a glass, here's a rhyming phrase that can save your ass:

Just say no to business lunchtime booze.

It's bad news,

Especially when you imbibe at restaurant interviews.

❖ ❖ ❖

Because lunch is not a good place to be interviewed, always try to schedule your first interview at the prospect's office. After preliminary interviews are over, you could be invited to lunch.

Some job candidates have asked if it's okay to order a drink if others do. According to a national survey of restaurant owners, lunchtime drinking is back in vogue. Business people have started bellying up to the bar again. So what could be wrong with a little wine at midday? There's plenty wrong.

Just one drink throws some candidates off their game when they're being interviewed. Heck, even if you have a job, drinking at lunch can get you in trouble. If alcohol hits you the wrong way on a bad day, you'll be left feeling tired and grumpy for the rest of the workday.

So if going to a restaurant is a part of your interview, keep in mind that it's part of the hiring process—not a social occasion.

55. Practice Makes Progress: Drill, Drill, Drill

Thinking you're going to give an outstanding interview the first time out is like expecting to play like Beethoven after your first piano lesson.

You'll achieve excellence in all areas of your job hunt only after practicing. That includes everything from interviewing and letter writing to telephoning your contacts and networking.

Nobody has to tell you that if you want to get good at anything, you have to drill at it. That's why you'll only begin to feel comfortable at interviews after making your way to a half dozen of them. The more you talk about yourself, the easier it will get, and the more believable your story will be. With practice, you'll get your presentation down pat.

Just as Broadway shows have out-of-town tryouts to iron out the kinks, conduct your own tryouts by interviewing for positions—ones light in salary and responsibility—that you would ordinarily turn down.

Another tactic for personal tryouts is to practice saying parts of your interview into a recording device. Your cell phone will do nicely. When you play it back, you'll hear how you sound to the interviewer.

Think of each interview, phone call, e-mail, letter, and networking experience as a practice session.

In your job search, as in all areas of life, practice makes progress.

❖ ❖ ❖

So you're not good at interviewing. Well, you didn't walk too well the first time either. The only way to become good at anything is to practice doing it.

After practicing, you'll do the same thing much better than you did when you started. Where do you think the sayings "practice makes perfect" and "habit is second nature" come from?

So just knowing interviewing techniques is not the same as having the habit. You must know and then practice techniques to get the skill. Practicing before an interview is an easy two-step process:

First, know yourself. After all, you're the product that needs to be sold. You—the product—are the sum of your achievements. They're listed on your résumé as bullet points. Practice talking about them as you would during an interview.

Second, know what a particular job requires, and then practice making the connection with your achievements as you would during an interview.

When you drill, drill, drill by practicing out loud at home, the words you need will come easily during the interview. On the subject of practicing, Writer Ed Macauley noted, "When you're not practicing, remember someone, somewhere is practicing. And when you meet him, he will win."

56. Interviewees Need to Do What the Best Actors Do—Rehearse

You can get ready to interview the same way actors prepare to go on stage. Rehearse the script for your one-person show that will be presented before audiences of prospective employers. The lines you deliver should present your background in the most favorable light.

Begin by rehearsing at home alone. Then practice bits and pieces of your interview material during normal conversation with family and friends. Ask for their input.

When you think you've learned your part—not perfectly, but well enough—you're ready for dress rehearsals. They're your chance to practice your performance in full costume—the interview outfit—in front of audiences that are not important. Your dress rehearsals will be interviews for jobs you don't want because of low pay, awful benefits, or a dreadful corporate culture.

Consider these dress rehearsals as out-of-town workouts to test response to your presentation. You'll need a number of dress rehearsals to perfect your performance and to develop confidence. Then you'll have the poise to show your skills in front of audiences who have those jobs you really want.

❖ ❖ ❖

To give good interviews, you need to learn your lines. That's the first thing actors do. They memorize their parts. There are predictable lines that you'll need to deliver in a natural yet convincing way, like when the interviewer throws you the cue, "Tell me about yourself."

Write down how you'll respond to this and other interview questions. Now, like the actor, you have a script to work from. That work is simply memorizing the words by rote. If committing words to memory isn't your thing, at least have an outline of what you want to say etched in your mind.

Actors first learn their lines, and then they rehearse. You'll make the job easier by using the nickel-and-dime method of rehearsing. Any time you have five or ten minutes to spare, run those lines over in your mind. You can do it while walking to the bus stop, waiting on a line, or waiting in a waiting room.

After you have mastered the material, you won't have to think about what you're going to say. Your only job will be to concentrate on what the speaker is saying. Then you'll react spontaneously with the words you've learned to whatever the interviewer says or asks.

57. The Most Important Part of an Interview

Whether you give a good interview is all in the mind. It's how you think about interviewing that makes you a winner. When you think you must win the interview, your nervous system takes a beating, and you will lose.

Winning is understanding it's unlikely you'll get an offer the first time out. Interviewing is a process—most often a long one. It usually takes numerous interviews with various companies before you're made an offer. But one thing's for sure. You can expect a pot of gold—that offer—to be awaiting you at the end of your interviewing rainbow.

So instead of trying to win an interview, just think about getting to the next interview. That objective is the most important part of an interview. And because this new mind-set also takes the pressure off of your having to win, you'll be able to relax more and enjoy the interviewing process as a give-and-take business discussion.

The key word is "discussion." You're not there to give a monologue about yourself. Hiring managers don't want to be on the receiving end of a brain dump. You'll do well at each interview when you wrap your mind around the most important part—being invited to the next interview.

58. Here's the Best Way to Learn How to Interview

What are you waiting for? No one is going to send you an engraved invitation to attend a job interview. Perhaps you're hesitating to hit the job marketplace because you're afraid to start your job-finding campaign.

If the shoe fits, think back to a time when you hesitated to jump into a swimming pool because you thought the water was too cold. Then your friend said, "Jump in—the water's fine." You did—and found the water to be delightful.

Now is as good a time as any to start your search. When it comes to interviewing, no one can teach you how to do it. Career counselors and self-help books only point the way. You need to learn by doing. So what are you waiting for?

It's easy to jump in when you stop focusing on having to get a job. That creates anxiety. Instead, concentrate on each step along the way. For example, don't make the goal of each interview to get the job. That puts too much pressure on you. Instead, just make your objective to get the next interview. Interviewing is a process. It usually takes a series of interviews before you'll get an offer.

A job search can be compared to eating a meal. You wouldn't think of shoving it all into your mouth at once. You finish lunch one bite at a time. Your job is to concentrate on each bite of your search instead of worrying about the whole process at once.

59. The Dirty Little Secret of Interviewing

The dirty little secret of giving an impressive interview is to tell your prospects what you think they want to hear. Your listener wants to hear how you can help satisfy his needs.

The easiest way to find out what those needs are is to ask questions. Ultimately, the best way to get information is to ask for it. That's why the early part of an interview or sales pitch should contain more questions than statements.

Once you've uncovered the requirements for a job, match your skills or selling benefits to what you think the interviewer is looking for. That's what he wants to hear. But just give enough facts to persuade your prospect that he's justified in hiring you. Keep your selling points brief. You can repeat them from different viewpoints as the interview progresses.

Asking lots of questions upfront to uncover key issues is the first step in a four-step process. The second step is to match your skills to what you think prospects want to hear. That's the dirty little secret of interviewing. The third step is to repeat your main benefits from different angles. And fourth, keep your selling points brief during the interview.

In order to tell prospective employers what you think they want to hear, it's essential that you perform the first step—asking questions—at the beginning of an interview.

60. How to Tell When You're Doing Well

Comedian Jerry Seinfeld said, "A date is really a job interview that lasts all night." An interview is a lot shorter than that. But the longer it lasts, the better it is for you.

The length of your meeting is one of the things that will tell you if the interview went well. Let's say it ends in fifteen minutes. That's a red light. It's a signal to stop, head for an exit, and move on to the next interview.

But if your interview lasts for a half of an hour or more, it's a green light that signals the interviewer likes you, is interested in what you have to offer, and wants to spend more time with you.

All in all, there are five green lights that indicate you could be moving toward an offer:

1. The interview lasts for a half of an hour or longer
2. The interviewer already has your résumé, and it's in front of her
3. The interviewer has made or is making notes as you speak

4. The interviewer asks her secretary or assistant to hold all of her calls

5. The interviewer wants to introduce you to someone else involved in the hiring process

So watch for the green lights. They're signals that your interview date might become a long-lasting business relationship. While a job interview might be compared to a first date, it's more like instant dating. You must woo an interviewer right away.

61. Signals That Indicate a Company Is a Good Place to Work

There are also red and green lights that indicate whether a company would be a good place to work.

Red lights include when employees with whom you interview reflect a lack of respect for you or their workers and when interviewers appear nervous, harassed, or down in the dumps. When a company's higher-ups don't have a life, neither will you. This red-light behavior signals a gloomy work environment.

Green lights that signal an inviting workplace include when an interviewer asks you questions about your life outside of work and shows respect for your answers. Other green lights are when a company makes a good impression on you. That shows it's a friendly and inviting workplace where you'd be happy to spend most of your waking hours. It's a good sign, too, when employees seem happy and friendly, make eye contact, or smile or say "hello" to you in the hallways.

Although you can get a feel for red- and green-light behavior during interviews and while observing the surroundings, another good time to test the waters is after you've been made an offer. Then you can talk to a few employees to ask what they like most about their jobs—and if they have a personal life.

If you get red-light answers ranging from, "It's a paycheck," to hysterical laughter, turn down the offer.

62. When Companies Test Your Testiness with Tests and Forms

Some companies—especially staffing services—require you to take tests as part of the interview process. You might not like the idea, but a prospective employer or temporary agency is simply trying to determine the best person for the job. So don't feel singled out. All job candidates are tested.

Some tests measure your typing speed. Others test your writing skills and proficiency in various software packages. When you're taking a test, don't worry about getting a perfect score. Just take your time. And do your best.

To determine beforehand if testing is going to be a part of the process, ask the agency recruiter or HR professional who is setting up the interview. When testing is a part of the deal, practice or study what you need to know.

Some temp agencies will not only test you but also train you on the software you'll need to know when you work with their corporate clients.

❖ ❖ ❖

There's nothing more frustrating than showing up for an interview and having an application form shoved in your face. That was the old-fashioned way of presenting your qualifications. Today, everybody uses a résumé. It contains most of the information requested on the application. So why do some companies require you to both submit a résumé and fill out a form?

A company has an easier time comparing candidates when each applicant writes down personal information under the same category. Other companies need to comply with the federal equal opportunity statutes. For that reason, you may be asked to volunteer information about your ethnic background.

An employer also needs to get information he thinks is important. Let's say you're applying for a sales position, but your management experience is not included in your résumé. Multiple skills could put you ahead of your competition. And the form shows how well you write, which is helpful when communication skills are required.

Filling it out is a pain in the neck, but do it with a smile. It's an extra opportunity to sell yourself.

63. How to Take a Reality Check

The only way to be happy in your next job is to look before you leap, says Bill Roth, a Connecticut-based executive coach who always advises candidates to make sure the position is right for them. "But they jump to a new job anyhow," says Roth. "A few weeks later, they're on the phone saying, 'Bill, I've made a terrible mistake.'"

You can avoid blundering your way into a dubious new job by accepting the responsibility of performing a reality check. You do it by determining if your skills match the job requirements and then making sure a prospective employer shares your values.

Roth likes using the acronym DATA—**d**esire, **a**bilities, **t**emperament, and **a**ssets—to describe a reality check that helps job finders take a look before they leap at an offer. A new job is right for you when it meets the criteria DATA outlines:

- The job reflects your **desire** about what you want to do in life
- Allows you to use at least five of your **abilities**
- Is the right corporate culture for your **temperament**
- Lets you showcase your **assets**

When you take the time to perform a reality check with the acronym DATA, you'll know what opportunities you are more suited for.

64. Create a Message for Your Campaign

"Your job campaign needs a message." That's the word from Bob Cuddy, the Connecticut-based executive coach we met earlier in this chapter. "The message is about what skills I need to talk about that match a job description."

Once your message is delivered, interviewers will catch the drift about who you are. Because employers will then know you're a good match for the position, job offers will start coming your way.

"You need to prethink the message," Cuddy advises. "It will be a little different each time because it's based on your interviewer's special needs—the requirements for the job."

The time to create your message is before each interview. The executive coach suggests you use a three-step process to prepare your communication:

1. Ask yourself, "What's the message I want to leave behind?"
2. Line up several values that both target your message and match the interviewer's needs. For example, "I'm a hard-working, experienced customer service representative who knows how to get results," and, "I've managed several internal projects that won accolades for their effectiveness."
3. Think about how you'll insert your message into the interview and how you'll repeat it during the interview session.

Delivering a targeted message at each interview makes a big difference. According to Cuddy, "When you create a theme before interviewing, you increases your chances of being hired afterward."

❖ ❖ ❖

CHAPTER 12

Interview Questions-How to Answer the Toughies and Strategic Questions You Should Ask

ANSWERING STRATEGIES THAT WILL MAKE YOU THE WINNING CANDIDATE

"DO YOU HAVE ANY QUESTIONS?" That's a question you'll almost always be asked at interviews. When you don't have any, you'll come off as a candidate who is not at all that interested in the job he's being interviewed for.

That's why it's so important to write down in advance a list of questions about the job and the company. Be sure to bring your list to the interview. Then when asked if you have any questions, you can answer, "Yes, as a matter of fact, I do." At that moment, you'll take out your list and fire away:

* Will you describe the position's duties and responsibilities?
* To whom would I report?
* What do you expect me to accomplish during the first six months?
* How will my performance be evaluated?

You'll come up with questions about a company by researching it at a business library and on its website.

Preparing questions in advance helps you give winning interviews for a couple of reasons. You'll have more to say at interviews, and because you'll be able to probe and get answers, you'll become more involved with prospective employers.

To sum it up, when you ask questions, you'll give the impression that you're a thoughtful, intelligent, and knowledgeable candidate who is interested in the job and the company.

❖ ❖ ❖

It makes no difference whether you're marketing a product or a service or interviewing for a job. Your mission is the same. It's to convince your prospect that she's justified in buying your services or hiring you for a job.

The dirty little secret of interviewing—and of making sales presentations—is to tell listeners what you think they want to hear. A prospective employer wants to know if you can satisfy her needs, and the way to discover what those requirements are is by asking questions. So the early part of your interview or sales pitch should contain more questions than statements. After all, the easiest way to get information is to ask for it.

So hold off presenting and solving a listener's problems until after you've uncovered the key issues or job requirements through asking questions. Then you'll have earned the right to try to persuade your listener to buy or hire by matching your service or skills to what your prospect wants.

❖ ❖ ❖

Interview questions don't get much tougher than "What are your weaknesses?" "You better not show a real blemish while answering," says career coach Sue Jones. "You might kill the interview deal by telling a prospect you don't communicate well or lack interpersonal skills."

A technique for answering the weaknesses question is to talk about a weakness that doesn't relate to the job you're applying for and then to explain what you're doing to correct it. Let's invent a couple of examples.

While you're being interviewed for an accounting position, you're asked, "What are your weaknesses?" You can tell the interviewer that you need to have a better understanding of all of the accounting software packages that are available in the market to better evaluate them. Then you can say you've enrolled at your local community college for a hands-on demonstration of the major software in your field.

Now let's say that you're interviewing for a job that requires certain technical skills. However, you lack a few of them. "If you say the missing skills are your weaknesses, you'll probably be disqualified," says the career coach. Jones suggests using the same answering technique and saying that you're taking courses to learn those skills.

We all have weaknesses. Still and all, discussing one of yours is a definite no-no. It might kill the interview deal. The way to get around discussing a real weakness is to talk about a shortcoming you're correcting.

❖ ❖ ❖

Let's delve a bit deeper into the question "what are your weaknesses?" If you answer the question honestly—by saying you've been trying to overcome a drinking problem, for example—you'll be out of there before you can say "downsizing." What you need to do is wiggle your way around the question.

You can tell the prospective employer, "I suppose everyone has weaknesses. I've always tried to focus on my strengths and make them even stronger. That's why I've been enjoying a successful career. Does that answer your question?"

If it doesn't, try this approach: "From what you've told me about the job, I'm sure I won't be required to use a weakness." Okay, that approach didn't work either, and your interviewer keeps pressing.

Because you're beginning to run out of wiggle room, "maybe it's a good time to interject some humor into the interview to lighten things up," suggests career coach Sue Jones. "Say you can't dance. Or don't play baseball well."

Either way, never use the *W* word at interviews. Try erasing "weaknesses" from your memory bank and replace it with "an area I've targeted for improvement." Then name the area and what you're doing to improve it.

❖ ❖ ❖

When it comes to answering the weakness question, you don't have to contrive a weakness in order to dance around the question. You'll respond nicely when you understand that the only weaknesses that concern your interviewers are those that would hamper your job performance.

Let's face it. If an interviewer thought you had weaknesses, he wouldn't have invited you to interview. Besides, an interview isn't a confessional. Then why do potential employers ask you to describe a weakness?

Some want to see if you'll confess to a shortcoming that will let them screen you out. None expect you to admit to an embarrassing weakness. They want to see how well you handle a tricky question.

You'll nail this classic question by keeping your cool while stating you have no doubts about your ability to handle the job. Then talk about a noncritical area you have targeted for development. That could be a technical skill not related to the position that you can easily learn. Then you can explain how you're working to improve a weak spot. Here is an example of a good answer: "I've gotten a bit rusty in my hands-on computer skills since becoming a manager, so I'm spending time each week doing hands-on work to stay on top."

In this example, the hands-on work is the noncritical area—the skill you wouldn't be required to use—in the technical job for which you're being interviewed.

Here's a similar approach to the weaknesses question: "I can't think of any weaknesses that would impair my ability to perform this job as you've described it. But an area I could develop in is learning a second language. Then I could communicate with a broader customer base."

In a nutshell, the best way to describe a fault is by talking about a shortcoming you're correcting.

❖ ❖ ❖

"Why is it taking you so long to find a job?" Now that's another tough interview question. A prospective employer will ask this question after some months have passed since you left a job. You have a choice of two ways to respond.

Finesse it. You can say that it was your first break in twenty years, so you spent time traveling—or that you took a time-out to enhance your computer skills.

Give the interviewer the facts. You can explain the reason you've not been working for six months is because jobs are tight in your field and it takes much longer to find a full-time position these days.

But you won't have to explain it away when you try to fill in your unemployment gap. What follows are creative ways to cover a gap:

* Consult in your field
* Help a friend who has his own business
* Take a temporary position
* Volunteer your services to a worthy cause

Even if you offer your services without pay, you're still the winner. You're maintaining your sills, and you're able to list consulting, volunteer work, or temp jobs on your résumé.

The average amount of time it takes to land is often based on how much money you make. The old rule was that it took a month for each ten thousand dollars of salary to find a new job. So if you earned sixty thousand dollars, a half of a year was about average.

But the old rule doesn't apply anymore. Although finding a job takes as long as it needs, plan on searching longer than you expect to.

❖ ❖ ❖

It's not worth losing your family over a job, so you'd better ask about the hours before you accept. The interviewer might say you'll work forty hours a week, but after starting the job, you might realize that means sixty hours one week followed by fewer hours and some downtime the next week. That's okay if you dig that kind of arrangement and it doesn't conflict with your family schedule.

But even among employees with expensive lifestyles, there's been a trend of viewing money as only one part of the equation. More important than salary is time spent on leisure and family activities. If you lose that, make sure you're compensated in some other way.

Time is not something you give away free. When you do, it's the equivalent of a reduction in pay. So before accepting a job, you need to find out about the hours. Talk to people who work there. Ask them about the corporate culture and hours.

If your family is important to you but your colleagues have no time for theirs, you'll be in conflict.

❖ ❖ ❖

If you were a fly on the wall at interviews, you would be shocked by the questions that are sometimes asked.

Naomi had a reentry interview with human resources when she returned from maternity leave. Although it's hard to believe, the HR representative asked, "Are you taking birth control pills?" Naomi said she was outraged by the inquiry. She replied, "That's a personal question."

Naomi shared her experience at an interviewing seminar. She wanted to know if she had handled her response correctly. Yes, she had. But Naomi's answer could have been less blunt. She might also have replied, "Does your question pertain to my job?" But that, too, is a crusty answer.

Naomi was coached on how to handle similar situations. When an unfair or illegal question is asked, pause for a moment by taking a breath and exhaling slowly. That buys you time to figure out why the question was asked.

Naomi's reentry interviewer was most likely concerned that she might get pregnant again and take a maternity leave…again. Armed with that insight, Naomi could have told the HR representative what she thought she wanted to hear: "No, we have enough children now."

❖ ❖ ❖

Another interview question guaranteed to make you fidget is "what are your goals?" Most job hunters either don't have any goals or are unsure about them.

That's the way it should be. In today's fast-changing job market, the position you hold today might not be there tomorrow.

While the inquiry about goals might qualify as a boneheaded question, it would be uncool for you to respond, "That's a dumb question. Can we go on to the next?"

So think about having a mission instead of a goal. Your desire to provide a quality service can be a mission. What propels you toward achievement is combining your mission with your strengths.

With that thought in mind, you can answer this question in terms of your strengths. You can say something along these lines of, "I'm not sure of my goals right now. Given the uncertainties of the economy, my job-market crystal ball is a bit cloudy. However, my mission is to provide quality service by continuing to make the best use of my major skills, which are program design, customer service, and sales. What that title will be in today's changing environment is anybody's guess. But those are the core skills I hope to continue using for now."

There's no need to fidget, fuss, or be fazed by the question about goals when you respond with your strengths that correspond to the job.

❖ ❖ ❖

As far as interview questions go, this one is another lulu: "What makes you stand out from other applicants?" You'll answer it satisfactorily by talking about your achievements that relate to the job.

An achievement is something you did well, enjoyed doing, and are proud of. It can be anything in your past that you performed at work, at home, or in the community.

Everyone can point to achievements. Have you written a computer program? Do you recall making a big sale? How about coaching little league? Or speaking before PTA meetings?

Here's how to prepare an answer to the question about what makes you stand apart from other candidates: Think about your favorite achievements and list them as one-liners. For example, your one-line favorite achievement could read, "Created and wrote a presentation for the Polytechnic Institute."

Now, turn your one-liner into an anecdote: "I created and wrote an industrial presentation for Polytechnic Institute that satisfied the need for a freshman orientation film."

So what separates you from other candidates? You'll ace the question by talking about anecdotes that link your achievements to the position. For the best results, keep your anecdotes to a minute or less.

The best way to sell yourself at interviews is to tell stories.

❖ ❖ ❖

"Would you tell me about yourself?" This artful question has been designed to show prospective employers how well you present yourself.

Although answering this question is your big opportunity to sell, too many candidates blow it by squirming in their seats and rattling on for several minutes about meaningless events guaranteed to put interviewers to sleep. Even when they're rehearsed, their answers sounds canned.

But if you've studied acting, go for it. You know how to make lines of dialogue sound spontaneous. The rest of you should try the positioned approach.

From your résumé, select three areas of your background that apply to the job. Then you can respond to "tell me about yourself" by saying, "I'm experienced in several areas that might interest you—computer programming, software design, and database management. Which category would you like me to talk about first?"

Your interviewer will normally select a category. If she opts for software design, you'll give a couple of brief examples of things you've accomplished in that area and their results.

Welcome the question. Your answer to "tell me about yourself" gives you four splendid advantages:

1. It allows for a two-way conversation between you and the interviewer.
2. It's effortless because there's nothing to memorize except for three preselected areas of interest to the employer.
3. You're allowing interviewers to participate in a two-way conversation about you.

4. You'll come across as a real person instead of just another interviewing robot.

When you're asked to "tell me about yourself," it's not a cue to tell your life story. Nobody cares. The answer is not really about you, but about your achievements and how they fit an interviewer's needs. That's what interviewers care about. That's why "tell me about yourself" is your opportunity to shine.

❖ ❖ ❖

Many job candidates find that questions about salary are the toughest to handle. It's like being caught between a rock and a hard place. If you give your salary first, you lose. You might be making too much or too little money to be considered as a candidate.

Every job you interview for has an established salary range, so it's a good idea to find out what the job pays before you go to the interview. While you won't always be successful, it's to your advantage to at least give it a try. Then when you're asked what kind of money you're looking for, you can quote a figure within the position's range.

Asking questions and using the Internet can uncover salary ranges. Ask the person who set up the interview—the agency, headhunter, or corporate HR recruiter—about the salary range. Ask people you know who are familiar with the business what they think the job pays. That's also making excellent use of your network.

When it comes to the Internet, salaries for posted jobs are often listed on a company's web page, and you can get information about what positions pay on salaries.com.

Trying to learn about salaries always needs to be a part of your research—that would be the homework you do in preparation for each interview.

❖ ❖ ❖

Some interviewers love to set this trap: "What do you want to be doing five years from now?"

You certainly don't want to say that you hope to have the interview's job by then. That would be a dopey answer. What interviewer in his right mind would want to hire a candidate who has just announced that she wants his job? But that's how some of you answer. If the shoe fits, the following coaching on how to handle questions about work aspirations can save the day.

You need to do some detective work in advance. Before an interview, investigate the job and where it might lead, or just think about the kind of things you would like to do along the way. Then you can explain your ambitions in a way that doesn't threaten the interviewer's job.

What do you want to be doing five years from now? Talk about a position similar to the one you're applying for that's a couple of promotions up the line. A positive statement would be, "I hope to move into management some day because I think I can manage people well."

Answer questions about goals in a way that shows the interviewer you've thought about your future. That's important. You'll be evaluated on what an interviewer sees as your future performance for the company.

❖ ❖ ❖

The more techniques you know for how to answer questions, the more successful your interviews will be. Question-answering strategies are all about keeping it simple and maintaining control.

Paraphrasing is a technique that can help you shine at interviews. When you're asked a question, simply repeat back or mirror the person's query without adding any thoughts of your own. That will help you to gain clarity about what the speaker is asking. With clarity, you can more easily discover what an interviewer is looking for.

Repeating another's question as you understand it gives you two more benefits that can make a big difference in the outcome of your interview presentation. First, paraphrasing gives you more time to think of an answer to a tough question. Second, it shows interviewers you're listening to them and understand what they're saying.

The paraphrasing technique is especially helpful during group interviews. That's because you need to make the questions public. Then you have a reason to answer everyone in the group instead of just responding to the questioner and inviting that dreaded follow-up question.

❖ ❖ ❖

You equate having to answer questions to being interrogated. You are correct. After all, the word "question" means, "to express a doubt about" the truth of something. So you are being cross-examined by someone who is searching for answers.

Interviewers seek information from you that will help them make hiring decisions. By understanding that, you can look forward to being asked questions. Answering questions gives you an opportunity to build credibility and to show off more of your stuff.

You need to prepare to answer questions by predetermining the tough and easy questions you think you might be asked about your experience and background. The four keys that follow will open the way to deliver your answers smoothly and fittingly:

The first key is to rehearse your responses patiently and enthusiastically instead of defensively.

The second key is to stay cool. That means resisting the temptation to interrupt, argue, or let the arrogance of an interviewer get to you.

The third key is to show interest in the interviewer's concerns or objections to your candidacy. Here, you can use the paraphrasing technique from the previous coaching vignette.

The fourth and last key on the chain is to keep your answers short. Under a minute will do nicely. Then, when you finish answering, stop talking. Shut up. And go back to your listening mode.

The way you handle interview interrogations will help you to become a more interesting and viable candidate.

❖ ❖ ❖

Because an interview is a two-way street, you're expected to ask questions in order to find out more about the job and the company. That's how you learn what your prospective employer is looking for. Then, as the interview progresses, you can match your skills and accomplishments to the interviewer's needs.

Before you have another interview, prepare a bunch of questions and bring them along. Questions can be about the job itself, the company, or the employer's expectations of his employees. Some questions are listed earlier in this chapter.

Job candidates often inquire if there's an appropriate time to ask questions. You can ask them either as they occur during the interview, or you can wait for the interviewer's cue. As a rule, you'll be asked if you have any questions. That's the time to take out the list you've prepared and fire away.

Prospective employers are impressed when you ask questions. First of all, you demonstrate interest in the job and the company. Second, your questions show that you care enough to have done some homework.

By the way, when you're asked a question, don't respond by saying, "That's a good question." The interviewer might think some of his other questions were not.

❖ ❖ ❖

When you don't understand a question, admit it. Don't fake it. You build confidence in what you're saying when you fess up to the truth. This coaching vignette will give you two techniques for coping with questions that you don't know how to answer.

The first method is to ask for an explanation by saying, "Let me see if I understand your question." That sounds better than responding, "Gee, your question is confusing."

The second tactic is to say outright that you don't know the answer and then offer to get back to the interviewer with a reply. That beats bluffing any day.

Now let's discuss what to do after responding. The idea is to keep the discussion moving. This is not the time to take a long pause. Doing so will make you seem unsure of your answer. Besides, pausing gives the questioner a chance to probe.

How do you keep the discussion moving? By answering a question and then proceeding to your next idea, or by popping one of the questions you've prepared to ask.

So after you've finished answering, use this transition: "Can we move on to the next point?" Or, "Wwould you like to hear about my experience in customer service?"

Remember not to grade someone's request for information. As stated in the previous coaching vignette, if you say, "that was a good question," you're suggesting some of the other questions were not so hot.

❖ ❖ ❖

Never let them see you sweat. Those six words from a series of old antiperspirant commercials can help you get through your next interview.

Some interviewers enjoy seeing you sweat—and squirm. You won't give them the satisfaction when you answer nasty questions in a way that reflects your self-confidence. Let's try on this interview zinger for size: rate yourself on a scale from one to ten.

You know you're a perfect ten. But tell that to a prospective employer, and you'll come across as cocky. Besides, your prospect might think there's no room for growth.

What if you offer a seven? That gives the impression that you lack confidence. You lose by giving yourself any number. You won't let them see you sweat when you respond indirectly by saying, "In my business and personal life, I've always believed in doing my best. So in everything I do, I'm always striving for a ten."

That's a safe answer. It lets the person know you're confident about your abilities, but you don't have to boast or lie.

❖ ❖ ❖

There's no need to shake in your shoes when tough interview questions are thrown at you. It's your opportunity to be the winning candidate.

The questions interviewers ask let you know what's on their minds and how they feel about you. That's why tough questions work to your advantage. You get to score more points, and your smart answers to demanding questions add to your credibility.

But you must prepare beforehand. You'll accomplish this easily by using the R&R technique: recall and rehearse. Recall the toughest questions you think you might be asked at your next interview. The Internet is full of them. Just type into your search engine "tough interview questions and answers." Then personalize responses to the questions you select. The trick is to keep your answers brief.

Rehearse by practicing solo. Then invite friends to lob those questions at you as you practice answering them. Finally, record your answers into your cell phone or telephone answering device. When you listen back, you'll experience how you sound to others.

The double-*r* technique for responding to questions will increase your self-confidence tenfold. Why? You'll walk into the office of a prospective employer knowing you have strong defenses against unexpected attacks from perplexing questions.

❖ ❖ ❖

There's only one reason you fear tough interview questions: you don't know the answers. While you can easily handle most interview questions, it's the zingers that throw you. You'll know when you get one. Zinger questions make you wince and feel anger. As a result, you'll answer defensively.

Think about questions as red lights and green lights. Zingers are red-light questions. Green-light questions are the ones you like and can answer in a cool way. The idea is to give a cool green-light response to the most hostile red-light question. You'll do so by keeping composed and providing information.

That's what General Norman Schwarzkopf did when he gave press briefings during the Gulf War, popularly known as Operation Desert Storm. The late general didn't aggressively defend his actions, but he patiently explained his strategy.

You'll act like the general of your own campaign by making your responses clear and confident. A practical technique to help you stay cool and positive while being interrogated is to repeat the question in a positive way before answering.

For example, when you're asked why you've been out of work so long, answer by saying, "Why have I been out of work for over a year? Let me explain what I've been doing." This is the reflecting or paraphrasing technique discussed earlier in this chapter.

Before attending an interview, anticipate red- and green-light questions, and be mindful to rehearse your answers to red-light zingers in a cool and confident green-light way.

❖ ❖ ❖

Most job candidates plan how the interview might go but just wing the question-and-answer part. That's a no-no. You must prepare talking points to the wide range of questions you could be asked. Then you'll have an advantage at any interview.

A question asked often is, "Why do you want this job?" You don't want to say it's because you hate commuting and the company is a short ride from your home. That's revealing personal preferences.

You should talk about how the job uses your talents and why it gives you an opportunity to contribute your skills. The question about why you want to apply for this job also translates to a question about why you left your last job.

Perhaps you were one of the victims of downsizing. Then explain what happened. But if you were fired, show proof of excellent evaluations from other bosses who liked you.

But under no circumstances should you bad-mouth the boss who canned you—not even if your supervisor was a scoundrel. When you criticize a former employer, interviewers will think you'll bad-mouth them, too.

So instead of bad-mouthing, bitching, and bellyaching, talk about the lessons you've learned.

❖ ❖ ❖

When you respond to an interviewer's question, turn around any of your blemishes so they appear to be positive. You can apply this technique to describing a weakness.

For example, you've been criticized for being overaggressive. You can describe that fault by saying, "I'm perceived as aggressive but find my less assertive style gets the best results."

You've ended the answer on a positive note. When you state the same answer but end it on a negative, it leaves the wrong taste in the interviewer's mouth. That's because the last thing you say tends to be the impression left in a person's mind. Therefore, you want to focus people on what you want someone to remember.

Examine these two statements:

First statement: "I'm a laid-back person who gets results, although I'm perceived to be not aggressive."

Second statement: "I'm perceived to be not aggressive but find that with my laid-back personality, I get results."

Doesn't the second statement sound more appealing?

Every statement you make needs to be positive or at least end on a positive note. In that way, you'll direct your interviewer toward the result you want.

So whenever you answer a question, start with the negative and finish with the positive.

❖ ❖ ❖

CHAPTER 13

Secrets of Negotiating Salary and Getting a Raise

How to Get the Salary You Deserve

A SECRET OF NEGOTIATING FOR a salary is your eagerness to get what you want. When you are eager to work in a certain field, you'll easily negotiate a salary because you'll have an idea about what kind of money the jobs in the field pay. But when you're vague about your needs, the techniques for negotiating will be obstacles rather than ways to gain control of the negotiating process.

You'll begin to gain control by never accepting the first salary offer. There's no reason to jump at it. That's because you're expected to negotiate.

Instead of labeling an offer as "low," present your prospective employer with additional selling points about yourself. Then ask the interviewer to reconsider a higher rate of pay. The more you get to talk about yourself, the more valuable you become in the eyes of a future employer. Besides, a recap of your values makes you look reasonable and allows you to gain concessions.

What if you don't get the salary you expect? You can trade stuff you don't care about for things you do. For example, the start date of a new job is important to the employer but not to you. So make a stink. Tell the prospect that you'll meet her schedule only if the company improves your relocation package. That's the issue you consider important.

❖ ❖ ❖

Many of you don't just say "no" to the first salary offer because you're terrified the company will withdraw its job offer if you ask for more money. You can eliminate the fear of asking for more money by equating negotiating for your salary with bidding on a new home. The buyer knows you'll bid lower than the asking price.

Similarly, your prospective employer is making a bid for your services. That's why a salary offer is a bid, not a demand. The reason you received an offer in the first place is because the company selected you as the best of all of the candidates. Therefore, it will not withdraw its proffer just because you're asking for more money.

Most jobs come with an established salary range. The person making you the offer wants to hire you at the lower end of the scale. That makes good business sense from the company's point of view, just as it makes good job-hunting sense for you to aim higher—at the midpoint or upper end of the scale. Then you and the company can meet at the midpoint.

Another technique to use when you're offered a salary that's lower than you had expected is to pause for a moment, explain that you need more money, and give honest reasons for why you do. That leaves the hiring manager thinking you are an employee the company must have.

Either way, negotiating begins by not saying yes too quickly.

❖ ❖ ❖

Thinking you have to accept a job offer right away is poppycock, especially when you're waiting for other offers to come through. "Candidates always feel pressured to say 'yes' because they think the offer will be lost if they don't," says Nancy Friedberg, a New York City–based executive coach.

But the opposite is true. If the company really wants you, they'll wait. "But if they pressure you, it really shows the establishment doesn't care about you, and they don't want to satisfy you for the future," Friedberg says.

When you need time to make up your mind, be upfront with the company that has just made the offer. You can say that while you're thrilled with the offer, you need to make a major decision and want to be sure it's the right one, so you would appreciate another week or so to figure things out.

In the interim, Friedberg suggests you use that offer as leverage with prospective employers when you think a job offer might be imminent. "Tell them you're really interested but are being pressured by three other companies, and they want you to start in two weeks."

Friedberg says a company that really wants you will get its act together and make an offer within a week. "If they don't, say goodbye."

❖ ❖ ❖

When you accept a job offer too fast, you might be the victim of an ambush! The surprise attack comes from prospective employers who offer a signing bonus if you accept the job offer lickety-split. Companies that are scrambling for employees will try to reel you in this way.

A sign-on bonus is a great recruiting tool. If a hiring manager wants you badly enough, you might be offered a few thousand bucks or an extra month's pay to come aboard. But there are drawbacks. There won't be much left after taxes and social security.

Whenever a company dangles a carrot, don't reach too fast. A good job-finding campaign results in several offers at once. You want to have a choice. Before accepting any of the offers, decide whether you can picture yourself working there and whether you'll fit in with the rest of the staff. Also, check out opportunities for growth.

So instead of grabbing an offer just because it comes with a signing bonus, accept the job that excites you because you like it. The money comes later.

❖ ❖ ❖

Don't even think about negotiating a salary or asking for a raise before you do lots of research. The more you know about how much a job pays or what others on the staff are making, the more likely you'll be to strike a good deal.

Homework helps you determine if it will be easy to bargain for more money or if you'll first need to hit your prospect over the head with facts. You can easily do your homework in three steps:

1. Try to discover the going rate for the job you're interviewing for.
2. Set your boundaries for how much you want and how little you'll take.
3. Ask yourself if it's worth less money because of the experience you'll get or if you'll take the job only if you get the salary you want.

Then when negotiating begins, try not to give your salary requirements first. Let your prospect make the first offer. The other side has information you don't—like how much they can pay.

No matter what the first offer is, reject it. Your prospect is also negotiating. What do you think he's going to do—open with his first offer? No way! So just say no. The other side will improve its bid.

Sometime you'll have to ask for a certain amount. When you name a figure, back up your request with sound arguments about why you deserve those extra dollars. Just throwing out numbers is second-rate.

❖ ❖ ❖

When you sell yourself for a cheap price by taking anything just to get a foot in the door, you could end up with a broken toe. Good companies are not looking to hire at bargain rates. Employers want candidates who are committed and self-assured. That being the case, your fear about negotiating for a higher salary is groundless.

When salary negotiations occur, you'll stand on solid ground if you enter the interview knowing the position's going rate. Salaries in your industry might be listed in *The Occupational Outlook Handbook* published by the Bureau of Labor Statistics, and on Salary.com. Your industry trade magazines might publish annual salary surveys.

It doesn't make sense to give up salary in exchange for a fuzzy likelihood of advancement. That's too uncertain. A new job is your chance to get a raise at the outset during salary negotiations. That jump in your pay will resonate for years. That's because raises compound—meaning they generate earnings from previous earnings—on the higher base you've negotiated.

Compensation experts say that when your pay starts high, you'll probably get a sizeable boost at your first salary review. But if you must accept a lower-than-expected offer, ask for an earlier salary review.

❖ ❖ ❖

Because salary negotiations are perceived to be the scariest part of the interview process, most job hunters are afraid to negotiate. "The minute an offer comes in, they get weak in the knees," says executive coach Nancy Friedberg. "As a matter of fact, they get concerned even before getting the offer."

Salary negotiations won't freak you out when you get used to the idea that dealing with salary issues is part of the interview process. But you should try to focus on the position first. "Save the salary negotiation process as the very, very last step," advises Friedberg.

On the subject of making yourself worth more as the interview progresses, Friedburg says, "He who talks about money first loses." That's because a company might offer you more than you expect.

In addition to knowing your minimum salary requirements and the going price for the job in question, you should also know your competitive edge. Throughout the interview, you need to talk about the qualities that make you stand out. Then you'll have the right hook to get the offer, the money, the position, the title, and whatever else you want from the company.

As Friedberg says, "It's a great feeling to get what you want after knowing your strategy and hanging tough."

❖ ❖ ❖

You can eliminate most of your fears about negotiating by learning how to do it before interviewing. This is especially important for women. Studies show many of you still get paid less than men for doing the same job. The reason? You're offered less to begin with. That's why it makes sense to take a class or read a book about how to negotiate.

Men are better at asking for more money. They've been raised to be aggressive—and negotiating is all about being assertive, because more firms are moving toward "merit pay," which is also known as "pay for performance."

Before you interview, try to learn what the position pays and what competitors at other companies get to do the same job. After you do the math, you'll be able to negotiate a salary that's either within the range established for the job or comparable to what others in your industry are earning.

But suppose the salary figure you mention is based on pay for similar jobs at other companies and your interviewer says, "Nobody in the department gets paid that much." That's your cue to explain that what you are paid is a private matter between you and the company.

The salary you deserve is based on your qualifications and performance. The best way to get that starting pay is by learning how to negotiate before the process begins.

❖ ❖ ❖

Most job hunters feel the toughest interview questions to handle are about salary. It's like being caught between a rock and a hard place. You lose by naming a salary first because you could be making too much or too little money to be considered a candidate. So what's an interviewee to do?

You'll recall that every job for which you interview comes with a salary range, so it makes good sense to find out what a job pays before going to the interview. Then when you're asked what kind of money you're looking for, you can quote a figure within the position's range.

Here are four ways to discover beforehand what a job pays:

1. Ask the agency or executive recruiter with whom you set up the interview.
2. Make good use of your network of contacts by asking people you know who are familiar with the business, industry, or company what they think the job is worth.
3. Visit the company's web page to see if salaries are listed for posted positions.
4. Uncover salary information on Internet sites such as salary.com and salaries.org.

Remember that part of the digging you do before each interview is finding out what a job is worth.

❖ ❖ ❖

It's especially important to dodge questions about salary when you want to start your next job at a higher rate of pay. And who doesn't?

Playing the dodge game is seldom a cakewalk since lots of companies are determined to find out how much you make. Why should a company offer you more money than you're used to making?

Your best shot at winning is getting the company's salary range first. Then you'll have an opportunity to negotiate within that range, bargaining for a better deal than the one you left.

When an interviewer probes you about salary during the initial phase of the process, try to defer discussions about money until you have both had a chance to focus on the job and mutually decide you're right for it. That also allows you to talk more about how your skills match the job in question, which increases your chances of a better offer.

Should the interviewer probe again about what kind of money you're looking for, nonchalantly ask, "What do you pay?" If the prospect doesn't answer and continues to press, give a figure within the range established for the position. But if you don't know the range, you'll have to give your salary honestly.

A company can check your past earnings in various ways, including by asking you to bring a W-2 to your next interview. If that's the case, don't even exaggerate a little.

❖ ❖ ❖

In the event that you bump into an interviewer who asks to see your income forms to prove your salary claims, consider the request off-limits. The company has reached beyond the accepted practice of asking for salary figures. The only people who are entitled to see your income tax forms are Uncle Sam and your accountant.

Job seekers should also try to avoid giving their salary history both when they're filling out an application form and are asked at interviews. You should consider a request for this personal data as what it is: garbage. You can reprocess and return the request by asking, "Why do you need to see it?" or, "What does it have to do with how well I can perform the job?"

Then follow up your questions by explaining that past salary isn't applicable to the position in question because it has no bearing on the job you'll do for the company Compensation is determined by your background, your on-the-job performance, and your potential value to the employer.

End your statement by explaining that you've researched salaries for similar positions in other companies. That's why your salary request is fair and represents good value for the money.

❖ ❖ ❖

If an interviewer asks for your minimum salary requirements, tell the prospect you're not interested in minimums—only in maximums. That would be the maximum use of your abilities and the maximum salary.

This technique worked well for one of my job-finding clients who was made an offer by a Japanese-owned bank in New York City. The position for a securities trader was advertised with a salary that was twenty thousand dollars below what Bob was used to making. The interviewer knew the candidate's previous compensation and offered a minimum salary.

"I'm not interested in a minimum salary," Bob replied, "because I'm offering you the maximum use of my skills and feel it's fair to ask for maximum compensation." The hiring manager said that wouldn't be a problem—and Bob got the salary he expected.

Be forewarned that this technique might not work at the entry level where some salaries are firm and therefore not negotiable because they're firm. As you move up the salary ladder, the range increases. But employers seldom lead with their best offer.

Like the securities trader, you'll conduct a successful salary negotiation by ignoring minimums and focusing on maximums: maximum salary and maximum use of your abilities.

❖ ❖ ❖

"How much vacation do I get?" is a question not to ask at interviews. Inquiring about fringe benefits before your interviewer gets to know you is like asking a first date, "How much money do you have?"

You'll find out about a company's vacation policy, and your date's financial status, when the time is right. And the right time to ask about your vacation is after you've been offered the job. Until then, your questions need to reflect interest in the position.

You could be offered a job but be unsure about whether you want to give up the month's vacation to which you were entitled at your old job. Then you can use it as a bargaining chip. Some firms that give out vacations based on seniority make special deals for new hires, so you might get the same number of weeks you previously enjoyed if it's not more that the firm allows its other workers.

But if you end up with less vacation than you had, figure out what your pay would be for the weeks you're not being allowed, and negotiate your new salary to reflect the difference.

❖ ❖ ❖

Negotiating consists of more than just talking about money. That's why a discussion about salary does not have to be only a money game. You can ask for other benefits.

But first, you must sell yourself by pitching for the job until your prospective employer agrees you're a good fit. The more convincing you are, the higher your offer will be.

However, when an offer is lower than you expected, present more selling points about yourself, and repeat the points you have already made about your ability to perform the job. Then ask your prospect to reconsider. This negotiating tactic softens a request for more money and makes you look reasonable while you gain concessions.

With salary out of the way, you can request other benefits like a signing bonus, a company car, a membership in a health club, and a salary review at an earlier time than usual.

Benefits add up, and there's more to a salary negotiation than just playing a money game.

❖ ❖ ❖

Companies used to offer signing bonuses—extra money upfront—only to big-shot candidates. Most firms will now present that incentive for executive-level positions to anyone who asks for it. Signing or "sign-on" bonuses offer benefits to both you and a company.

For you, a signing bonus can bridge the gap between your salary requirements and what's being offered. That gives you extra money without disturbing an established salary scale. After getting the sign-on bonus, you'll be making the same as everybody else, and nobody will be the wiser.

For a prospective employer, signing bonuses are a tool that can help him compete for good talent and keep accomplished employees. The tool is also used to recruit graduates with high potential.

The time to ask for a signing bonus is after the job is offered and the salary is discussed. You could get from a couple of thousand dollars up to five grand or more.

Regardless of the amount you negotiate, be forewarned that you might not get your signing bonus on the day you start. Some firms want you to become vested first. That means you need to stay with the company for about a half of a year before they'll show you the money.

❖ ❖ ❖

When the good times roll, low unemployment informs you that companies are often competing to hire the same talented candidates. Therefore, prospective employers with whom you interview will be more willing than ever to give you other benefits as a part of your compensation.

But you need to ask for these perks after negotiating for pay. A nice way to segue into this subject with your interviewer is to say, "Now that salary is out of the way, can we talk about a signing bonus?" This perk is not just for top executives anymore. Signing bonuses are usually available at all levels. Along with the benefits discussed earlier, the perk also covers your job-search expenses and the strain of adjusting to a new job.

Other extras you can try to get include beefed-up retirement plans, stock options, and reimbursement for school tuition.

When you're a working mom or a job candidate who's going to school, request flexible hours.

But don't expect your new employer to give you these goodies right away. Remember that you need to be vested. The company will let you enjoy some of the perks agreed to after you've worked for six months to a year.

❖ ❖ ❖

Negotiating a salary, let alone those extra benefits, can be an uphill battle when the job market tightens.

The result of conducting an active job-finding campaign is getting several offers at once. That is the rule of thumb for any job search in any kind of job market. It's especially important to have a choice when there aren't a lot of other jobs around. That's because a choice allows you to select the best deal.

When you're offered a salary that you think is fair, take it. This isn't the time to play games. The time to let the games begin is after you've done homework about salaries for the jobs you're going after and before the company makes you an offer.

When the interviewer asks about how much money you're looking for, it's important to ask for the salary range. But that technique might not work all of the time. There are lots of employers who keep salaries a secret. Unless the company has a union, ask friends in the same field what the salary range is for their job. Perhaps you know somebody who works at the company you're about to interview with. Ask that person if he can find out what the job pays.

After obtaining this information, you'll have something to work with. Then you can start to negotiate at the middle of a salary range instead of at rock bottom.

❖ ❖ ❖

When you consider life's most stressful situations, asking for a raise ranks right up there with getting a tooth pulled. You'll suffer less pain when you carefully plan for the big event by gathering evidence to prove you're worth a raise.

Such evidence might include figures of increased sales, examples of your accomplishments since your last salary review, and ideas you proposed that were successfully implemented. In the event that you received positive feedback from colleagues, customers, or supervisors, present that evidence, too.

Before you walk into the meeting, know what you're worth by learning what people with similar backgrounds and experience earn at other companies. You can also discover what your dollar value is in the job market by checking out classified ads and recruiters at employment agencies.

Now that you have the ammunition to justify a raise, all that's needed is an appointment with your boss. The verse that follows suggests an easy way to get it:

Preparation for the big day is complete,
When you finesse the best time to meet.
Early mornings are best
Because both of you are fresh
With the boss more likely to say "yes."

❖ ❖ ❖

Few employees know how to ask for a raise without begging. You become like Oliver Twist, who pleaded with his master for food by saying, "Please, sir, I want some more!" Everybody wants a raise. But there are two requirements for winning it.

First, you must have earned the right to ask for the raise by being an excellent performer. When excellent performers finish an assigned task, they don't just sit there waiting to be told what to do next. They determine what else needs to be done and volunteer to do it.

Second, you need to know how to present your case without whining. You can accomplish that by explaining what you've been doing to help your department. That shows that you're an excellent performer. Then ask for his input.

Why sell yourself to your boss? You're barking up the wrong tree if you think a supervisor will notice your good work. How often do you notice his? That's why you need to build a relationship with a manager before asking for more money.

You could make a boo-boo by equating petitioning your superior with kissing up. An employer will not take care of you, so you must act.

The time to act is after showing your supervisor that you're an excellent performer. Then and only then are you ready to present your case for a raise without having to beg.

❖ ❖ ❖

You can wipe out the anxiety associated with asking for a raise by showing the boss you have earned it. Just make sure the timing is right.

A choice time is after you have completed a successful project or have scored points with a client. Another choice time to ask for a raise is when your supervisor compliments you on a job well done. Thank her and say you would appreciate a meeting to discuss your performance and salary.

A company cannot always give you the raise you deserve for reasons discussed earlier in this chapter. But most employers have the option of granting you other forms of compensation. Executives can ask for bonuses, stock options, and profit sharing. Lower-level employees can ask the company to pick up the tab for a corporate credit card, offer reimbursements for travel, or pay for a cell phone or a pager if the job is in the field where there's no cell phone reception.

When you can show you have contributed to the success of a department or its top dog or have helped to improve the company's bottom line, you don't need to be afraid to ask for more money. You have earned the right.

❖ ❖ ❖

Perhaps you think asking for a raise guarantees a transfer to Siberia. You might feel that way because cutting a deal for money intimidates you. Fear not. There is a principle for getting the salary or raise you want. It's knowing what you want before asking.

When you want a raise, have a clear idea about what you deserve based on your contributions over the past year or since your last pay hike. When you've recorded those contributions in a success notebook, you can back up your request for more money by explaining some of those contributions and their results.

Whenever you accomplish something you feel good about, write down the details in your success book using the SIR format: situation, input, and the result.

In a nutshell, relate the situation or problem surrounding an achievement and then describe your input (i.e., what you did to bring about a successful resolution to the situation). Finally, talk about the result in terms of how your achievement benefitted your boss, department, or company.

Different kinds of achievements include completing a successful project, training a new hire, solving a tricky problem, or making a tough sale.

Remember that you won't become spooked about asking for a raise when you know how much you want and can show that you've earned it.

❖ ❖ ❖

Now that you've been coached about how to get a raise, what do you do when you're turned down? Needless to say, throwing a temper tantrum or threatening to quit will only prove that you are expendable. This holds true unless you already have an offer from another company. In that case, you possess leverage to try to get a raise if you would rather stay put than join the other company.

You can explain that you love your job and want to stay but are sitting on an offer that's going to be hard to turn down. Then ask your boss for advice about whether he thinks you should take the offer and whether the company is in a position to make it worth your while to stay.

But when the boss says no and you have no place to go, leave the discussion open to further negotiation by asking if you can meet again in several months for a salary review. During the interim, you need to show you've got what it takes. In doing so, you'll also demonstrate that rejection won't prevent you from being an excellent performer.

Part 2: How to Manage Your Life and Career

CHAPTER 14

Taking Care of Number One

Your duty is to yourself.

—PSYCHOLOGIST DAVID SEABURY

LOOK OUT FOR NUMBER ONE. This is a dynamite principle to apply when you're creating and developing an important project. Taking care of your needs first is considered selfish. You've been conditioned to believe that selfishness is wrong. Get over it.

Successful people understand selfishness in a different way. Being excellent or creative at any task requires you to be selfish. That's because you need to focus. Being selfish means concentrating on your own well-being without regard for others. So what's wrong with that during a time of personal need?

Be selfish. Experiencing how delightful it feels to be good to yourself is as easy as one, two, three:

1. List several things you really want but have not given yourself permission to have.
2. Decide you deserve them.
3. Now go for it—one item at a time.

When something is good for you, it'll benefit others, too. Being selfish isn't really selfish at all when you understand it's easier to be of help after you've taken care of number one.

❖ ❖ ❖

"Your duty is to yourself," writes American psychologist David Seabury in his book *The Art of Selfishness*. So you must learn to muster up the courage to just say no to people or situations that interfere with your time.

Society has conditioned you to believe that selfishness is wrong. That's why you feel guilt and fear if you don't jump in when asked. The result of fear is failure. "Someday, in an urge to conquer trouble," wrote Dr. Seabury, "we shall learn the part unselfishness plays in hindering us."

To protect your time, free yourself of the guilt and fear of being selfish. How? By using selfishness as a defensive weapon to see you through the times when a job and career depends on focusing on number one for a while.

On the one hand, it's difficult to say "no" to someone. On the other, difficulty is a part of life. Besides, when it comes to protecting your time selfishly, what's good for you is always good for others.

Should a persistent, bumptious, inconsiderate infringer of time question why you said no to a request, feel free to use the well-worn phrase, "I use the word 'no' as a complete sentence. Which part of 'no' don't you understand?"

❖ ❖ ❖

Corporate America broke its employment contract with workers years ago. Today's employees have lost their naivety about expecting to stay with a company until their retirement.

Today, you can find yourself beached in a New York minute through no fault of your own. Maybe the company downsized, merged, or outsourced the job you held. You are forced to move on.

That's why your commitment is to yourself. If you don't take care of numero uno, who will? Not the corporation.

The only job security you have is knowledge about how to change jobs. For that reason, it helps to bone up on the subject through reading, taking a course on job finding, or taking advantage of an outplacement package if one has been offered.

Taking care of number one enables you to stay marketable throughout your career, so it's vitally important to keep your network green, especially when you're working.

Keeping your network in place will serve as a bridge to your next position if you lose the one you have or decide to change careers. By reaching out, you'll learn what's going on inside and outside of your company. That will inform you of two things: the direction your employer and industry are headed in so you can determine where you'll fit in down the line, and what skills you need to develop in the changing marketplace.

If you can deliver what the job market needs, finding your next position will be no big deal.

❖ ❖ ❖

Your career and job hunt begin with a dream. You have to dream it before you can do it. Holding that model in your mind is like sending an advance scouting party to check things out.

The next step is to begin speaking your dream out loud. Tell yourself that you think you can see yourself doing it. Give birth to your dream by telling yourself you know you will do it. Now you've committed yourself to making it happen. That's a necessary element.

Without committing your will to achieve your goal, nothing will happen. You will lack the willpower to express your vision in the world if you don't have a strong desire. Those who desire but have no will to work are the ones who always talk about starting the business that never happens.

The crucial step on the path to getting what you want is making the decision to act and then making a plan to achieve your dreams within a specified period.

You might have to learn new skills to make it happen. But you have given birth to your project.

❖ ❖ ❖

You can dream the possible dream of the perfect career, but you had better make that dream a beaut. You rarely exceed your own dreams. That's why it's a mistake to set your goals too low. You won't be strongly motivated to move toward your dream when you do that. On the other hand, be careful not to set your dreams too high. You would be creating negative instead of positive reinforcement in that scenario.

When it comes to dreams, goals are the stepping-stones. Your dream is on the horizon. The stepping-stones are directly in front of you. To prevent your dream from becoming a nightmare, don't try to leap from the first to the last stone. Be realistic. You can't really become chief executive officer of your company by the end of next year when you're just a salesperson now, so that isn't a sound or realistic goal.

The CEO's slot may be your dream, but don't attach a date to it. Dates should be attached to your goals, not to your dreams. But dream you must. American poet Carl Sandburg understood this well when he wrote, "Nothing happens unless first a dream."

❖ ❖ ❖

You must have energy in your life to accomplish tasks. "Energy" means the necessary strength and vitality required for a mental or physical activity.

How are you going to perform your job or search when your batteries aren't charged? You can draw energy from your physical environment. Messy surroundings can drain your strength. Charging your batteries by revamping your office and home will make what surrounds you more restful and nurturing.

And when something doesn't work, fix it now. Oil that squeaky office chair, and don't blow up at the computer when it crashes and the project you've been working on vanishes into thin air. That's enough to take the charge out of anyone's batteries.

You won't be the victim of computer glitches when you use any one of the following four tips to keep your cool at the keyboard:

1. Train yourself to save every ten minutes.
2. Back up your computer regularly by saving your stuff to CDs or DVDs.

3. Attach important files to your e-mail.
4. Store online with a site that offers storage on a cloud.

People are part of your environment, too. They should add energy to your life. When someone bugs you, talk things over. And if your dog barks every time you pick up the phone, train Fido.

When you manage the surrounding people and things, you'll have all of the energy you need to accomplish important tasks at home and at the office.

❖ ❖ ❖

The key to succeeding in your career is taking action on what you know. While information is vital to your success, knowledge is power only when you take action on it.

You can discover the knowledge you need in order to get there from here in a public library, online, and at book and video stores. Success is possible when you act on what you've learned. Only action will produce a result. So the saying "knowledge is power" is also baloney unless you take action. After all, the definition of "power" is the ability to do something that produces a result.

The winners in life have that ability to get themselves into action. For example, other people had the same knowledge that Steve Jobs acquired, but Jobs got rich building computers because he acted on the information he had.

It's the action taken on knowledge that's the key to your success. The Greek playwright Sophocles put it this way: "Knowledge must come from action."

Knowing this is a gift—a gift you can develop.

❖ ❖ ❖

To be a winner, "you've gotta have heart." So say the lyrics from the musical comedy *Damn Yankees*. Successful people need to have "miles 'n miles 'n miles of heart." That's why passion is a main attribute of people who get ahead.

"All you really need is heart" to decide to do something you're passionate about instead of just settling for a paycheck. What does it mean to have heart? It means that you are strongly devoted to a certain activity. But passion alone isn't enough. You also gotta believe you can do it—or else you won't.

The goal you're passionate about had better match your values. Your "values" are your personal concept of what's right and wrong. When you want something that goes against your grain, even the best plan won't work. That's because the emotional and physical issues that surface can sabotage your success.

After determining that your passion matches your values, you need to create a written plan in order to take action on your conviction.

When it comes to planning a project, building a business, or finding a new career, remember "that first, you've gotta have heart."

It's the only way to make your dream a reality.

❖ ❖ ❖

When it comes to writing down your goals or mission statement, allow Rudyard Kipling's short poem to help you. In his *Just So Stories,* the English writer and poet wrote,

> I keep six honest serving-men
> (They taught me all I knew);
> Their names are What and Why and When
> And How and Where and Who.

The poet's six *W*s are used by students, writers, and journalists as a formula to tell stories. You can task the six honest serving-men with helping you tell your business stories in e-mails, letters, reports, and telephone scripts. Before you do, allow the six honest serving men to assist you with the first step: writing down your career or business goals.

First ask yourself **what** kind of job, career, or business you want. Then ask yourself **why** you want to do it. You'll get the answer by figuring out how your skills link to what it is you want to do.

Then ask **when** you want to start and select a target date. Next ask how you are going to conduct it. Here, you'll select the steps you need to take. The fifth *w* stands for **where** in the world, country, or state you want to do it. And finally, **who** do you want to work for?

Rudyard Kipling's six honest serving men—or the six *W*s—are taught to high school and college students and used by journalists and advertising and public relations writers.

Kipling's six *W*s can also serve you by helping you get your job campaign off to a flying start and keeping it airborne with well-written job-search literature.

❖ ❖ ❖

Well, don't just sit there—do something! What do you do when you hear rumors that your company plans to slash jobs? Most of your coworkers will just sit there and do nothing except keep their fingers crossed, hoping their jobs will be spared.

But when you want to do something about an impending employment collapse, set a personal goal beforehand. Career experts agree that you must have a goal. Working toward one brings out the best in you and helps you land the job you dream about.

What follows is a powerful way to set goals by asking yourself three questions:

1. What would you like to be doing in a year from right now? Write down the answer. This is your long-germ goal.
2. Where do you need to be in six months in order to achieve that ambition? Consider this your medium-term objective. How about three months from now? That's your short-term goal.
3. Make a list of things to do today or this week to get you started toward your three-month target.

If you create your personal career goal now, you won't have to just sit there waiting for the other shoe to drop.

❖ ❖ ❖

Setting goals and striving to meet them doesn't work for everyone. How do you feel when a goal cannot be reached? Disappointed. Confused. Baffled.

However, some goals can help you. A case in point is setting daily goals by making a to-do list and checking off completed items. But when it comes to your big ambitions—like deciding on a career—many of you focus obsessively on your goal's external requirements.

Let's say your mission is to become a doctor. Since you lack the grades to get into medical school, you feel like a loser and forget about your dream.

By focusing on your goal's bench marks—like getting into medical school—you've missed all the other kinds of healing work you could do in the health care field. Rigid thinking prevented you from considering social work, becoming a nurse, or becoming a nutritionist.

Obsessively focusing on your goal means you're always thinking ahead. You're not present in your life. Successful people forget about what they're trying to achieve and concentrate on what they're actually doing in the present moment.

It's okay to set a goal, but try not to make its requirements the meaning of your life.

❖ ❖ ❖

The paradox of setting goals is that you cannot live in the present while thinking about the future. Living in the here and now is where it's at. According to the British writer and social reformer Havelock Ellis, "It is not the attainment of the goal that matters. It is the things that are met with by the way."

Handling things you meet with along the way to a goal is like keeping your eye on the ball. A batter focuses on whacking a pitched ball rather than on the bases he hopes to race around when and if he should hit a homer.

That's why setting goals and striving to meet them doesn't work for everyone. Where is it written that you have to set a goal and then feel defeated when you cannot reach it?

An alternative to goal setting is creating positive statements and repeating them often. Rather than saying "the goal of my business is to net eighty thousand dollars next year," try an affirmation like, "I'm in the here and now, generating successful strategies while handling important details."

Now your proclamation has come to pass. Writing and repeating positive statements can change your behavior as you start acting like the winner you introduced in your positive statement.

❖ ❖ ❖

You need to steer clear of the goal-setting trap. Business is changing so fast that the job you're dreaming about might not even be there in the future. So wake up! You need to succeed in the work you do today.

It all comes down to knowing your values instead of setting goals. A value is something you appreciate and naturally gravitate toward. You can consider values to be the themes in your life that attract you. For example, your values could include having adventures, creating, learning, or nurturing.

"The supreme value is not the future but the present," wrote Mexican poet Octavio Paz. "The future is a deceitful time that always says to us, 'Not Yet,' and thus denies us. What man truly wants, he wants now."

In order to get what you want sooner, make a list of your values, and then get involved in activities that let you express them. If creating or designing is a value, find a job that has a creative aspect to it, or build some creativity into whatever it is you do.

Rather than being seduced by goals, learn to lean on your values. They'll guide you to the right opportunities.

❖ ❖ ❖

There is no need to strive for a goal, struggle for a peak performance, give yourself pep talks, or swim with the sharks. That's motivational junk that can stress you out. There is a better way.

Just take care of the present. Goals are all about your hopes and dreams. They lie in the future. So setting goals is like dreaming about Bermuda instead of making travel plans to go there.

When you're more interested in the future than you are in today, you lose the present. That's how the trouble starts. You spin your wheels while wondering what to do with your life. The answers can be found right here in the now. That is where the action is and where opportunities—chances that can lead you to the future—are uncovered.

With that aim in mind, concentrate on today's activities. Instead of fiddling around with goals, know your values. A goal is worthwhile only if it's based on values, because those objectives come more naturally you.

❖ ❖ ❖

When you think about why people work, you'll understand what motivates you to tolerate long hours and crazy politics. It's not the money. You're convinced the work is worth doing and that something good will come out of it.

Survival is a basic instinct, but a sense of purpose reduces anxieties related to survival. That sense of purpose can only be expressed and fulfilled through work. Your work is what ties you to the real world. It's work that tells you whether your ideas make sense.

Work demands you discipline your talents and master your impulses. Work makes you feel needed by providing recognition for your effort.

Your work lets you ventilate and satisfy some of the basic emotional instincts like self-expression and mastering a task. Only work lets you express the forces that drive you. Studies show that people who are satisfied with their lives are involved in some kind of work, idea, or objective.

When your job is cut, find another work assignment or volunteer position, and soon. It's your work that makes you tick.

❖ ❖ ❖

"Decide what you want to do with your life. Then go at it with all your energies." According to former New York State Governor Mario Cuomo, that's how to succeed in business or politics. He ought to know.

While he was the governor of New York, Cuomo became a national figure in the Democratic Party. He was on the short list for president and he gave the keynote address at the Democratic National Convention in 1984.

After being defeated for his fourth term as governor by Republican George Pataki, Cuomo successfully changed careers by applying the same principles that made him a hit in politics to business.

Cuomo told a reporter about the five ingredients that contributed to his success:

1. Decide what you want to do, and then go after it with all your might.
2. Stay persistent even if you've been turned down a hundred times.
3. Never make excuses or whine.
4. Learn how to write well. Practice your writing every day by keeping a journal
5. Learn how to speak well in order to make your ideas sound more forceful and convincing.

The late governor practiced what he preached even after he lost the governorship. Mario Cuomo wrote books and many essays, and he spoke before organizations all over the country for thirty thousand dollars a pop.

Like father, like sons: Andrew Cuomo is the current governor of New York, and Chris Cuomo is a television journalist on a cable network.

❖ ❖ ❖

Trying to become like somebody you admire will stunt your growth, yet surveys show that a whopping 40 percent of you compare yourself to others—and think they're better than you are.

It's normal to want to become accomplished, but comparisons hurt. That's because you can always find someone who does something better. The antidote to false comparisons is to look at people as role models you can admire.

There's nothing wrong with being inspired, but you'll never feel good about yourself when you focus on what others do better. You pay a high price when you strive to be like somebody else. It costs you opportunities in the present. You cannot see them because you're riveted to someone else's present than to your future.

Always focus on what you do well. No one else can duplicate the person you are, just like you can never duplicate whoever it is you respect.

People of style and accomplishment can be admired. But don't aspire to grasp on to their coattails.

❖ ❖ ❖

Your career, business, family and social life will succeed when you begin where you are and take baby steps to where you want to go. That's the first part of the secret for getting what you want.

The people who you contend have better chances—because they've attended college or know more than you do about technology, for example— also had to start from somewhere. You have the same chance to advance.

So begin where you are and move forward with baby steps. When you face a barrier, remove it. For example, if you are somewhere without a college degree and that bugs you, become a part-time student. Or if where you are in technology makes you feel like Dumbo compared to your colleagues, take courses.

Beginning where you are is just the first part of a lovely quartet that constitutes the secret of getting what you want:

1. Begin where you are.
2. Do what you can do gracefully. (Take those baby steps.)
3. Step out in faith.
4. Expect God to help.

You can apply the secret whenever think you're not good enough to get ahead.

❖ ❖ ❖

Aristotle said that the most distinctive human activity is planning one's life. And while the ancient Greeks of the philosopher's day structured their lives by dividing them into seven-year periods, it's amazing how most people today fail to think about planning their careers.

The productive people you know participate in career and life planning. When you're considering going Greek, your plan begins with a dream, and you must organize that dream in your mind. That allows it to develop like a baby grows in its mother's womb.

After selecting a realistic goal, you need to plan how to achieve it. You can create a plan in three easy steps:

First, ask yourself what you imagine doing seven years from now. Second, determine what steps are needed to accomplish what you've imagined. And third, work on each step to completion.

You might need to initiate a self-help program to conclude one or more of the steps. Let's say one of them is to become a computer administrator. In that case, you'd need to become certified in computer administration by taking courses.

Benjamin Franklin expressed the gist of this coaching vignette about planning when he said, "When you fail to plan, you plan to fail."

❖ ❖ ❖

It's possible you're unproductive because of a bad attitude about time. Everybody has exactly the same amount of time, but productive people don't waste their time on trivial activities.

Your greatest resource is you. When you waste time, you waste yourself. Here's a time-management technique to help you find the time you're wasting: give yourself sweet-talk instead of a pep talk.

Make a deal with your yourself to work on an important project for a short period—perhaps an hour. When you sweet-talk yourself into this deal, your mind will allow the hour.

You turn off your mind and create anxiety when you give yourself a vague pep talk such as, "I'm going to write this letter if it takes all day." With an attitude like that about time, it probably will take all day.

Becoming more productive is not a question of managing your time. The issue is planning that time to accomplish important tasks. That involves sweet-talking yourself about not wasting time with trivial pursuits and instead focusing on the steps needed to achieve your goal.

❖ ❖ ❖

The process of making a career transition—moving from one field to another—can be an exciting opportunity to follow your dreams and to learn more about yourself.

Because your transition might take a number of years to complete, you'll manage it most easily with a written plan—a list of tasks that are necessary to complete your career veer.

The thought of writing a career-transition plan won't freak you out if you consider what Chinese philosopher Lau-Tzu meant when he said, "A journey of a thousand miles began with the first step."

What's your first step? To find the first step. Most likely, it's to define your career goal.

The second step is to get in touch with your personal contacts to seek information about new fields you're considering.

The third step is to conduct research using a library and the Internet to read trade journals, articles, and books about fields of interest.

The Encyclopedia of Business Information Sources indicates major periodicals and recent books in each field. That knowledge is power you can apply to network meetings and, ultimately, at interviews.

Speaking of power, you can facilitate your transition by harnessing the power of momentum. The beginning of a project is always the hardest and most time-consuming. Your project will become almost effortless after a while as momentum builds inside you.

It's the powerful force of momentum that will move you forward to completion.

❖ ❖ ❖

The best time to start looking for your next job is the day you begin your new position. "That's the new attitude these days," says Kate Wendleton, the president of The Five O'Clock Club.

Companies don't give a second thought about pulling the plug on your job. "The onus is on you to start taking care of yourself," Wendleton says. You can take care of number one by talking constantly to your contacts. This isn't the kind of friendly conversation where you're just keeping in touch. Wendleton calls this "directed networking."

The purpose of "directed networking" is gathering information about your industry and bringing it back to your employer. So when you talk to a counterpart at another company, probe to see how her job is done. The process will improve your current position. You'll be valued more and get to keep your job longer.

In a nutshell, directed networking is of vital importance to your continual job hunt. While you're gathering intelligence, you'll also be able to keep your network green.

❖ ❖ ❖

You'll raise the odds of surviving a purge by job hunting all of the time. The continuous job hunt described in the previous coaching vignette is not as exhausting as it sounds.

Government studies show the average employee keeps a job for only four years. So you need to hold onto that job longer and be ready for your next position by always keeping your eyes and ears open for opportunities to gather information about market conditions inside and outside of your company.

When you know what's going on in your industry, you can examine what you have to offer to current and future employers and then increase those skills you need to survive.

Then you'll fit into the new direction your company and industry is going in. That will make you more useful. As a result, you'll hold onto your job longer. That's important when jobs are being slashed left and right.

You'll go with this unfortunate flow by developing a new attitude about finding jobs. It's the mind-set of Kate Wendleton's continual job hunt.

❖ ❖ ❖

You must keep your next career move in mind all the time. You can never tell when your company will merge or sell. That's why you must be on the lookout. Perpetually.

Do you expect your employer to take care of you? To decide where you need training? To calculate your best career path? Get real! A company's main concern is the people who hold its stock.

You are responsible for planning your career and staying employed. You can do so by looking at your work life from the viewpoint of serving your company's current and future needs.

Ask yourself how and where can you best fit. At the same time, use your network to constantly gather information about your industry. Then if you need to jump ship, you'll know where to jump and who to contact.

For that reason, your perpetual job search will pay off. Your job performance will improve, and you might get to keep your job for a longer period. That's because you'll have added value to your work.

❖ ❖ ❖

You need to be on the lookout for your next gig even when your job is hot. It's foolhardy to wait for it to cool down before deciding if that's what you want to do for the rest of your working life. You never can tell when your job will be cut, so be at your mental observation post at all times in order to spot your next job inside or outside of your company.

You'll find it much easier to recognize a good opportunity after deciding what it is you want to do and what you're good at doing. Listen to your feelings. The answers are always inside you.

You can see what lies inside by taking your own career MRI:

* **M**ake note of your dreams—especially your daydreams. What you dream about all day indicates what you should be doing.
* **R**esearch articles that pique your interest online and at libraries. Save and refer to them twice weekly.
* **I**nquire about fields and job of interests from people working in your areas of interest.

Within a few months, your MRI will show you a pattern of interests. The best time to take a personal career MRI is while your job is still hot. Who knows how long it'll last or if your industry will stay dominant?

When your job search is a constant process, you'll be able to keep a couple of steps ahead of those job-cutting bogeymen.

❖ ❖ ❖

The time to think about finances is when you suspect your company will be chopping heads and yours might be one of them.

Whether you plan to look for another position or go into business for yourself, there are three principles of financial planning to consider:

The first is to prepare a budget designed to get you through the period of time it will take to land your next job or to start the business you've always dreamed about. You probably won't have to match your current paycheck.

The second principle is to aim for your net income minus the discretionary spending you can eliminate. That means cutting out optional items, avoiding impulse buying, and postponing major expenses.

The third principle of financial planning is to line up your resources, including your savings, investments, and severance pay.

You need to think about money before beginning a job search or starting a business. Money might not be the biggest issue you'll face. However, financial planning will put your mind to rest so you can focus on getting your work life back together.

❖ ❖ ❖

When you separate your life and career goals, nobody is going to tell you to "get a life." You'll have already balanced your life by planning some personal long-range goals based on your values.

Life planning is not about what to do for a living. That's career planning. What is life planning? It's planning to achieve those personal long-range goals based on the dreams that are close to your heart.

You should begin by choosing some broad categories under which you'll list a few goals. Categories might include "physical," "spiritual," and "financial."

It's best to list just a couple of goals for each category and to accomplish them rather than note lots of goals you may never get around to. Under the "physical" category you might list a weekly exercise program and weight goals.

Next, assign priorities to what you have listed under each category by asking yourself a couple of questions:

Which goals most support my highest values? And which goal would yield the richest reward if I only accomplished one of them?

Finally, create intermediate goals that will help you reach your personal life plan. Under the goals concerning your weight, you might list and prioritize eliminating breads and desserts, weighing yourself each day to track progress, and looking into an exercise and aerobics program.

Then while you're working on your daily career or work agenda, include a couple of those higher-priority lifetime goals on your to-do list.

❖ ❖ ❖

Parkinson's Law says, "work expands so as to fill the time available for its completion." And that's reason enough to make scheduling a regular part of your daily routine.

Planning your time doesn't take much time. But no time is better spent than intervals used to examine and schedule your time. That's because it results in immense amounts of time saved for leisure activities. Unless your downtime is also scheduled, you'll live in a constant state of anxiety due to not being sure you'll ever find time to relax.

What follows are a few time-management tips that will help you get the most out of planning:

- Plan your day's activities in the early morning. You're the freshest then.
- Stick to a schedule as best you can.
- Let this old adage be your mantra: "Plan your work, then work your plan."

There's no need to be ashamed of guarding your time. Napoleon Bonaparte wasn't ashamed when he said, "You may ask me for anything you like except time!"

Your time to complete a project is all the time you have. You can make the most of it by setting time limits for each task. And feel sorry for people who interrupt you, because they don't think of time the way you do.

Benjamin Franklin hit the nail on the head when he said, "Lost time is never found again."

❖ ❖ ❖

It is possible to keep your work life exciting by knowing the difference between what you want and what you need.

Your needs must be met. They include having enough income and decent living conditions. Because your wants are never the same, you can change them. It's all about life planning. The ABCs of life planning are figuring out what you want out of life, what kind of job will satisfy you the most, and how to uncover both of those things by listening to yourself as a child would listen to himself.

An infant who cannot form thoughts or use words knows he wants a bottle or a ball by listening to his body.

So when it comes to planning a career, listen to your inner self. That's where answers to those two questions already reside—in the secret recesses of your mind. You need to reveal those answers, not by forcing them out but by coaxing them out.

You can persuade your mind in a couple of ways. You can observe yourself as you daydream about the things you'd love to be doing. And you can doodle on a pad to draw, diagram, or rough out the qualities of the job and career you want.

Your work life will be kept exciting and ever more meaningful if you can know your needs and uncover your wants.

❖ ❖ ❖

If you're successful at work but your life is out of whack, you might be suffering from baby-boomer anxiety. That's when you perceive a gap between the achievements in your career and personal fulfillment.

Perhaps you experience this void because you actually believe that whoever ends up with the most toys wins. Your generation focused on material things and status symbols like sports cars and trophy wives. Then you realized happiness couldn't be found through ownership.

That's why today's trepidation is more about having pleasurable careers, meaningful relationships, and time to enjoy the results of your sweat.

When it comes to your career and establishing a work-life balance, you always have a choice. The angst you suffer is caused by not liking the choice you made.

You can choose to design a second life. The time to do it is after you've won the game you're in. Then it's time to stop playing.

Simply acknowledge you've won and move on to the next game. You'll have a better chance of winning it when you stop living in the past. You can stay focused by visualizing the future and aiming toward that.

❖ ❖ ❖

Be suspicious of anyone who offers a quick fix to your career crisis. Unless you're fortunate enough to have a career counselor by your side, making a career switch is a do-it-yourself project.

You say you're unhappy in your work? Your employer isn't going to figure it out for you. Career planning is your responsibility.

Let's say you work for a company of any size or are looking for a new job, even in another field. You probably don't think you're in business for yourself. So change your mind, and consider yourself an independent entrepreneur.

Entrepreneurs need to sell their services. The reason you detest selling is because you've been a buyer most of the time. Nevertheless, a career veer requires you to sell your services to someone—a prospective employer.

You can prepare your sales pitch by writing down your answers to two questions: How do I translate what I want to do into something people will pay me for doing? And how do I package myself as a product an employer will buy?

From the answers you've written, create a sales strategy statement. It should be short—no more than seven lines of typed text. Your statement needs to describe both the service you offer and its benefit to a potential employer.

After editing and polishing your strategy statement and rehearsing it ten times, you'll almost look forward to delivering your pitch.

Focusing on what you can do to fill a need or solve a problem is the most exquisite way to sell.

❖ ❖ ❖

The purpose of life is finding out what you want to do and then doing it. Instead of doing what you love, too many of you are working at jobs you think you should be doing.

Unfortunately, you were programmed with those "shoulds" at a young age in order to accommodate what others expected of you. That was then, and this is now, when we have some career management tools to discover our purpose in life.

You already know what it is you love doing. If you don't, tapping into your hidden wisdom is easy. Just examine your daily experiences.

At the end of each day, ask yourself two questions: What did you enjoy doing the most today? What did you dislike doing the most? After a month of performing this exercise, you'll notice a pattern of likes and dislikes. This pattern often points the way to your purpose in life—the hidden wisdom mentioned earlier.

What gave you joy today? Do more of it. And what drained your joy away? Avoid doing that. So examine yourself each day. Those daily experiences will uncover your purpose in life.

As the old proverb states, "Experience is your best teacher."

❖ ❖ ❖

When you're at the point of beating yourself up over not having the necessary skills to do your job well or to find another one, don't rage—engage. There is a way to engage in a method that will allow you to target and to acquire those skills while greatly improving your performance at work. It's a three-step process:

First, decide which skills are important to your work, or establish those talents you think are critical to your future.

Second, talk to some friends and business associates about the talents you've selected for self-improvement and ask for their feedback. You'll learn a lot. They might suggest areas of improvement you haven't even thought about or inform you about weak parts of your personality you thought were pretty good. Feedback from friends and close business associates informs you about how you really come across. If that doesn't sharpen your focus, nothing will.

Reactions from friends and associates enable you to build on your strengths as well as to learn about skills that need to be improved. Then you can research self-help materials in areas where you need to concentrate.

Finally, the third step is to coach yourself on improving the skills you've tagged.

Whether your goal is to become a star at work or an accomplished entrepreneur, you can achieve your objective by following this method for transforming yourself into an outstanding performer on the job.

❖ ❖ ❖

Being a manager these days ain't what it used to be. Managers have more to do with less authority to do it, and the compensation might not be worth the hassle.

That's why you might have thought about jumping off the management track in order to return to your original position—the hands-on job you loved before you started to climb the corporate ladder.

But nobody has to tell you that after a quick peek at your résumé, a prospective employer might say, "Gee, it's been a long time since you've done hands-on work." Consequently, you need to recover your former skills before making your next move.

As a frustrated manager who is still working, start doing some hands-on work right now. That will awaken old skills. Then add that experience as bullet points to your résumé.

If you're on the beach, figure out what skills you'll need to qualify you for the new job you want, and then take courses that will help get your act together.

Then you'll be able to confidently tell job prospects that you were a player-coach and can offer the hands-on experience they're looking for.

❖ ❖ ❖

A date on your calendar that you'd probably love to forget is the date of your annual performance evaluation. It's almost a no-win situation. You're probably being evaluated by somebody who is doing the thing he's worst at while trying to determine how well another person is doing her job.

The best way to ace an annual review is to prepare for it in advance. You can accomplish that by keeping a notebook all year. Write down evidence of the tasks you performed well; for example, write down how you streamlined a system or how you saved your company lots of money.

The reasons for keeping a journal are twofold. First, you cannot expect your boss to remember all of the good things you've done, so you must remind him during the review. And second, having that evidence to present is a reminder that you won't die at a performance review.

Many go into it thinking they're going to be fired. Yet statistics say that not a lot of people are actually sacked...except during downsizings, where firings can bear little relationship to performances.

You need to present useful information at the review about how you achieved goals, and then ask your boss how you can do an even better job.

❖ ❖ ❖

Instead of waiting for a performance review, monitor your own track record by keeping a performance notebook. You should always be on the lookout for the wonderful things you're accomplishing for your boss and customers, and you should enter each achievement into your performance book.

Write a paragraph about what you did and describe the result. Then use that material at your next performance review. It'll knock your boss's socks off!

To get even more material for your performance book, ask your supervisor what she considers to be your major contributions. That's also a good way to suck up without being too obvious.

And the next time somebody compliments your work, ask him to put it in writing. Seeing a testimonial increases an interviewer's confidence in wanting to hire you, because a testimonial is evidence that what you've said about yourself is true.

A performance book will also help any time your confidence evaporates. Just reading through it will recharge your batteries.

❖ ❖ ❖

When you hate to drag yourself out of bed to go to work, it can mess up your whole life—business and social. Your attitude will be miserable, and you won't be that much fun to be around. So if you don't love it, leave it.

Your whole life will change when you like what you do. That's because it will give you a purpose for living. Also, you won't feel like you're stagnating personally or professionally.

People who love their work say they would pay someone so they could do it, and their jobs are fun even when the work is difficult.

There are five other big benefits you'll receive when you like what you do:

1. Time will pass faster.
2. The love for what you do will return when you're able to use your best skills on the job.
3. You'll awaken feeling eager to get back on the job.
4. You'll consider it an opportunity to use your God-given talents to express yourself.
5. You'll be motivated you to do an even better job.

The message here is loud and clear: discover what you want to do, and go for it.

And when heavyhearted colleagues who also hate their jobs surround you, get rid of them. Hang out with friends who love their work.

You'll discover that the enthusiasm that radiates from love is contagious.

❖ ❖ ❖

The conventional wisdom about selecting a career is that if you do what you love, the money will eventually follow.

But when a job hunter named Brian heard this unscientific expression for the first time, he challenged it. "You can do something you love," he said, "but if the job pays little money, it ain't worth nothing." Brian had a point.

Let's say you love making miniature figures. It's your hobby. But as a livelihood, it doesn't pay the rent. Then you must hunt for a practical career that comes closest to what you love doing. That kind of search revolves around three steps:

First, investigate several fields that make use of your manual dexterity and ability to create. Second, get firsthand knowledge about each career by talking to people who do that work. And third, select the field that comes the closest to matching your interests, aptitudes, and skills.

Career selection is not a science. That's why choosing one is a gut decision. Make the final judgment based on how it feels. When it feels right, it probably is right.

❖ ❖ ❖

Many of you decide to try a particular field because it's well publicized. Sometimes, going to law school is the thing to do. And every so often, getting an MBA is a prevalent trend.

That is no way to pick a career. It's like trying to make a killing in real estate in an area that's just been written up in the Sunday papers. By then, it's too late.

It's a blessing to know exactly what you want to do from an early age. But as a rule, most people muddle around trying to find themselves instead of eliminating options early.

You'll eliminate the muddling-around part by choosing a career based on your values—the things that you're attracted to. That's how to determine if a certain path is worthwhile.

Why not pick a field no one is talking about and learn it well? You can take a lesson from beginning sailors. While they learn how to take account of prevailing winds, nothing substitutes for setting their own course and striving for it...regardless of which way the wind is blowing

❖ ❖ ❖

It can be harder to stay at a dead-end job than to look for a new position. Many of you decide to just grin and bear it because the job market is shaky. But there are jobs out there in any economy.

You'll know when it's time to go when you see these telltale signs: You got chiseled on your recent performance reviews. Your last raise was a joke. You're not getting promoted. Someone from outside filled the job you wanted. Also, you're being left out of the loop by not getting important memos—and no one asks your opinion anymore.

But don't be too quick to jump ship. Perhaps you can save your job for a while by energizing your career. Find out what your company's needs are. When you can use your current skills or pick up new ones in order to fill a need, you have a chance to get a better job where you are.

If you choose to try to stay put, tell your boss about your interest in improving your situation, and then explain how you can help the department by filling whichever need you've targeted.

Scoring with that pitch means your career decay will become an opportunity to stay. Failure to score means it's time to move on. Nothing lasts forever.

❖ ❖ ❖

Sometimes a job isn't worth the hassle. When you're not a happy camper, prepare to change jobs, but hold on to the one you have.

Even if you can afford to jump ship now, it makes sense to hang in there until you find a better position. Prospective employers might question why you left the job. Besides, bailing out might be considered a weakness.

What follows are four job-changing strategies you can apply while still employed:

1. Talk with people outside of your company about jobs that are similar to the one you're doing. Then you'll always know where you fit and what you're worth.

2. If your networking uncovers a need to develop additional skills for the job you want, obtain the new talents while doing the job you have.

3. Should you decide to jump ship after all, contact employment agencies and executive recruiters. They're experts at matching people to jobs.

4. Consider registering with temporary employment agencies. They're also known as "staffing services." The option of temping is a great way to try out new fields while bringing in some income as you research permanent choices.

Even if your job isn't worth the hassle, consider putting up with it awhile. You'll have a much better chance of being hired when you're still employed.

❖ ❖ ❖

When you're successful at something you like, just keep doing it. That's how to perpetuate success while earning a reputation for being one of the best at what you do. Then your services will always be in demand.

Whether you play tennis, fly an airplane, or program computers, you'll keep improving the more you do it. That's the way to get ahead—with practice. If you're picking up a new skill to enter another field, the golden rule of business applies: the person with the gold rules. The gold here is "training."

The repetition of practice over a period of time is the basis for developing any skill. You won't become proficient with computers just by taking a course and listing it on your résumé. You're only fooling yourself. You need to buy a computer and practice, practice, practice. A skill doesn't come from reading a book or debating it.

There is a distinction between knowing and doing. It's the difference between talking and taking action.

❖ ❖ ❖

You're barking up the wrong tree if you try to figure out what you've learned from the mistakes you made. That's the word from Bernard Haldane—the late granddaddy of career consulting—who said you learn from your successes, not from your failures.

On one hand, admitting your mistakes is an age-old custom. It shows you're willing to learn. On the other, Haldane contends that the more time you spend analyzing mistakes, the more mistakes you'll make. That's because analysis leads to paralysis when you overstudy what went wrong.

You limit yourself when you try to strengthen weaknesses or avoid making mistakes. Wise up! Open yourself to studying achievements. Successful flight was accomplished by accumulating achievements and strengths, not limitations.

Companies that enjoy success grow by focusing on the most profitable products—not the least profitable stock. You can imitate excellent corporations by concentrating on applying your most profitable qualities or talents.

Succeeding in business is a no-brainer. Haldane's advice is to study your most rewarding accomplishments, and then to go with your strengths.

❖ ❖ ❖

You have the potential to be more successful than you've imagined. Yet you're not the hotshot you're capable of becoming because you are afraid to succeed.

While some of you are both attracted to and repulsed by succeeding, your ambivalence toward success is different from your fear of failure. Fear of failure causes you to withdraw from competitive situations.

Those who fear success welcome success-oriented activities. Yet when progress is made, they feel compelled to hit the brakes and to find ways to sabotage further success.

You can liberate yourself from fearing success by recognizing three of its symptoms:

1. Your job is going well, and you become uneasy because you know it won't last.

2. It's important for you to be liked by people with more status than you.
3. You criticize yourself about your inability to succeed.

These are also three reasons why you achieve only a small part of what you're capable of.

Study the symptoms in order to decide how to work with them, and then learn to accept compliments—and stop acting like a doormat!

❖ ❖ ❖

American Industrialist Henry Ford said, "You cannot petrify success by humoring the lazy side of your mind." When it comes to careers, lazy people try to set their success in stone by thinking that's all there is to do. Then they wonder why they experience downfalls.

"When you begin to think you have at last found your method," wrote Ford in his book *My Life and My Work*, "you better begin a most searching examination of yourself to see whether some part of your brain has not gone to sleep." To keep your brain awake and success alive, you must respond to fresh challenges. Otherwise, you risk becoming stale.

In order to grow, "you must wake up anew every morning and keep awake all day," advised Ford. Easier said than done? Not if you stay alert to the fresh ideas this day offers rather than slavishly relying on what worked yesterday.

Ford would most likely consider the loss of any monotonous job as a stroke of good luck for the worker because it would give him the freedom to "wake up anew every morning" to locate fresh opportunities.

❖ ❖ ❖

You have a dream and have set a goal to manifest it. Now you need to see if you're waking up to that same dream or to a nightmare. You might discover the dream is different from what you had thought.

You can only make a dream come true by testing your strength to do it. The way to examine your resolve is to accept the fact that there are always problems connected to any dream. Problems must be solved quickly because they keep on coming.

It's like pulling tissues from the top of a Kleenex box. As soon as you pull one out, another tissue pops up to take its place. Your job is to overcome the hurdles that block your route

They usually manifest as delays and doubts. So you need to ask yourself if you really want to make those changes in your life in order to chase that dream. A positive answer means you'll enjoy achieving your goal all the more. A negative one informs you to move on to the next dream.

Successful business owners tried and failed many times before they scored. You can only attain dreams by trying them out—and by continuing to try until you can make one of those dreams come true.

❖ ❖ ❖

A key ingredient in your life is having goals. That's what Dr. Milton Erickson believed. The late American psychologist was one of the most influential psychiatrists of modern times.

Setting goals was Erickson's favorite prescription for enjoying life—and even for prolonging it. "Always look to a real goal in the near future," Erickson said. "It's not necessary to have a reason for your goal. But it is critical you set goals that are immediate and easy to achieve."

This applies especially to your job campaign. You need to have a goal or an objective. Define the job you're looking for. Are you unsure of what it looks like? Then talk to people who are doing the kind of job that interests you.

After you've set a goal, write down the steps necessary to achieve it. Some goal setters work backward, beginning with the last step—the one right under their goal—and then listing the steps before that right down to the very first.

That's the step you can take today. It's immediate and achievable.

❖ ❖ ❖

Grabbing an early retirement package too quickly could be a huge mistake. Generous severance packages will make your first several years of early retirement a financial breeze. But your long-term fiscal stability might be at risk. That's because you face two dangers: lower social security benefits and reduced private pensions.

That means you won't have enough money to retire. Forget about having a comfortable income if you want to stop working before turning sixty-five. You can expect to live longer these days. When you retire early, it's possible to spend almost half of your adult life in retirement and to run out of money.

Corporations have been pushing early retirement for many years to cut costs. That is why it's a good idea to try to resist an early retirement package and to hold on to your job for as long as possible.

But what if you turn down a package, knowing the next offer could be a lot worse? You wouldn't have faced this dilemma if you had been working on the continual job search described earlier in this chapter.

In any case, you need to be sure that you have enough income to live on during the golden years.

❖ ❖ ❖

"Problems are only opportunities in work clothes," said American Industrialist Henry J. Kaiser. When you can look at problems as opportunities, you'll be more successful. Problems come with the territory.

Whether complications arise in your career, job hunt, or family life, your task is to solve them quickly. That's how to eliminate worries caused by problematic situations.

Worry means "strangled" in Old English, and nobody has to tell you who it is you're choking. Successful people like Kaiser tackle a problem like a project by breaking it down into small, manageable pieces.

You're more likely to come up with answers when you look at a dilemma objectively. There is a simple formula for solving problems has worked well for me over the years. Ask yourself four questions, and jot down the answers:

1. What is the problem?
2. What caused the problem?
3. What are the possible solutions?
4. What is the best possible solution?

You should generate possible solutions because most problems have more than a single remedy. Problem solving becomes easier when you have choices. And by selecting the best possible choice, you can rest assured that you've done everything possible to successfully handle any issue.

The formula just described will help you not only to solve problems, but also to solve them quickly. When you're going through turmoil, don't stop to take pictures.

❖ ❖ ❖

When you need to find a new job or keep the one you have, follow Aristotle's advice. The ancient Greek philosopher said, "Education is the best provision for old age." His words of wisdom apply especially to older workers. You need to update your skills in order to keep pace with younger employees.

After all, you're competing for available slots not only with younger workers, but also with a huge amount of workers your own age. For a ten-year period of your life beginning at age fifty-five, you're part of the fastest-growing segment of the workforce, according to government statistics.

Because of your age, it's helpful to be familiar with the Age Discrimination in Employment Act. This legislation protects most employees forty and over from age-related discrimination.

Violations of this act include being passed over for promotions despite nice job evaluations, or being told you're overqualified for a job. Of course, that could mean the boss thinks you're too old. When you believe you're a victim of discrimination, your state's human rights commission are the folks to contact.

Lots of workers believe they were shown the door because of their age when in fact they were dumped for not keeping up with technology. So regardless of what kind of work you do, take Aristotle's advice to heart. The safety net for older workers is continuing education. That means studying and working to keep your skills up to date.

❖ ❖ ❖

You can survive your company's next purge by understanding this fact of corporate life: when jobs are cut, new positions are created. That means you need to position yourself to get one of those newly created jobs.

To use this survival technique, be aware of what's going on inside and outside of your company. Try to stay abreast of market conditions and how you measure up to them. Then you'll know what skills you need to learn, increase, or update in order to make sure you fit in to the new direction your company and industry is going in.

Always gather information about what's going on out there. Then apply that intelligence to improving the job you do. In that way, you'll be considered a more valuable player and get to keep your job longer.

To become a survivor, protect your job by finding out what part of your company is growing—and where senior management is placing its bets.

Then hitch your wagon to that star.

❖ ❖ ❖

You don't get to be a hit unless you take a risk. You might be giving up big opportunities and resting in your comfort zone. There is a way to determine if you're wasting your time by staying on the same job and are ready to move on and take that bet.

Ask yourself why you're sticking around in the first place. Perhaps it's because after all these years, you're still hoping against hope to get promoted. That's what headshrinkers call "magical thinking."

You need to take a reality check. Think about staying on the job only if there's more to learn. If not, get out. If you chose the latter, decide what skills you need to add to your repertoire. Then you can expand your responsibilities for either a better job or a career veer. And there's no need to take a time-out for self-improvement—just add more layers of skills as you go along.

If you're resting in a comfort zone, you might be so comfortable doing the same work in familiar surroundings that it's easier to stay than to switch. Change is never easy. Besides, the unknown can give you the creeps.

Nevertheless, you'll never know the success you might enjoy if you don't take a calculated risk. That means going for it only after thinking carefully about that risk and estimating its possible outcomes.

This coaching vignette began with the admonition that you won't get to be a hit unless you take a risk. The ancient Greek historian Herodotus put it more eloquently when he wrote, "Great deeds are usually wrought at great risks."

❖ ❖ ❖

A big reason companies decide to terminate an employee is because that person failed to keep up with technology. You need to make a commitment to understand both the new and the most advanced technology in your field. Computer science is making the world go round.

The skills gap in America is partially responsible for tens of thousands of jobs going overseas. This skills deficit is the modern equivalent of running out of iron in the middle of the industrial revolution.

Notwithstanding, the demand for technical skills in the United States is growing by leaps and bounds. The fastest-growing information technology (IT) jobs run the gamut from mobile application designer, technology manager, and database administration to software engineer/developer, video game designer, network administrator, and systems analyst.

This growth in demand for technical skills is the result of the high-tech industry creating new jobs faster than companies and schools can train people to handle them. So there are plenty of opportunities for you to become skilled, not stuck, in the new economy.

Job applicants who offer one or more of the skills just mentioned will always find jobs—and so will applicants who know how to design web pages, become web masters, or administer for any kind of network, whether it's on the World Wide Web or a corporate network.

The technical skills you lack need to be acquired. It's what you know, sweetheart.

❖ ❖ ❖

You gotta be wary of myths surrounding your career plans. Take the notion that everyone goes through a midlife crisis at forty. Baloney! You can have critical personal problems at any age and in all areas of life. Career problems are often the result of personal difficulties, or they can stem from a specific obstacle at work.

Now take the misconception that you must jump through lots of hoops in order to make a midlife career change. Double baloney! You don't always have to go back to school or start at the bottom of a new field. Career veers can be facilitated outside of the system.

Instead of responding to job postings and contacting human resources departments, focus on your network of personal contacts. Read the chapter titled "Networking: The Quickest Way to Get Interviews."

And how about the old wives' tale that you'll always have more than one kind of position? People tend to continue doing the same work. For example, most former Catholic and Episcopal priests go into social jobs like teaching or counseling. You don't see them becoming construction workers.

The late Arkansas senator James William Fulbright taught his colleagues to be wary of cock-and-bull stories when he said, "We are handicapped by policies based on old myths rather than current realities."

So before you leap, take a reality check.

❖ ❖ ❖

It's getting harder to make your retirement dream come true. The word "retirement" is becoming obsolete. Because life expectancy is rising, you might not have enough money to retire on.

Ask yourself the following question: if you want to call it quits after sixty-five, will you have enough money saved up to last twenty or more years? Retirement planners say the solution to this problem is saving 10 percent of your income. Most people find the money by cutting back on expenses.

The modus operandi for building up your retirement income is paying yourself first. The first check you sign is to your retirement plan.

However, slicing that much out of your budget at once can be a tough nut to crack. Start out by saving the first 5 percent of your income, and then add a percentage or two each year. You can make your retirement dreams come true, but you need to start saving somewhere.

This method for building your retirement savings is simple enough to seem trite, as is this worn-out expression, "A penny saved is a penny earned." Trite but true.

❖ ❖ ❖

CHAPTER 15

What to Do for an Encore Now That You've Landed

HOW TO BE A BETTER EMPLOYEE

NOW THAT YOU'VE LANDED, WHAT do you do for an encore? Some career counselors suggest beginning to look for your next position the day you start a new job.

This is especially good advice if you landed through networking. You've allowed your friends, business associates, family members, and professional contacts to advise or help you. Perhaps a referral enabled you to land your new job.

The network of personal contacts that guided you to a happy landing can also assist you again when you begin to look for your next position. So keep your network permanently activated. You'll find opportunities to do so by dropping contacts a line, sending an article you know will interest someone, making a call, or just sending a Christmas or Hanukkah card once a year.

To assure that your network remains in place permanently, remember to thank each person on your list after you've landed. This is important. People want to know how your search turned and the role they played in your success. That's because networking is about people wanting to serve their fellow man.

❖ ❖ ❖

You'll succeed at your new company by knocking 'em dead during the first week on the job. You might feel like a blockhead at first because you think everyone knows more than you do. Not to worry. All new employees feel that way at first. You can appear cool by putting a smile on your face.

You'll be noticed favorably when you come in early and stay late.

New tasks require more time to master. When you give yourself more time during the first week, it'll be easier to climb the learning curve and to become more productive.

You'll also get off to a good start when you don't ask lots of questions. You'll drive everyone crazy by bombarding your coworkers with too many of them. You'll manage to keep questions to a minimum by applying three rules:

1. Inquire only about what you need to know to do your new job.
2. Avoid asking questions that can wait.
3. Avoid asking questions you can investigate.

The time to notice how to dress for the new job is during interviews when you can observe what employees are wearing. However, when your office allows casual dress, make sure you are not the most casual.

❖ ❖ ❖

If you make the first week at your new job the most important, you will have the chance to make that crucial good first impression at work. So you had better hit the street running in order to make sure your first week isn't your last.

You'll make a good and lasting impression by confirming that you and your boss are on the same page. It's helpful to review your job description with the supervisor and to talk to others who have performed the same job.

The time to develop office relationships is during that first week at work. But you must not share your intimate secrets. Coworkers are also your competitors. When a dozen of you are in a training program, for example, only a few may end up getting supervising positions.

You'll also impress your boss by carrying a pad so you can take notes at meetings. Your manager will consider it a sign of respect that her words are worth writing down. When meetings have been concluded, take a few minutes to review what you heard. Then chat with the person who led the meeting to restate your understanding of the action plan.

❖ ❖ ❖

You'll need to keep on truckin' during the first month on your new job because it's much like the first week. Your supervisors are still watching. Because you continue to be the new kid on the block, keep coming in early and staying late. It is the fastest way to learn more and to start becoming more productive.

You'll also make your mark by raising your hand a lot. But you need to understand that if there's a sudden deadline and you have a date, the date gets cancelled.

You can breathe easier after several months on the job. You've come through the probation period with flying colors. So why not ask your boss for an unofficial evaluation of your performance to help clarify items that need to be addressed?

This is the time to review your accomplishments during your first few months at work and to ask for input—information your boss can provide to help you improve your work.

There are two kinds of input. Positive input informs you to do more of what has been good about your performance. Negative input informs you about what needs to be improved in order for you to become even more efficient.

❖ ❖ ❖

You will ace your new job by setting goals for it. Select your work goals by first identifying your job—what you get paid to do—and then by breaking down your job into categories.

A sales manager's position could be broken down into three categories: becoming proficient at Microsoft Word and Excel, writing management reports, and budgeting and forecasting.

Categories provide a balanced method for writing goals. If you ignore the Microsoft Word and Excel category, how can you write and illustrate management reports that reflect budgets and sales forecasts?

Here's a simple way to set goals for your new job:

* Plan lots of time for writing and polishing your plan.
* Assign a priority and deadline to each goal.
* Wrap up your goal by writing a brief statement about how you'll accomplish the task. For example, you could write "I'll select several computer training classes in my area, obtain information from each vendor, and enroll in a class for training."

Employees at all levels need written goals. They support your personal development and help you to become a star at work.

❖ ❖ ❖

People will like you less, not more, when you put on airs. You pay a price for adopting the mannerisms of others because you come across as a phony-baloney.

You will attract more people when you drop the pretenses. That will let your real self shine through. When you pretend to be more than you are or will ever be, you erect a temporary defense to boost a weak self-image. Besides, the result of acting all the time is emotional exhaustion.

You posture because you don't realize business colleagues and friends find you attractive just as you are. So you can discover the real you by accepting yourself just as you are. You don't have to like what you see. But when you think you're a loser, admit it. When you believe that sometimes you act like a fool, accept it. The concept of accepting yourself just as you are is the best way to uncover your defects so you can overcome them.

More character defects are built into your personality because you tried to act or sound like somebody else. It's easier to expose your shortcomings and to master them than to try to imitate someone you're not.

❖ ❖ ❖

Humor in the workplace has become more popular. Studies show that humor at work lightens moods while improving morale and performance.

A sense of humor is good for your soul and body. That is what health professionals have long believed. The late neuropsychiatrist Dr. Abraham Low maintained that "humor is our best friend, temper our worst enemy." Seeing humor instead of anger in a situation can prevent you from flying off the handle.

But you need to be careful how you use funny business at work. Telling a dirty story or making an off-color remark is not politically correct. There are rules against making your coworkers feel uncomfortable with the words you use.

Critics of the let's-have-some-yucks-at-work theory think tickling funny bones can get out of hand, specifically when someone who feels uncomfortable complains to the boss. When that complaint has a chance of involving legal problems, your boss might tell you something that's not so funny: "you're fired!"

❖ ❖ ❖

Your chances of becoming a star at work increase when you try to avoid getting romantically involved with anyone you work with.

There is a big problem with office affairs: they're not always between two people on the same level. When one is a manager and the other is not, coworkers will grumble because one of their peers is being treated with favoritism. But who cares? You are in love and bursting with excitement. Besides, it's your business.

But it might not be your business for long. Don't believe for a New York minute that you can keep an office romance secret. When management finds out, one of you will be transferred or pressured to quit.

The employee who suffers the most will be the person with the lowest rank. That's often the woman involved. Even if nobody finds out, what will you do when your office romance ends? You'll still have to deal with each other while you're nursing your wounds.

"Love is a wonderful thing," as the lyrics to one of Michael Bolton's songs suggests. But an office affair is not so wonderful when it wrecks your job.

❖ ❖ ❖

You have been told it's wrong to indulge in office gossip. That's nonsense. The need to tell stories is a basic human instinct. Henry James wrote novels based on anecdotes he heard at dinner parties. So why not admit that it's fun to gossip? Besides, gossip can advance your career.

Gossip is news. You learn about most of the good jobs through the grapevine, not from classified ads. And you can understand what is really going on in your company through office gossip, not from official memos, e-mails, or press releases.

Gossip can make you feel connected to the rest of the world because an exchange of information about others might inspire you. Their experiences may be similar to yours, and you may learn that your secrets are not so tarnished after all.

While it's okay to listen to gossip, it's not kosher to become a gossip—someone who reveals sensational details about others told in confidence. Malicious gossip diminishes the person who is gossiping along with the person who is being gossiped about.

❖ ❖ ❖

When you are invited to play a round of business golf, don't tee off your boss. There is no need to worry about beating him. Your boss will respect you for giving your best effort. But a golf game is the wrong time to talk about work, unless your boss mentions it first. And good golfers should forget about giving bosses advice on how to improve their swings—unless they ask for it.

Also, be sure to dress right. Many golf clubs expect players to wear slacks. If jackets are required to enter the club's dining area, be sure to bring one along. So inquire beforehand about the proper golf attire.

You also need to be concerned about social skills. You are on display at any informal business situation. The ability to handle yourself smoothly contributes to your business success. A sociable worker makes bosses feel comfortable, so an employee who is more congenial is often promoted over someone with more experience.

When you cultivate social skills, it's possible to have a good game of golf and to help your career.

❖ ❖ ❖

You have landed a job as manager. But do you know how to manage a staff? In order to stand out in your job, help each staff member to succeed in his job by developing a strategy to guide your team.

Managers who succeed use this simple three-step method of leadership:

1. Hold individual meetings with each employee. Half-hour meetings will do nicely to keep each staff member's assignment on track.
2. Ask to hear about project updates; congratulate your employee on what is going well, and target areas where a staff member needs your help.
3. Have an open-door policy so you can respond to employees' questions that only you can answer. You can accomplish this by inviting your staff to drop in for a quick meeting—anytime. (But remember that a "quick" meeting means getting to the point in a couple of minutes and then getting out.)

You'll become a mentor to your staff when you apply these methods of individual meetings and an open-door policy to your new management position. In turn, staff members' improved performances will make you look like an excellent leader.

❖ ❖ ❖

A Georgia-based hospitality business hired a general manager who fit the job specifications to a tee. "Tom is just what we wanted," said the resort's owner. "He has energy, enthusiasm, and is great with guests."

But the new manager had just one problem that got him fired. Previously, Tom had served in the military, and some of the resort's staff resented his militaristic approach. Tom needed to develop a softer side to his personality.

Today's competitive job market doesn't lack for good talent. So domineering managers need to hold on to good workers—and to their own jobs—by smoothing out their personalities.

When you land a new job as a manager, you'll earn your staff's respect and support when you develop your compassionate side by writing down the good things each of your employees has accomplished and what you value about each person.

This technique will enable you to help your employees fix their problems, and to avoid criticizing workers who make mistakes.

The manager's old theme song, "it's my way or the highway," is no longer on the charts. Unless you stop treating people simply as instruments to use to get things done, you'll be on the highway.

❖ ❖ ❖

Your chances of becoming a hit early on will be enhanced when you perform a couple of personal assessments. The first is a reality check on what to expect from your first position.

It's obvious you won't be starting at the top. Your first job could be a rock-bottom position. Even a college intern with a bit of experience could be given assignments that a company won't let a new worker do at first. So ask for a job description from the person who hired you, and begin thinking about how you can contribute to the company.

The second personal assessment is an attitude check. Your goal in college was to enrich yourself, and you were looking forward to joining a company where you would be given opportunities for growth.

The company that has hired you doesn't give a tinker's damn about your personal desires. The folks who run it are interested only in what you can do for them.

To get promoted, you need to convince your supervisors that you can help them more than any of your fellow workers can. But don't make a complete fool of yourself trying.

❖ ❖ ❖

While it's illegal for your company to listen to your personal phone calls, it has the right to monitor your e-mail and web surfing, so you'd better start minding your e-mail manners.

Over twenty employees of the *New York Times* wish they had been more careful. They were fired for sending potentially offensive e-mails. Similarly, Xerox canned forty workers for excessive surfing on websites unrelated to work.

The practice of firing or reprimanding employees for negligent web use is common. When you're wired at work, inquire about your company's policy pertaining to Internet and e-mail use.

Companies are liable for everything that happens in the workplace—especially on computers—and it's scaring them. Sexual harassment or offensive jokes are abuses of a company network that could result in lawsuits.

So act as if anything on your company network can be monitored. If you wouldn't yell it over the company's intercom, don't write it in an e-mail at work.

❖ ❖ ❖

When you're entering a new field, consider writing a consultant's résumé, which is written around a list of your skills and services. A consultant's résumé differs from the chronological format. A consultant's résumé emphasizes special skills and describes client assignments rather than listing former employees in reverse order as the chronological format does.

When you are a new consultant with no client experience, list your prior employment until your client list grows. Then you can update your résumé by adding names of new clients and eliminating previous nonconsulting employment.

The format of your consulting résumé can be as easy as one, two, three:

1. Start with a list of areas of special service you performed as an employee. That will tell prospective clients what you can do to help them.
2. List your clients and name several former employers.

List your education credentials last. Your consultant's résumé needs to be easy to read and kept short. As already mentioned, you'll keep it short by deleting less important assignments as you add the more significant ones.

❖ ❖ ❖

CHAPTER 16

Getting Ahead at Headquarters While Protecting your Hindquarters

HOW TO PROTECT YOUR JOB AND SURVIVE THE NEXT DOWNSIZING

YOU SURVIVED YOUR COMPANY'S DOWNSIZING and still feel stressed out. "One of the things that's going on," says Dr. Stephanie Gannon, "is what's called the 'survivor syndrome.' Part of you is wondering 'why me?'"

Although you are relieved that you didn't get the ax, "there's often guilt and anxiety about being one of the people who manages to keep their jobs," says the Hartsdale, New York–based psychologist.

The best way to handle the survivor syndrome is to understand it. While it's normal to experience guilt and anxiety, "you have to keep thinking about it so you are not overwhelmed by those feelings," says Dr. Gannon, who specializes in work and career issues.

When colleagues lose their jobs and you keep yours, it's not your fault. You have no control over what happens to them. That's simply the way things are these days. You can only hope the colleague who lost a job might wind up with a better one. That's also the way things often go these days.

The way to smite the survivor syndrome is to recognize what's taking place. "Then call on your inner resources to cope with it."

❖ ❖ ❖

Another reason you experience stress after surviving a downsizing is that you have too much work to do. That gives new meaning to the phrase "lean and mean." You are part of a lean staff that's expected to turn out the same amount of work. That's mean, all right, and it can make you feel overwhelmed.

One way to regain control over your life is to participate in personal activities you love. "And that might be something you do at home that you are going to commit to," says Dr. Stephany Gannon. You might want to commit to playing tennis a couple of times each week or to working in your garden. "Do something that's yours—something you feel good about."

You have little control over what you're required to do on the job. "But when you perform personal activities at home, you get back that sense of control over your life."

Feeling overloaded is a wake-up call that you need to add a personal activity to your list. Whether it's playing golf, reading a book, or listening to music, you have to begin doing something to deal with stress. "The key to managing your stress is to notice it," says Gannon.

❖ ❖ ❖

You can become stressed out when you lose a job and when you find one. That's because stress is also attached to the good things that happen, like getting what you wished for.

Any situation that requires you to adjust your behavior causes anxiety. Examples include switching from being unemployed to employment and from ending a relationship to starting a new one.

Another circumstance that produces anxiety is squeezing in more work than you can handle. Management gives you the impression that if you're not constantly busy, you're not being productive. That's the downside of today's downsized environment.

Poor mental health is the consequence of getting to the point where you can no longer distinguish what you must do from trivial stuff that can wait.

So when you've got too much on your plate, analyze your daily to-do list by distinguishing between tasks you must do today from stuff that can

wait. Then move tasks that can wait to the bottom of your list—or eliminate them.

❖ ❖ ❖

Corporations that have downsized are finding that the employees who remain are
stressed out. That's having a negative impact on bottom lines. The consequence
of having extra work on your shoulders is extra stress, which can make you sick

That's why many companies are helping employees to cope with stress
through exercise and nutrition. Some employers provide state-of-the-art
gyms with qualified trainers on site. While many corporate health centers
have closed due to financial restraints, almost every company cafeteria offers
some variety of healthy low-fat meals.

If your employer offers amenities like these, take advantage of them. If
you prefer not to, develop your own nutrition and exercise program to reduce
your stress level.

You'll also feel more relaxed when you stop drinking coffee. Caffeine can
give you a lift, to be sure. But it also can give you the jitters. Why not consider
getting your physical lift from breakfast, which is a meal that can also provide
extra energy to get you through the morning?

And consider using a to-do list at work. It will let you focus on your tasks
one at a time. When your most important work is completed, much of your
stress will be eliminated.

❖ ❖ ❖

When all of the people around you are losing their jobs, and you're afraid you'll
be next, count your blessings. Gratitude is an effective antidote to fear. Religious
teachings about being grateful for what you have already can help you to experience
the good that's always going on in your life. That in turn can help you to maintain
a more positive attitude that will contribute to better emotional well-being.

Another technique to help you get through changes is to take your mind
off of yourself. Constant analysis causes paralysis. You can neuter self-absorp-
tion by giving some of your energy to others.

Maybe a colleague needs your help. That's also the golden rule—doing unto others as you would expect them to do unto you—in action. But do for yourself first. Then you'll have more energy to help a friend.

But you also need to schedule private times on your calendar in order to do what makes you happy, whether it's meditating, jogging, or browsing a bookstore. It's easy to forget who should come first when you use a major to-do list. So avoid waiting for your schedule to settle down. It never will.

❖ ❖ ❖

You'll experience less stress at work by understanding that your work will never be finished on time. Work is infinite, but time is limited. Therefore, you must manage your time, not your work. Remember the fact that work expands to fill whatever time is allotted to it and that your work generates more work if it's successful.

As a result, the concept of finishing all of your work is a paradox so sinister that it can lead to burnout. That's because it puts unnecessary pressure on you. It's important to remember that work is infinite and will continue forever unless you slap time limits on it.

Disciplining yourself to manage your work, not your time, will help you to develop better work habits. You don't need more time but more discipline to use the time you have.

Satisfaction comes from knowing that you're allotted time each day for the work you love to do. So instead of trying to finish your work, just find time to do your work. Then focus on doing your best.

❖ ❖ ❖

Becoming burned out is serious. The term should not be used lightly because "burned out" used to be called "a nervous breakdown." That's when you feel depressed, lack physical energy, and become cynical toward life.

What follows are three strategies for dealing with the symptoms of burnout.

The first strategy is to organize your workday in a way that lets you perform more of those tasks you enjoy doing the most. You can determine what they are by listing work activities that give you the greatest enjoyment. Then do more of those tasks and delegate or eliminate the rest.

The second strategy is to do tasks at home such as volunteering for household chores and incorporating activities you love into your daily life. They might be listening to music, working on a needlepoint project, or reading.

The last strategy is to make exercise a part of your routine. Aerobic and bodybuilding activities are known to reduce stress and to energize people.

Those three activities will enable you to prevent or to deal with burnout symptoms while becoming more proficient at work.

❖ ❖ ❖

You must try to eliminate stress, not just to reduce it. When you focus only on stress reduction, you may not get enough benefits to make a difference.

This recalls the inscription on the Hopkins Memorial Steps at Williams College in Massachusetts: "Climb high, climb far. Your goal the sky, your aim the star."

There are a few methods that will help you point yourself higher than your goal so you can at least reduce anxiety. For example, you can be neat by not tolerating clutter or mess, and you can identify several sources of your current stress—whether they're people, places, or tasks you perform—and eliminate them. You can also identify and eliminate at least a dozen promises you have made to others that are causing stress.

And your important obligations can be fulfilled in alternative ways. Perhaps your job makes you feel so stressed out that even reducing tension won't help. Then quit. Sometimes there's no other choice.

Former President Harry Truman said, "If you can't stand the heat, get out of the kitchen."

❖ ❖ ❖

Sometimes you have to say "no" to people. It's another good way to prevent yourself from becoming stressed out. Until you've built a solid base of what you need, don't give yourself away. How can you carry the burden of responsibility for other people before you're ready?

You possess special gifts and talents that need and deserve nourishment. Because your skills won't blossom without nourishment, create a setting where you can grow. Should someone try to interrupt your flow, learn to just say "no." That's a powerful word—and many of you feel uncomfortable saying it.

So give yourself a practice session right now by repeating "no" over and over again for a couple of minutes. Doesn't that feel good? You'll feel even better when you say "no" to someone who tries to take advantage of your time. But what if that someone persists? Then it's time to assert yourself by saying, "I use the word 'no' as a complete sentence. What part of 'no' don't you understand?"

❖ ❖ ❖

Another way to beat office stress is to get organized. Everybody wants to have some control over her life and you'll take control when you use the principles of self-organization on the job.

A good way to start is by establishing deadlines for projects. When you set time limits, you'll be motivated to work only on the priorities and won't need to bother with those unnecessary tasks. That's why working under the pressure of a deadline helps you to complete a project faster and with less stress.

Another principle for getting organized is not sweating the small stuff. Most of what comes across your desk is small stuff that can be handled quickly. Those items won't pile up when you do them now.

And do the worst first. When you put off doing a difficult task it makes getting started that much harder. Procrastination causes you to feel anxious. It's much easier to jump in and do something than to worry about why you can't. You need to take the *t* out of can't and just get started.

❖ ❖ ❖

Most business people, including top executives, are concerned with the problem of getting organized and managing their time. "The problem is almost always the paper," says organization expert Stephanie Winston.

People become overwhelmed with paper. That includes e-mails, faxes, and everything else you might categorize as information. Most of you think it's all that paper that causes a lack of neatness. Winston disagrees. "Messiness is a problem of decision making," she says.

The organizational expert calls it "Chinese water-torture decision making" because every single piece of paper and every message scribbled on the back of an envelope requires a decision to be made. That's the bad news.

The good news is there are only four things you can do with a piece of paper: you can throw it away, refer it to another person who's involved, act on it personally, or file it.

Winston uses the acronym TRAF to describe her system for **t**ossing, **re**-ferring, **a**cting, and **f**iling. "Papers must move. What comes in must go out," Winston says.

❖ ❖ ❖

You have checked off a lot of items on your to-do list but still feel a lack of accomplishment. So why bother to make a lengthy list and then to proceed to scratch your head at the end of each day, wondering why you haven't accomplished the important tasks?

There is a reason. You think much has been accomplished because you've crossed off so many items. Those items are usually the quick and easy calls to make, the memos and e-mails to write, and the errands to run. You focused on tasks rather than on goals.

You need to stop spending time on things to do right now and focus instead on where you want to go and how you plan to get there. When you write down your top several goals for the year and list the most important tasks you can do to achieve them, you'll have a plan.

The ingredients of this plan will become the main items on your itinerary, but you're not expected to do everything on your list. The secret is to prioritize the tasks that dovetail with the goals written on your plan. That way, the insignificant items will fall through the cracks.

❖ ❖ ❖

You'll give your best job performance by streamlining your work. When you apply the three ideas that follow, you'll create more free time so you can either work on another project or enjoy outside activities.

1. Stop addressing envelops by hand. Use a computer program that will allow you to quickly print mailing labels that can be slapped on to correspondences. If you're computer literate yet haven't used this method by now, slap yourself. And get with it.
2. Save lots of time by avoiding routine business meetings. Let your colleagues sit through those long and boring sessions while you get a lot of work accomplished. Check with your coworkers later to catch up on what you missed.
3. Make yourself more efficient by taking a lunchtime exercise break. A brief workout doesn't have to make you sweat. A stroll around the block will get your energy flowing.

The most important timesaving tip is to know what things not to do. They're the mechanical parts of the job that you can easily delegate.

❖ ❖ ❖

Those long hours you work could be a wake-up call that you're not efficient. There's more to living than working, so you need to get or develop a life outside of work. According to a study conducted by the productivity expert Robert Kelley, when you balance your life with spare time, you'll achieve more.

Professor Kelley's book *How to Be a Star at Work* gives tips about becoming a better performer on the job. Do you want to be a star? Try these tactics:

* Get the big picture of your work. It's easy when you see your product or service through the eyes of your customers. Then you can give them what they want.
* Learn to delegate as much of your work as possible. Carve out more time to enjoy your life by taking on a supervisory role.
* Make an appointment with yourself each week just to think about your business or job and to do strategic planning. When you have a plan, your career or business or project will go a lot smoother.

When you're able to get a life outside of work, life is lived to the fullest.

❖ ❖ ❖

The easiest way to get that life outside of work is to set limits on your workweek by working shorter hours. That concept is hard to digest after you've been programmed by bosses who cling to the ancient idea that time worked is equal to output. You just assumed you have to put in longer hours than everybody else.

Professor Kelley, the productivity expert mentioned earlier, believes that you'll improve your performance when you shorten your hours at work. You can accomplish that by following the critical path of your project. You should follow the critical path method when you're scheduling all of the activities necessary to complete your project.

When you're planning a program, looking for the critical path will let you solve your problem in the quickest way. That's because it allows you to concentrate only on those tasks that are essential to finishing the job and prevents you from getting sidetracked with time-wasting obstacles.

Nobody has to tell you that the shortest distance between two points is a straight line. The straight line that lets you save time at work is the critical path.

❖ ❖ ❖

While the critical path method is an effective tool for project management, you'll automatically develop a system of links whenever you work on a big project. You cannot just write a book, build a house, or find a job. You write one page at a time. You lay one brick upon another. You discover your skills and find a job that links up to your interests.

Any big endeavor is accomplished in small segments. And the more carefully you develop each segment, the greater the whole work will be. Each segment is like a link in a chain. A chain is no stronger than its weakest link, as the saying goes. So if you make each link or segment strong, the links will be connected as though they had never been detached.

The cement that holds everything together is linkage, and the habit of linkage will help you to overcome your daily anxiety of restarting your project. Linkage causes you to move into productive action. Your project's momentum will build because there will be a connection between today and tomorrow.

❖ ❖ ❖

The expression "put a lid on it," is a kinder way of saying, "Shut your mouth. You're talking too much." But sometimes you need to shut your mind; you're thinking too much and are not able to concentrate on the tasks that are important.

When you think too much, put an uncompleted project in a cardboard box and put a lid on it. Closed boxes in your workplace will let you concentrate on the project at hand. Once you put a top on the box, that project will be out of your mind.

It's like relegating a thought to the back of your mind, where it will continue to percolate. The quality of your current projects and output will improve because you'll be working on your priorities before you take the lid off of the box.

Then you'll discover that some of the items no longer have to be done and that the world hasn't ended because you didn't get to them. Box management is putting all but your priority projects in a box and putting a lid on it.

❖ ❖ ❖

You can use the same mental-training methods to succeed in business that athletes use to achieve peak performances in sports. Athletes who excel in their sports make complete visualizations of what they do. Many coaches and athletes agree that the ability to reach optimal performance in sports is 90 percent mental, according to a report in "Athletic Insight, The Online Journal of Sport Psychology."

When you see yourself doing all of the functions leading to any achievement, you'll also succeed. That includes planning your career, advancing it, and landing a job. You must program activities in your mind before it's time to do them. That's what imagination is for. Just imagine yourself doing a sports, business, or personal project, and action will more easily follow.

If you cannot picture yourself clearing the hurdles or speaking before a group of several hundred people, you won't be able to do it well. Research literature on the neurophysiology of exercise establishes that the mind and body are inseparable. Thoughts and feelings affect every cell in your body.

In his book *Peak Performance*, psychologist Charles Garfield says our bodies tend to do what they're told if we know how to tell them. Learning how to tell your body through visualization is the trick.

❖ ❖ ❖

You are ill advised to equate peak performance in your job or job search with always having to jump over hurdles. If you spend all of your time putting out fires, you'll get burned out and will be no good to yourself or to your current or future employer. Besides, you'll find that some of those business and job-hunting fires extinguish themselves.

You need to get a life! It's what you do outside of your work life that helps you achieve balance. That doesn't mean balancing yourself on the sofa to watch TV and become a couch potato.

You need challenges to get your adrenaline going. An exercise program does the trick. So does taking a course you need to bring your skills up to speed and working on that home remodeling project.

While you don't always have to jump over hurdles at work, giving yourself hurdles to leap over outside of work will balance your life. Tackling challenges outside of your career will help you to become more poised and emotionally stable.

❖ ❖ ❖

You'll never give peak performances when you fear making mistakes. Even after you visualize performing all of your project's steps with ease, you will have a blunder once in a while. So remember the cardinal rule for doing your best: have the courage to make a mistake.

Anxiety about messing up paralyzes your ability to make decisions. The spontaneity needed to innovate is reduced. You need to be loosey-goosey to innovate. That's impossible when you fear making a mistake. When you have the courage to make one, you won't try to avoid something because you fear making a blooper and being punished for it.

After you've made a boo-boo, ask yourself what the worst thing that could happen is. Could you lose your job? Chances of getting fired for making a mistake are practically zero. But if worst comes to worst, you can talk at upcoming interviews about the lessons you learned from the situation.

Your fear of making mistakes will be removed only when you're daring enough to make them. Just draw some lessons from your bloopers, and you'll reach future business decisions with more ease.

❖ ❖ ❖

When you are wrong, quickly admit it. Listen to how this tried-and-true Dale Carnegie technique of enthusiastically admitting your mistake produced astonishing results.

Chris was a customer service representative at a major bank for a big international customer. He made a big mistake. So the customer went over Chris's head to a high-level vice president and demanded to know why his service representative had blundered.

When the VP questioned Chris at the customer's request, the customer service rep quickly admitted that the mistake had been his fault, called the customer to take responsibility, and explained how he would fix the problem.

After the dust settled, the VP said to Chris, "It took a lot of guts for you to take it on the chin and fix the problem without pointing a finger at anybody else. I respect you for that."

Self-help guru Dale Carnegie said that when you quickly admit to having made a mistake, most people will have a forgiving attitude, minimize your error, and even come to your rescue.

Chris learned that admitting a mistake right away was more impressive than trying to defend himself.

❖ ❖ ❖

Interpersonal relationships can get mean in today's lean-and-mean work environment. People are overworked. That's the reason companies emphasize conflict resolution as a way to help you and your fellow workers get along better. When tempers flare, you can be compatible with difficult colleagues by using the Two-C formula: communicate and compromise.

First, you need to communicate by listening to your colleague's words and then repeating them back in your own words to make sure you understand the message. Now you can speak openly without accusing or blaming your coworker. Just avoid using the word "you." Instead of saying, "you hurt me," it's better to say, "I felt hurt."

When you express, yourself honestly, you can still experience anxiety because you fear others won't like what you say. But suppressing those feelings can make you tense and filled with resentment.

Second, you need to compromise. Your goal is to get along with others, not to win arguments. The question to ask yourself is, "How can we resolve this conflict so both of us feel good?"

Nobody said conflict resolution is easy. But you'll master it by practicing the Two-C technique: communicate honestly, and compromise.

❖ ❖ ❖

You need to resist the tendency to approach your job with a what's-in-it-for-me attitude. Instead, consider what makes you a good employee or candidate for a promotion or a better position.

Bill Gates once listed the qualities he finds in the best and brightest employees. You need to be curious about your company's products. "Talk to customers about how they use your merchandise," Gates wrote in a syndicated column. "Then you'll understand customers' needs and be able to serve them better."

You also have to enjoy thinking through how a product can help make peoples' lives or work more interesting, says the Microsoft chairman.

And good employees focus on personal long-term goals. For example, your goal could be developing skills because you must have specialized knowledge or talents in today's workplace. "Never assume the expertise you have today will be good enough for tomorrow," wrote Gates.

Whether you have a job or are looking for one, keep the qualities that can make you a good employee in mind. Then you always will be good enough for tomorrow.

❖ ❖ ❖

A good employee can become a better employee by remembering a slogan posted on the bulletin board outside of the Park Avenue Methodist Church in Manhattan: "When it comes to giving, some people stop at nothing."

When you stop at nothing in order to give of yourself at work, nothing will stop you from receiving the recognition and success your efforts deserve. That's the benefit of going beyond what's necessary to get the job done.

Any time you interview for another job, internally or externally, be sure to talk about how you walk that extra mile for your company and its customers. The expression, "When it comes to giving, some people stop at nothing," can also be called "value-added marketing" because it makes customers, bosses, and potential employers feel they're getting more value for their money.

Giving exceptional service always needs to be your top priority. With so many people, products, and services competing for attention, it's getting more difficult to make yourself stand out from the crowd. You will be noticed when you remember to stop at nothing "when it comes to giving."

❖ ❖ ❖

When you look forward to Monday morning the way others look to Friday afternoon, you are a workaholic. Don't brag about it, and don't tell a prospective employer, "I'm a workaholic" as if it were an asset. You have a compulsive disorder that can get out of hand. Workaholics set especially high standards for themselves. That factor alone can drive you nuts.

You are a workaholic when you rise early and can't wait to get started, prefer labor to leisure, and get depressed on weekends and holidays. Workaholics also work long hours seven days a week and consider sleep a waste of time. They don't take vacations—or they cut short their trips after a few restless days.

But workaholism has a bright side. Psychologists say workaholics are happy because they're doing what they love, which is working at what they do best—and they can't get enough of it.

How does one handle this condition? At least plan a short vacation. A week will do nicely. Be sure to pay for it in advance, and leave your laptop behind.

❖ ❖ ❖

Some employees get to keep their jobs because companies provide executive coaches to help them identify and strengthen the skills that will give them more pizzazz.

You can coach yourself. "You take the initiative to identify, develop, or improve certain skills you believe are going to be critical," says psychologist and career coach Randy Ruppart.

His job-search candidates learn to coach themselves with a method called Self-Directed Development. It begins with asking some of your contacts to answer questions about what you perceive to be your strengths and weaknesses. "When you ask them to rate you on a scale," says Dr. Ruppart, "you'll know how you're really coming across."

People who know you might disagree with your perceptions of yourself. Perhaps you decide you're a good listener, but feedback indicates that what people tell you goes in one ear and out the other.

Their opinions should go into your plan for self-development. You'll then be in a better position to target a skill for development and to research self-improvement strategies by reading a book, buying a self-help cassette, or taking a course.

The critical difference between self-help and Self-Directed Development is the feedback element, which can be uplifting. "Most people discover they have far more strengths than they do development needs."

❖ ❖ ❖

Everybody is concerned about the lack of job security. Although nobody ever promised you a job for life, it's still disorienting when your company downsizes.

Because capitalism exists in a sea of change, jobs have always been cut. New products have always replaced old ones. Similarly, workers with updated skills have always displaced employees whose talents have become obsolete.

You'll know that your skills need updating when the jobs you're after require skills you don't have. Then it's time to learn new ones so you can offer your next employer a bigger bag of tricks.

What's your bag? It had better be filled with skills that are marketable. The new meaning of "job security" is having the right skills and knowing how to market them to prospective employers.

There are many courses out there where you can learn new computer skills, for example. If you're getting unemployment benefits, ask about courses you can take at no cost.

Speaking of free courses, perhaps the company where you work offers professional training. Your signing up for some training could make the difference between getting the boot and keeping your job during a future downsizing.

❖ ❖ ❖

The best time to develop new skills is before your company dumps you—not when you're worried about losing a job within the next few weeks. When you find opportunities to learn while you still have a job, you'll always be prepared when you need to make a change.

As your career unfolds, keep evaluating which aspects of your job you need to know immediately and which you'll need to know down the line. Then you'll be ready to find out if the company you work for offers courses that will provide the skills necessary to protect your position.

Many large companies have a training and education department that offers a catalogue of courses. When that's not the case, or if you've lost a job, look for classes in your community that will teach you what you need to know.

You can find training to fit every budget. Community colleges are probably the least expensive, and many offer classes over a several-week period. You might also find the right course in your community's continuing education and recreational programs.

You can keep ahead of the downsizing wave by looking at your business training and education as an ongoing experience you'll commit to for the rest of your career.

❖ ❖ ❖

Many companies are firing with one hand and hiring with the other. Your head need not be on the chopping block when the ax falls if you acquire the technical skills needed for your job.

Employers create almost as many jobs as they eliminate, according to The American Management Association. New positions are created for people who offer an updated range of technical skills. Jobs requiring those talents don't need as many supervisors. That's why so many middle managers get the old heave-ho while professional or technical people are in better positions to either keep the jobs they have or to find new ones.

Are you a middle manager worried about your job being cut? You need to talk to people in your organization about technical needs and the background required to fill them and to then take courses in the technical aspect of your business.

While some jobs aren't technical, most have technical aspects (like using computers) associated with them. One of the easiest ways to bring yourself up to speed is to acquire the basic computer skills needed for your current or next job.

❖ ❖ ❖

You got a promotion but don't feel ready for it, so you wonder how you'll handle the title you just earned. Most employees are ready to move up the corporate ladder before they think they are, according to a published report. Yet once they're promoted, workers tend to doubt their abilities and to believe they won't succeed in the more important job.

Those negative thoughts need to be dumped in order to dig into your job with the confidence you'll need to succeed. Remember that you earned the promotion. The higher-ups at your company selected you because they know you're a capable hired hand. A good manager knows that once you've mastered your job, it's time to move forward. Because that is the reason you were promoted, you need to trust the management's judgment.

While employers will almost always promote you before you think you're ready, you will be ready when you start with what you know you can do. Then you'll make instant contributions while you grow into the new job. So what if you make a mistake or two? Just go back and correct them.

❖ ❖ ❖

After you get promoted, don't lean back on your cushy, ergonomically designed chair, put your feet on top of the desk, and clasp your hands behind
your head. You might fall off the promotion ladder while kicking back.

You'll keep your feet on the ground by keeping your mind on the reason
you were promoted—the boss noticed your strong points. Be sure to use those
strong points a lot in your new management job, and don't enter the new job
without a clue about what you should do. You want a job description—plus a
description of the parts of the job management didn't tell you about—from the
person who held the job before you.

Moving up the ladder is also a chance to learn more. You can learn
more about spreadsheets, web design, or PowerPoint by signing up for
classes.

As you delegate authority to the talent below you, keep an eye out for
somebody who can fill your shoes someday. Your next promotion will come
faster when you have your protégé waiting on deck.

❖ ❖ ❖

Are employees motivated by fear or affection? That was the old management
dilemma that no longer holds water. That's why your approach to managing
people should not be like the old bull in a china shop.

Managers who bullied ruled American businesses for decades. "It's my
way or the highway" was their anthem. But products of the information
age come not from assembly lines but from employee's heads. That means
successful managers today find that showing a compassionate side works
better—and means they get to keep their jobs longer.

Instead of treating your employees merely as tools to get things done,
respect their feelings. You'll get more out of them. To increase your empathy for fellow workers, make a list of what you value about each staff member, and help them fix problems instead of condemning those who make a
mistake.

❖ ❖ ❖

When your boss is driving you crazy, chances are you have a crazy boss. Kooky supervisors come in three colorful varieties:

There's the bully boss. Leona Helmsley was an example. In order to handle the bully, you have to be an apple polisher. But keep your dignity while doing it.

Up next is the paranoid boss, a perfectionist who suspects you and your fellow workers are plotting against him. The icon here is former US President Richard Nixon. You cannot argue with a paranoid, but you can let the manager vent his rage, and then walk away and have a good laugh—or a cry.

Finally, there's the bureaucracy boss. She's a wimp who loves endless meetings, takes all of the credit, and then gets lost when it's time to share the blame. A bureaucracy boss goes by the book to cover her tail. If you work for a bureaucracy boss, make the hard decisions yourself.

It can be tough working for a nut case. But when the going gets tough, tough employees either go shopping or job hunting. It's your choice. But either way, you'd better learn how to deal with your maniacal manager.

❖ ❖ ❖

You have three choices for dealing with a bully boss: you can quit, go job hunting, or confront the person. When you take it on the chin day after day, you'll continue to be demoralized.

Ever ask yourself why you continue working for a bully? If the reason is because you make good money, think about spending some of it on a career counselor or a therapist. They'll tell you not to allow a bully to chop away at your self-esteem.

When you choose to confront a bully boss, be nice about it. You'll only release pent-up emotions when you blast a bully. But if you still have a job by the end of the conversation, you can kiss your raise goodbye.

A technique that works well when confronting a dreadful boss is asking him to repeat a statement. The bully will often water it down because when you stand up, bullies back down. And never tell bullies they are wrong.

Bullies get revenge, and they're cowards who attribute to others their own hang-ups.

Whether you quit, job hunt, or confront, the message you want to convey to a bully boss is, "It's not okay to mess around with me."

❖ ❖ ❖

When you work for an incompetent boss, it makes you wonder how the blockhead could have ever been given a supervisory position in the first place. Who said life is fair? But you still have to deal with the schlemiel.

Let's say you work for someone who never praises your work. You need to set your own goals and reward yourself for achieving them. You empower yourself in the process.

But you might have a boss who praises you to the skies but doesn't deliver on his promise for a raise, a promotion, or support for you projects. Your boss is a wimp! He fears sticking his neck out. How do you deal with a candy-ass?

It's a mistake to push the wimp, because he might jump ugly on you. He's less afraid of you than he is of approaching his boss. If you want a raise, for example, take a roundabout approach by sending the wimp a memo describing the reasons you deserve the raise. Then all the milquetoast has to do is route your memo to his boss after attaching a note that reads, "She makes some good points here."

Bad bosses help you understand the important fact that you are in charge of your career.

❖ ❖ ❖

You are sick and tired of your job as a manager and aren't going to take it anymore! Before you decide to jump off the management track, improve your managing style by following three techniques used by excellent managers:

1. Give employees authority. According to a study, this is the top quality that good managers have in common. Supply your staff with the tools, and then stay out of their way. When your staff takes responsibility

for assignments, they assume ownership of a project and do a better job.

2. Set objectives. Make a list of activities needed to achieve your project or goal.

3. Get your priorities straight. The study also points out that excellent managers put their families first. The job comes second. Outstanding managers balance careers with a strong commitment to family, friends, and community.

You'll experience less stress when you try to manage better and fuss less. Who knows? You might even get to like your management position.

❖ ❖ ❖

So you've landed a job as manager. But do you really know how to manage a staff? Your team will make you look like an excellent manager when you help team members succeed in their jobs. You can accomplish this by using a two-step strategy to guide them:

First, hold individual meetings with each member of your staff. Half-hour meetings will do nicely to keep each employee on track with assignments. You can ask to hear project updates, target areas where a worker needs your help, and congratulate your staff on what's going well.

Second, have an open-door policy. That makes sense because an employee may have a question only you can answer. Remember to tell your team they can drop in anytime for a quick meeting. That means they must get to the point in a couple of minutes and then get out.

When it's applied to your management position, this two-step strategy will allow you to become a mentor to your staff. In turn, they'll make you look good. That's how to keep your management job longer.

❖ ❖ ❖

You've heard the definition of managers. They're people who are good at something else!

Managers and middle managers have been forced to look for something else as skilled administrative assistants are filling positions that used to be considered middle management.

Today, we're talking about a new breed of manager. That tough boss who ran the show without any lip from you is gone. Who replaced those head-strong bosses? Computer whizzes who use and explain the latest information technology to the rest of the company.

If you aspire to be a manager someday, do your current job well. Then you'll gradually be given projects to manage—especially if you stay on the cutting edge of computer technology your entire career.

And that much-discussed master of business administration (MBA) could be a big-ticket item on the road to management success. However, it makes good sense to start earning your MBA after you've held a job awhile, so you can better understand what to major in. Besides, your employer might pay for your studies. That would be quite an advantage because a part-time MBA program can cost up to one hundred sixty-five thousand dollars.

❖ ❖ ❖

There is a downside to being a manager. Just when you think the new job is going well, you could get the boot. About 40 percent of management jobs only last a year and a half or less. That statistic is according to a survey of human resources executives. The study also indicated a couple of ingredients that determine whether new managers make the grade.

The first component is personal chemistry. The second is your ability to fit in with the company's culture. The study shows that a whopping 80 percent of new managers who get pink slips after a short stint failed to build strong relationships with their peers and subordinates.

That goes to show that bonding with your fellow workers is even more important than bonding with your boss.

❖ ❖ ❖

Most executives fear making mistakes. You have been conditioned at work to not admit to making them. But rapid change is the name of the game in today's business environment, so it's next to impossible to not make a mistake.

For that reason, job experts have started to change their tune. Go ahead and talk about your blunders. Your boss—and even your hiring managers—will like you more. Admitting to a mistake and explaining what you did to correct it shows you can take risks to deal with change.

Everybody makes mistakes, and successful people rebound from them. Take Babe Ruth. He also broke the major league record for strikeouts. Babe felt it was smarter to make bold moves and to sometimes miss than to always hit singles. And how about Walt Disney? He was fired from one of his first jobs because he couldn't draw.

Business people who rebound from failure have learned that defeat often foreshadows success. If this is true, perhaps Susan B. Anthony was right. The turn-of-the-century women's activist said, "Failure is impossible."

❖ ❖ ❖

Your peak years for earning money are also the years your job is most at risk. When you hit fifty, you're at the point in life where you may be laid off because of your high salary. At best, you'll qualify for a package. Either way, your job will be gone.

Getting a pink slip is always a shock, even if you had suspected it could happen. You're shocked because it's harder to find a new job at your age—and you'll probably discover that some of your skills are outmoded.

The key to protecting your job is sharpening your skills. As you get older, keeping a job means having skills that are in demand. So identify the skills you know your company will need. Either learn them or get additional training and education in the skills you've identified.

But it's not enough to sharpen and update your talents. You must let your boss know about it. Lots of people lose jobs for no better reason than the downsizing committee wasn't aware of what they had accomplished both on the job and in business education.

❖ ❖ ❖

A good nap can help you work better. According to a sleep expert, dozing off is a tool that can increase your productivity. According to Dr. Martin Morre-Ede, "A 20-minute nap can help you gain up to four hours more of peak alertness without the crash you suffer when a caffeine buzz wears off."

But don't tell that to your boss. While siestas are a way of life in some European countries, they're considered sleeping on the job in the United States. The self-employed don't have to hide their napping. But when you work for a company, coworkers will raise their eyebrows when they see you drop your eyelids. So it's a lame idea to sneak a nap in the lunchroom.

However, you can make your cubicle a resting place by turning the back of your chair to the aisle so passers-by won't catch your eye or catch you napping. In order to complete the deception, place a newspaper opened to the business section on the desktop in front of you.

The best time to find a place to rest is after lunch. That's when you feel most drowsy, and you're not going to be productive anyway. So what the heck—why not grab a power nap? You don't always lose when you snooze.

❖ ❖ ❖

When your voice sounds like fingernails being dragged across a blackboard, you can turn off business contacts and interviewers. Who wants to listen to a hoarse voice?

When you're attacked by hoarseness, heal yourself by following four methods suggested by specialists who treat voice problems:

1. Drink plenty of water. About a dozen glasses a day keeps your throat and your vocal chords moist. On the other hand, milk and dairy products can increase the mucus in your throat.

2. Rest your voice completely. Hoarseness usually disappears after a few days if you stop using your voice for a while.
3. Inhale steam for five minutes every several hours.
4. Suck on soothing lozenges.

Most vocal problems can be averted by not abusing your voice in the first place. You can strain it and injure your vocal chords by talking in noisy places and by speaking in a lower-than-normal register. When your voice sounds grating, abandon the affectation and use your normal speaking voice.

Other habits that will give your voice a raucous sound are smoking cigarettes and repeated attempts to clear your throat. Try swallowing instead.

In a nutshell, you can treat hoarseness with rest and patience.

❖ ❖ ❖

When you consider leaving a dead-end job to peruse your dream, it's much like dating. You might think you're head over heels in love. But after the first date—well, maybe not.

So check out your dream job to see if moving into it is worth the effort. If you go back to school and earn another degree or certification, you'll most likely have to start again from scratch. And chicken scratch is what you'll make.

As you think about your dream job, determine if that dream just interests you or if you feel passionate about it. There is a difference. Being interested means you are ready to consider something. But being passionate means you have a strong liking for doing something.

When you're motivated by passion, meet people who work in the business you want to enter in order to learn what a workday is like. Then consider keeping your dead-end job for a while and taking classes at night. That's how to make sure your interest has evolved into passion.

❖ ❖ ❖

When you have a job and decide either to make a move or to just check around to see what's out there, you must be careful when responding to classified ads in the newspaper or job postings on the web. Most ads are straightforward. A company lists qualifications it thinks are important in order to attract qualified candidates.

But your company might place a blind ad to see if any of its employees are peeking on the outside. You're justified in being suspicious when you do not see an organization's name on the newspaper ad and are obligated to respond to a box number.

Companies might also run blind ads for a few other reasons:

* To stop you from calling or dropping by
* To prevent employees from knowing they're looking on the outside
* To keep the competition in the dark

So when you have a job, you'd better think twice about answering blind ads. Your résumé and cover letter could end up on your boss's desk. That'll cut you out of the loop, stop your promotion, or get you fired. But when you don't have a job—hey, you've got nothing to lose.

❖ ❖ ❖

You will increase the odds of surviving your company's next purge by job hunting all of the time. "The continual job search," which is a term coined by career coach and author Kate Wendleton, "is not as exhausting as it sounds." Wendleton's advice for keeping your job longer and for being ready for the next move "is to just keep your eyes and ears open."

A continual job hunt happens when you're inclined to continually gather information about market conditions both inside and outside of your company. "When you know what's going on in your industry," says the career coach, "you can examine what you have to offer your company and prospective employers." That will inform you of the skills you need to increase in order to survive.

Presuming your company will take care of you by deciding where you need training or what you must do next to improve your career is outdated thinking. You're responsible for taking care of yourself.

When you fit into the new direction your company and industry is headed in, your employer will value you more. Then you'll get to keep your job longer.

❖ ❖ ❖

CHAPTER 17

When You're Sick and Tired of Being Sick and Tired of the Corporate Rat Race

Working for a nonprofit organization can be very rewarding.
—SALLY SKIDMORE

YOU'VE HAD IT WITH THE corporate rat race and are "as mad as hell and… not going to take this anymore," to quote Howard Beale's rant in the movie *Network.* Now you want a job that'll give you a purpose in life. Chances are you won't find your heart's desire in the corporate world.

"If you're having problems landing in the private sector," says career counselor Sally Skidmore, "try not-for-profit organizations. There are lots of jobs there."

Each not-for-profit institution exists for a special purpose. The reason could be for education, religion, mental or physical health, or land preservation. "They offer a wealth of job opportunities where your skills might fit," says the Connecticut-based career counselor who specializes in nonprofits.

Yet this is an employment area that's highly overlooked. Maybe it's because you equate this kind of activity to volunteer work where there is no pay. Nevertheless, nonprofits offer administrative and professional jobs that pay well. You can direct programs, raise money, write proposals, or run membership activities. Salaries can range anywhere from thirty thousand dollars a year to eighty thousand or more. According to the Bureau of Labor Statistics, jobs for administrative assistants pay between twenty thousand and forty thousand dollars a year.

While "there just might be a not for profit that suits your passion," Skidmore suggests you must first decide what part of a foundation you want to be involved in. Do you want to raise money? Be an administrator? Or offer accounting and financial skills for managing the assets, funds, and expenditures of an organization?

Either way, Skidmore maintains working for a nonprofit organization gives you a wonderful feeling to share with others in the same dedication. "It's very, very rewarding."

❖ ❖ ❖

When you're sick and tired of being sick and tired, you won't get a new life by doing the same old same old. That's looking for work with companies in the same old industry that you find so disagreeable. That's why an increasing number of you have explored the more laid-back world of not-for-profit.

Foundations offer a different environment from the corporate rat race. "To work for a nonprofit offers the chance to tap into things that matter to you," says Sally Skidmore, the career counselor we met in the previous coaching vignette. "You can discover an organization's special meaning by sharing in its spirit." Associations put their assets to work for humanitarian efforts or for the benefit of their communities and states.

You can make good money and work at wonderful jobs in the not-for-profit world. How do you find work there? Make it a part of your regular job hunt. "Networking techniques provide a wonderful way to become informed about which area of not for profit to focus on," Skidmore advises. So ask your contacts who they know in the nonprofit world, and then talk to people who work in it.

Outside of networking, you can mine for job leads in your local paper where foundations often advertise. You can also check out job boards on the Internet and in *The Chronicle of Higher Education* and *The Foundation Library*, two helpful publications. Check your public library's business section.

❖ ❖ ❖

When the job market shatters, you can increase job prospects by turning to the nonprofit sector. "I'm noticing more and more job hunters say they want to have additional meaning to the work they're doing," says nonprofit career specialist Sally Skidmore. "I encourage them to explore the wealth of opportunities in the nonprofit world."

Maybe you assume only a couple of people make up an agency's administrative staff. That isn't the case. Nonprofit workers serve both as volunteers and paid staff. Large foundations—museums, not-for-profit hospitals, educational institutions, and community service organizations—have extensive paid staffs.

You can find public-spirited community organizations right in your own backyard. Just use a search engine to look for nonprofit organizations in your community.

When it comes to reasons that you might be interested in working for a foundation, look into your own values for the answer. From Skidmore's experience, employees should feel in sync with their foundation's worthwhile cause.

And while nonprofit environments are often superb in terms of people having a spirit for the organization, not-for-profit organizations provide another nice perk—more vacation time upfront. Corporations give new employees only a couple of weeks starting out while nonprofits have a more generous approach to personal time.

❖ ❖ ❖

Even when you're not sick and tired of the corporate rat race, high unemployment rates can force you to seek alternative areas of opportunity.

For example, many job candidates I've coached were left holding the bag because the job they had held wasn't available elsewhere or was outsourced to Bangalore, Mysore, or Thiruvananthapuram. Nonprofits were only one of the many areas available for exploration.

Richard and Ann obtained teaching certificates. Art went into real estate sales. Dick and Reggie took the CDL exam in order to drive school busses and trucks for the duration. Bob made a successful career veer from a position as a banking executive to one as a legal administrator with a major law firm in

New York. And Terrance took the LSW exam, was admitted into law school, and became an assistant district attorney in Florida.

Speaking of the legal field, attorneys who seek alternative opportunities can offer excellent writing skills. Even if you're not John Grisham or Scott Turow, two lawyers who transformed their writing abilities into best-selling courtroom dramas, you can transfer your writing skills to other kinds of businesses. Books about how to study the law are always in demand.

Some lawyers have formed temporary employment agencies to help other out-of-work attorneys to become freelance lawyers. JuriStaff in Philadelphia and Lawyer's Staffing in Virginia are two examples. Those staffing agencies specialize in helping paralegals find temporary jobs.

There are unlimited alternative fields that you can explore. Just let your imagination guide you. If you're good at something like carpentry, have been complimented for your cooking, or enjoy working with animals, create a job for yourself.

❖ ❖ ❖

CHAPTER 18

How to Get a Job through Staffing Agencies

LET EMPLOYMENT AGENCIES AND RECRUITERS BEAT THE BUSHES
FOR YOU

EMPLOYMENT AGENCIES COME IN A variety of flavors—contingency employment agencies, retained search firms, temporary staffing agencies, and niche recruiting agencies.

Contingency agencies are for most workers—white collar, blue collar, and pink collar (secretaries)—and are paid a fee by the hiring company only if you're hired. That fee, a percentage of your first year's salary, can range from 25 to 75 percent. It's unethical, and even unlawful in some states, for a staffing agency in any category to charge you a fee. If you're required to pay one, walk away. Then call the authorities!

Retained search firms called "headhunters" keep their fee or retainer whether or not they find somebody with the experience and skill to fill a specific job opening. Professional executives go to retained firms. But when they're selecting executives to work with, headhunters are picky, picky, picky.

For that reason, it's best to network your way into a retained search firm by getting an introduction from a friend. If you don't know anybody who can refer you, attach a brief letter to your résumé and send it to the director of research. That method will get your résumé into the retained agency's database from which résumés for searches are pulled.

❖ ❖ ❖

Temporary (temp) staffing agencies fill jobs for all manners of occasions. Temp workers are needed to cover vacation periods, to help out during seasonal

increases in business, and to surround permanent staffs that have been se-
verely downsized.

As a matter of fact, companies save money by dumping you and hiring
temporary employees to fill in, so there are countless part-time jobs you can
apply for. That is true no matter what you do.

Temp agencies also offer "temp-to-perm" positions. That means you start
as a temp but could become permanent. Either way, a survey of five hundred
employee benefit specialists showed that most of their companies used contingent workers.

Unlike contingency and retained services that cover a variety of jobs in
a variety of industries, niche recruiting agencies hire specialized workers,
including doctors, lawyers, architects, and engineers.

❖ ❖ ❖

The easiest way to find reliable agencies is to ask your friends and colleagues
for the names of staffing services with whom they work. Your former boss
might be willing to recommend you to the agency her department uses. Sign
up with at least three of them.

And when it comes to your first meeting with an agency recruiter, "cut
to the chase and tell them what you want upfront," advises Brandon Thimke,
a staffing professional with a Cleveland-based staffing company called the
Reserves Network.

Marketing your part-time service has never been easier. According to a
survey of five hundred employee benefit specialists, more companies planned
to hire temporary and contract workers in 2014 than during the previous
year. It showed most companies used contingent workers.

In a study by CareerBuilder, 42 percent of employers surveyed said
they planned to hire more temp and contract workers in 2014 than during the previous year. That percentage is a five percent increase over the
previous year.

Many corporations are hiring more temps while reducing the number of
full-time workers in order to avoid changing healthcare options because of
Obamacare going into effect.

Computer-related skills are especially in demand. This category is in the list of the top ten highest-paying temp jobs. Staffing agencies place programmers, systems analysts, and software developers in well-paying temp jobs ranging from thirty-three to forty-five dollars per hour.

❖ ❖ ❖

When it comes to working with retained search firms, you need to have a strategy for developing a relationship with them. Retained search firms are also known as "headhunters." They hate that term. Members of retained firms consider the word "headhunter" to be as demeaning as "quack" and "shyster" are to other professions. For that reason, they would prefer to be called "recruiters," "executive recruiters," or "executive search consultants."

Executives earning over seventy thousand smackeroos a year can register with headhunters. Only a few companies retain most of the executive recruiters. That's why it's wrong to assume you've covered all of the bases by sending your résumé to a single firm. So register with as many retained firms as possible.

You'll find listings in *The Directory Of Executive Recruiters*, the bible of the headhunting industry. It can be found in the business section of your local library and online. Each firm has a website to help you research. Online or off, this directory lists firms—permanent and part-time employment agencies along with executive recruiters—geographically and by specialty.

You can let the firms you select use their creativity and relationships with the companies they represent to help you market your talents to their clients.

❖ ❖ ❖

The best time to contract an executive recruiter is before you lose your job or want to make a career change. Search firms can help your job-finding campaign and career by keeping you informed about the latest developments in your industry while updating you on skills you need to pick up in order to become an even more attractive candidate.

When you're leaving your current job, contact as many executive recruiters as you can. It makes sense to cover all of the bases, especially when jobs are scarce.

You'll find a listing of executive search firms that focus on your industry in *The Directory Of Executive Recruiters*. That's the so-called bible of the headhunting industry you read about in the previous coaching vignette. In addition to looking for a copy in a business library, you can order the directory from publisher Jim Kennedy in Fitzwilliam, New Hampshire.

Remember that when you work with an executive recruiter, it's a two-way street. The recruiter can help your career, and you can help her career by recommending people you know for positions. That is how a good relationship with a search firm is developed.

❖ ❖ ❖

There are a couple of ways to approach executive recruiters and employment agencies: the passive approach and the expert method.

The passive approach works best for most job hunters. That's because it uses the recruiter's judgment to match your skills with the search firm's job assignments.

To use the passive approach, write the recruiter a cover letter with your résumé; just write a few paragraphs to introduce yourself and to give a brief description of your background.

Your letter can end with a statement like, "If you feel my background would be a good fit with one of your corporate clients, I'd love to get together with you. With that thought in mind, I'm looking forward to calling you in a few days to follow up."

The second approach, which is the expert method, gives you more control because it allows you to show the recruiter how you can help him. Again, you start with a letter. But instead of just covering your background, explain how your background satisfies a current business need in the marketplace, and then follow up with a phone call to schedule an appointment. This kind of letter is based on your research and knowledge of your field.

With the expert method, you—not the recruiter—are the judge of your rightness in the marketplace.

❖ ❖ ❖

When executive recruiters fail to stumble all over themselves to respond to your résumé and cover letter, don't take it personally. Headhunters are not working for you but for companies who pay them to fill a position.

The best way to contact an executive recruiter is to mail your résumé with a cover letter. Executive recruiters are interested only in candidates who fit their current openings. However, if your résumé impresses a search firm, it might add you to its database of executives by scanning your résumé into a computer. For that reason, you need to use standard typefaces and résumé formats so it can be read easily.

And you'd better think twice about following up by phone or e-mail. You risk alienating a recruiter who might have an opening for you someday by taking up his valuable time now. You'll be contacted when an executive search firm has a position that fits your profile.

When a recruiter calls, you'll be asked to talk about an open job or to recommend someone who you think fits the bill. Either way, you've started to build a relationship with a recruiter who can help your career.

❖ ❖ ❖

Executive recruiters and agencies can help you get jobs, but you need to be careful when dealing with them. You'll find some to be honest and helpful. Others are sneaky and devious.

Just because a recruiter agrees to a meeting doesn't mean he has a job prospect for you. The headhunter might just want to network for job openings by pumping you for information. He'll ask for the names of places where you've already interviewed. It's important not to tell him. The recruiter may call the company, send another candidate to interview, and beat you out of a job.

So when you talk with recruiters, just discuss the job they're recruiting for and how your skills match up. Then shut up. Recruiters are not your friends. They're your competition because they don't have jobs either.

Remember that executive recruiters are paid by management and earn their living by finding openings at companies who retain them and then filling those openings with candidates who match the job descriptions.

That's your job, too. You're trying to find an opening and fill it with yourself. How do you deal with recruiters? Carefully.

❖ ❖ ❖

When you send a résumé to an executive recruiter, you probably won't be called for an interview unless that recruiter has a specific job in mind.

Most recruiters won't even acknowledge your résumé or file over-the-transom résumés on your behalf. So resubmit your document in six months if you're still in the job market. However, if you're lucky enough to have qualifications that match a recruiter's current assignment, you'll be invited to interview straightaway.

Following up on your résumé submission by telephone is unwise. It's a waste of your time, and you risk annoying the recruiter. For the same reason, you should not walk in and expect an interview.

When you get the opportunity to talk to a recruiter by phone or in person, be honest when you're asked to give your present or expected salary. These experts are professionals and have a way of zeroing in on the truth.

Finally, recruiters must respect the confidence of your situation. If you have any doubts, think twice before venturing out. There's always a remote possibility of a slip-up, but that's a chance you need to take once you've decided to make a change or to test the job market.

❖ ❖ ❖

Who loves ya, baby? Not the executive recruiter. When dealing with recruiters, understand you are not the client. Recruiters and employment agencies serve their customers, who are companies with openings that recruiters are asked to fill. They find people for jobs—not jobs for people.

Don't think even for a minute that the recruiter is your friend. Some can be quite devious. For example, a recruiter might agree to meet with you not to discuss a position but to pump you for information about job openings you might know about. That's why it's important to not tell headhunters where you've been interviewing. They may call the company and send another candidate for an interview and beat you out of a job.

If you're asked what companies you've interviewed with, say, "While I'd prefer not to discuss who I've seen so far, if you let me know to which companies you intend to submit my résumé, I'll be happy to inform you if I've already established contacts there."

And if the agency representative asks you a question in confidence, keep your guard up. Remember that you're always being interviewed. Your objective is to find out if they have assignments—job openings—that match your skills. Then convince them you're a great fit.

So, who loves ya, baby? Your spouse or lover, maybe. But certainly not your recruiter.

❖ ❖ ❖

CHAPTER 19

Temping as a Way of Life

JOIN THE CONTINGENCY WORKFORCE AND GET YOUR FOOT IN THE BACK DOOR

THE CONTINGENCY WORKERS ARE COMING! As a matter of fact, they've been coming for years. That's why the contingency workforce is the fastest-growing phenomenon in the job marketplace. "When you're a part timer, freelancer, subcontractor, or job sharer, consider yourself one of them," says Anita Lands, a New York City–based career specialist who helps workers over fifty.

This is an option many senior job hunters select. It's easier to become a part of the contingency workforce than it is to get a permanent job. Freelancers of all ages make up 30 percent of America's workforce. That's over forty million people. And according to a survey by the software company Intuit, by the year 2020, contingency workers will compose over 40 percent of the workforce. That's over sixty million people.

While finding a job can be difficult for candidates young and old, it's much tougher for workers over fifty. Older workers are also more expensive workers. So when you choose to temp, the hiring odds are in your favor.

That isn't to say that older workers who have been downsized should stop trying to get back into the corporate world. "If an older worker has developed a very good skill set," Lands continues, "they have something to offer, and that facilitates their being hired."

Whether you choose to stick with corporate work or to try freelancing as a temp, it's important you value this proven fact: as an older worker, you've developed a work ethic and first-rate habits that come from experience and training. That's a benefit younger workers cannot offer.

❖ ❖ ❖

When you get sick and tired of working for someone who could care less about your career goals, create your own job. Millions of Americans are free-lancing as temps for a variety of reasons:

* They've not been able to find full-time work.
* Their money is running out.
* They want to keep their skills honed.
* They want to control their work life and career.

Temping can satisfy those needs. Outside of the call for income, the need to keep your skills honed is the most important of all. As the old saying goes, "if you don't use it, you'll lose it." That applies to skills in any field.

Some workers choose to freelance. Others pick this alternative because they've gotten the ax. Either way, millions of Americans prefer working part time.

Having control of your work life and career is just one of the benefits you get as a freelancer. Listing a temporary job on your résumé is another. Then you won't be embarrassed when you're asked, "What have you been doing since you left your last job?"

A lame response is, "I haven't been able to find anything after all these months." But with a temp job listed on the résumé, you can explain you've been working part time in order to bring in some income while looking for full-time work in your field.

Even when you're forced into self-employment for the first two reasons listed above, take a positive approach. Instead of thinking of yourself as being between jobs, look at each freelance assignment as an opportunity to learn something new. That will make you a more marketable candidate for the full-time job you want.

❖ ❖ ❖

A buzzword often used in place of "temping" is "interim." Professional workers who are hired on a temporary basis prefer that word. It sounds much better to say "I'm an interim lawyer" than "I'm a temp attorney."

Regardless of which way you put it, there is a boom of professional white-collar workers making careers out of temporary work. While temps answer phones and operate computers, they also practice law, engineering, and architecture. Top industries represented by freelancers include information technology (IT), health care, advertising, graphic design, film, and television.

It's true that many of you temp because you cannot find jobs. Nevertheless, an increasing number of contingency workers prefer the lifestyle. Some of you actually enjoy the adrenaline rush that comes with starting a new job.

Downsized corporations are hungry for temporary talent of all kinds. You'll find interim positions through employment agencies like Manpower Inc. The agency's main business had always been filling pink-collar slots. Now Manpower and other staffing agencies also place professional workers in the top industries.

You'll find the names of agencies that specialize in placing interim professionals in your field by consulting *The Directory of Executive and Professional Recruiters* in the business section of your library. The directory is a bit pricey. Amazon sells it for around forty-five dollars.

❖ ❖ ❖

Instead of knocking yourself out to find a job, let temporary employment agencies beat the bushes for you. Sign up with a few of them. Among the top bananas in the national staffing world are Manpower Inc., Olsten, Adecco, Kelly Services, and Robert Half.

After you get an assignment, the staffing firm will take care of billing and tax withholding—and your paychecks will arrive on time. Some are quite impressive.

According to an industry association, the most seasoned pros can earn over one hundred bucks an hour. The association also found that a technical writer can earn over twenty dollars an hour. An engineers can earn up to thirty, and the hourly rate for a graphic artist is almost twenty dollars.

More temp agencies now offer benefits like 401(k) plans, time off with pay, and health insurance. At the time of this book's publication, health insurance offered by corporations is in question due to Obamacare.

The cut that agencies take from your work is a closely guarded secret. Typically, the employer is charged around 30 percent above what you get paid, but that can go as high as 50 percent. Although there will be room for negotiating before you accept the assignment, you'll have a better chance of bargaining for a higher hourly rate after you've proven yourself.

Let's say you wow a couple of employers and that it helps your agency place more temps. Then you might get a raise.

❖ ❖ ❖

As companies continue to dump over fifty million employees each year, corporations are hiring more temporary workers to support the meaner and leaner staffs left behind.

When downsized companies begin to hire again, guess who has the inside track? Contingency workers, of course. Companies tend to hire from their pools of interim workers.

Unfortunately, the percentage of temp workers who become full-time workers has fallen considerably. "Companies are in a holding pattern because of Obamacare," says Brandon Thimke, the director of communications for The Reserves Network, a Cleveland-based staffing service.

Only 30 percent of industrial part timers have been offered permanent positions during the past year, Thimke says. Compare that to 70 percent of full-time workers who were offered permanent jobs prior to the recession of 2007.

"Health care turned the staffing world upside down," Thimke continues, "because of how poorly Obamacare was rolled out. It has frozen all the businesses."

Nevertheless, hiring at The Reserves Network was up almost 3 percent in the third quarter 2013. "It would have been a lot higher if it weren't for uncertainties Obamacare brought about."

Finding a temporary assignment in a dicey job market is a numbers game. The more staffing agencies you contact, the better chance you'll have of being called back with a temporary gig.

So touch bases with oodles of temp agencies in order to make known your availability. Then sign up with at least five of the staffing services you deem to be the most reliable.

Some ways to determine reliable and undependable temp agencies are discussed in the next couple of sixty-second coaching vignettes.

❖ ❖ ❖

You'll stumble upon both reliable and unprincipled agencies during a search. All industries have ethical issues. The staffing business is no exception.

It's easy to separate the wheat from the chaff by observing some red and green lights. Red lights inform you to stop and walk away. You need to be aware of four of them:

The first red light is when the agency tries to charge you a fee. The company, not the applicant, pays agency fees.

Red light number two is when a recruiter asks what companies you've been talking to. The agency is frisking you for leads it can use for its other applicants. Accordingly, you'll damage your chances if you tell.

The third red light is when the agency asks for references during your first meeting. The recruiter is more focused on getting leads from your contacts than on your needs. Tell him you'll be happy to provide references when there's a mutual agreement you're a good fit for a particular assignment.

Red light number four is when a recruiter wants you to embellish your résumé. While it's okay to make yourself look better than you are, embellishments on a document often cross the line and become lies. Should a company discover you lied on a résumé, you can kiss that relationship good-bye.

Green lights—signals to proceed doing business with the agency—are outlined in the next coaching vignette.

❖ ❖ ❖

Reliable temp agencies will help advance your career goals instead of just filching your leads and floating your résumé. What follows is a trio of green lights that signal that an agency is reliable:

The first green light is the number of years an agency has been doing business. "An established agency will have better relationships with hiring managers with whom you'll work," says Brandon Thimke, director of communications at the Reserves Network.

The second green light is when a staffing service asks lots of questions about your skills, where you are in your career, and especially where you want to go. That indicates they're focused on your needs and how they can help.

The final green light is when an agency offers specific placements for professionals in law, medicine, engineering, or IT. The agency should be wired into employers with the specialized needs you can fill.

Passing through the three green lights in order to identify and interview with reputable outfits is only the first step. You need to sign up with a handful of agencies. That increases your chances of landing an assignment as quickly as possible.

Because an agency probably won't have an assignment for you right away, follow up frequently to let recruiters know you're still available.

When a green-light agency comes up empty-handed for two months, cross it off your follow-up list.

❖ ❖ ❖

You probably bristle every time you read about another corporation slashing its staff—especially if it's your company that has downsized. Nobody says you have to like today's trend. But lots of job hunters are taking advantage of it. An old saying applies here: when someone hands you a lemon, turn it into lemonade.

A part-time job—the lemonade—could be as good as it gets. That's because companies have been shrinking to 75 percent of their former full-time staffs and filling them out with part-time workers.

They aren't just clerical and unskilled workers anymore. Professional people have joined their ranks as the fastest-growing category of part-time employees. Among them are doctors, lawyers, human resource and labor relations specialists, accountants, and software developers. Temporary employment is also a good option for middle managers whose full-time jobs have vanished.

While a large number of contingency workers have been hired full time, don't get your hopes up. Remember that companies want a quarter of their staff to always be part time.

Also, when a hiring manager claims your part-time job could go full time, take it with a grain of salt. While some 30 percent of all part timers are offered permanent gigs, an unscrupulous manager could sucker you into believing that might happen in order to persuade you to take a second-class assignment.

To prevent yourself from falling into a pit of depression when that doesn't happen, keep two things in mind. Understand there are no auditions in part-time work. Act as if it is possible for the assignment to go full time, but stay anchored to reality. You'll probably move on.

❖ ❖ ❖

The reason doors are being slammed in your face is because companies aren't replacing jobs they've cut. Therefore, you cannot find another job like the one you lost. That's one reason why careers in temp jobs are the wave of the future.

The best place to look for a temp assignment is with your previous employer. After all, she knows your work and will be more comfortable with you than with some stranger a temp agency sends over.

When your former company doesn't have a temp job for you, ask for the name of the temp agencies they use. You can also ask HR professionals in other corporations about which staffing outfits they use to fill temporary positions.

As a temporary worker, you'll need to buy your own benefits. You can accomplish that by breaking down your former salary into an hourly rate and then adding 30 percent more per hour for your benefits package. Remember to include insurance and a pension plan. There's a reason why it's important to design a benefits package. When you work as a temp these days, you may be on your own for good.

❖ ❖ ❖

Don't give up the search for a full-time job. While temping has its benefits, there is a downside. What do you get in return? Low pay. And in most cases, no benefits.

Why do you think companies hire temp workers? So they don't have to pay benefits. That's what a survey of five hundred employee benefits specialists showed. Some 70 percent of companies surveyed said temporary workers were hired to avoid paying employee benefits costs.

Despite that, the contingency workforce has gotten so competitive that the demand for temporary workers has forced temp agencies to offer some perks. They include 401(k) plans, unemployment benefits, disability compensation, and professional training. Agency hires may also be entitled to federal family and medical leave benefits.

You'll notice health benefits are not mentioned here. Some agencies had offered medial insurance. "We tabled health benefits because of the uncertainties cased by Obamacare," says Brandon Thimke, the spokesperson for The Reserves Network, a regional staffing service based in Cleveland.

Alice in Lewis Carroll's *Alice's Adventures in Wonderland* alludes to uncertainties by saying, "How puzzling all these changes are. I'm never sure what I'm going to be, from one minute to another."

Obviously, you are going to be more secure working at a full-time job. Remember that part-time work equals part-time pay—and few benefits.

Unless you've consciously chosen to freelance for a career, are among America's 1percent, or have inherited a bundle, don't give up your search.

❖ ❖ ❖

Some temporary workers feel miserable on the job. That's because some employers treat contingency employees the way drivers treat rental cars. They drive you into the ground.

The next time you're sent out by a temp agency to interview at a company, you'd better ask lots of questions in order to determine if you'll be happy there.

At the interview, demonstrate you can do the job. Then try to determine whether you would enjoy working there by asking these questions:

1. Are temporary workers made to feel like a part of the business family?
2. Would you please describe my duties?
3. If there's a learning curve, is the company willing to give me time to catch on?
4. Can I meet other temps who work here?

It's not important to meet fellow temps for a brief assignment of a measly week or two. For a longer stretch, it pays to make the request. Ask temps you'll be working with how they like their job, the company, and its supervisors.

While it's important to ask questions during all interviews—for contract, temporary, or permanent jobs—it's especially vital to query a temporary prospect. You don't want to be treated as a rental car or as a discard.

Just because you're called "temporary" is no reason to work in an environment where you'll be abused.

❖ ❖ ❖

A phrase taken from an old Alka-Seltzer commercial is, "Try it—you'll like it." A waiter gave that advice to a customer suffering from acid indigestion.

When it comes to trying temporary work, you might like the batch of benefits you'll receive:

* You'll be able to list temp assignments on your résumé. Because a temp job looks like all of the other jobs on your document, it makes you look like you have been active since you left your last full-time job.
* You'll learn some new tricks while expanding your skills and learning new ways of doing business. That could make you a stronger candidate for a full-time job somewhere else.
* You could impress your employer so much that he offers you a full-time job. As stated earlier, take this one with a grain of salt, but act as if it could happen. Companies like to hire temps for a couple of reasons. Managers are familiar with their skills, and they've already developed a relationship with you.
* Temping is like auditioning for a role. It's a chance to strut your stuff before a company and to show them what you have to offer.

❖ ❖ ❖

Temping is also called "the try-and-buy method" of finding a full-time position. You let a company try your wares in the hope that it will like and buy them.

You'll motivate managers to do so when you demonstrate four qualities of great employees. You can easily accomplish that by working with the acronym IDEA:

Initiative. Take the initiative to learn things about your job. Rather than wait around to be assigned a task, take the initiative to see what needs to be done, and then volunteer to do it.

Dependable. Show up on time. Be the first to arrive. Be the last to leave.

Eagerness. Show excitement to be a part of an organization and for tasks you're assigned.

Animated. You've heard the expression "Don't just sit there—do something." Doing something means becoming physically animated. When you believe what you have to offer is of great value to an employer, you won't have to bother acting animated. You'll automatically become so. Would you hire you? Make a list of reasons why and burn them into your mind. Then your enthusiasm will be contagious.

You need to demonstrate the four qualities of IDEA right away. Unlike the full-time worker, you're more expandable. A hiring manager can simply call the agency to send someone else over to take your place.

That won't happen when you take initiative. It's the most important of the four qualities of IDEA. Employers love workers who can manage themselves instead of needing to be micromanaged.

❖ ❖ ❖

If you scoff at the idea of working part time because you think it's beneath you, it's time for an attitude adjustment. Shame is not the same as guilt. When you feel guilt, it's about something you did. But when you feel shame, it's about who you are.

Perhaps you're a lawyer who needs to work part time in order to make ends meet. That's who you are—temporarily. Where's the shame in doing an honest day's work?

True, you might feel underemployed for the time being. Nonetheless, you still need to build relationships with your fellow temporary colleagues. So you don't want to give the impression you're unhappy by saying, "I'm really not a clerical worker. I'm a lawyer looking for a job." If you do, you'll have erected a wall between you, fellow employees, and customers.

You can take down that wall while building relationships with fellow workers and supervisors. Tell them that you're investigating other ways to better use your skills and because that might take a while, you're exploring various fields while making a decision.

That statement is who you are—temporarily. And it creates the impression you've planned to take time for some research and are making a serious effort to arrive at an intelligent decision. Isn't that the truth?

Renaissance writer Francois Rabelais said, "Speak the truth and shame the Devil." Because there's no shame in doing an honest day's work, don't let evil throw a monkey wrench into doing what you gotta do for now.

❖ ❖ ❖

You'll pay a price for your freedom. Temporary workers are often placed under tremendous pressure. You'll need to meet tough deadlines while working alongside an overwhelmed full-time staff. There's no time to climb a learning curve.

If you can withstand pressure as the price for freedom, temping could be the answer. Many job seekers in specialized fields are working in interim jobs while awaiting permanent ones. Others are making careers out of freelancing.

There are employment agencies that place temporary workers in their specialties. A company called Accounttemps works with accountants throughout the United States. System One in Tampa, Florida, places communications experts. Robert Half, Kelly Law Registry, and Special Counsel find jobs for lawyers. You need to sign up with several specialized agencies to increase your chances of finding interim work.

You can also make careers out of freelancing. A public relations executive in the Midwest earns some income from his own clients; he earns the rest from placement firms such as Paladin, an agency that places advertising and PR types.

By accepting temp jobs, you can shorten the dry spells while building a more impressive résumé.

❖ ❖ ❖

Temporary workers need to mind their manners. Conduct that's accepted in a full-time position might not be appropriate during an interim assignment.

There's a protocol that temp workers need to follow, so you need to be on your best behavior.

For example, it's inappropriate to get too familiar with supervisors, so don't make your networking too obvious. That means you shouldn't push for a full-time job in the corporation while you're engaged there. You should wait until the assignment ends. Then you can ask your supervisor if there's anyone else at the company you might talk to about a job—full or part time.

Chances of being offered full-time status increase when you mind your manners. After all, you are in the spotlight, and you're on trial. Supervisors are judging you to see if you'd make a good employee someday.

Look at a temp job as an opportunity to show off more of your skills, and be mindful of the fact that you'll give your best performance when you're on your best behavior.

❖ ❖ ❖

CHAPTER 20

Flying Solo

Tips for Going into Business for Yourself

If you are sick and tired of being told to clean out your desk, that's reason enough to decide to go it alone. How sweet it is to avoid commuting so you can stay home and take care of your children.

But your decision to start a home-based business represents a big change in your lifestyle. You don't get to schmooze with your fellow workers anymore. According to studies, feeling isolated and lonely is the biggest challenge you'll face working out of your home.

The remedy is to see people. Be sure to work a game of squash or a trip to the newsstand into your schedule, and attend meetings of your professional support group.

Your home-based business will run a lot smoother when you mentally separate your office and home. Many home workers say it helps to get dressed in whatever you would normally wear to the office and to set up office hours that you'll keep.

That means getting to work on time, quitting on time, and not lingering over problems at dinnertime.

❖ ❖ ❖

Many of you have thought about starting your own business for a couple of reasons. You're tired of eating all that corporate baloney—and you've heard about the legions before you who have successfully made it on the outside.

But self-employment isn't for everyone. There are a couple of reasons for this. First, you need to have the opportunity to transfer your corporate skills into your own business. And second, you must also be blessed with the right temperament. Your answers to the questions that follow will determine if you have the right temperament:

* **Can you live a work life without the support and insight of colleagues?** You'll recall that's what small business owners miss the most—rubbing elbows. Although coworkers may drive you nuts, at least they're around you.
* **Are you willing to take risks?** You are used to minimizing risks when you work for a corporation, yet it's a main ingredient when you strike out on your own.
* **Are you ready to do away with your regular paycheck?** You're expense account will be gone, and you'll be forced to accept a more humble lifestyle while you get your business up to speed.

To sum up the coaching in this vignette, let's reflect on this verse:

So consider first, if you feel like a wreck,
If it's best to stay put and draw your paycheck
Or to venture out into the world alone,
Only to miss all that money you've blown.
Few of the legions before you launched a successful gig,
Yet many who did have made it real big.

❖ ❖ ❖

Despite the hardships of going into business for yourself, gazillions of would-be entrepreneurs start their own businesses each year. The majority of them fail. Yet those who succeed have some qualities in common: they are in good health, have a desire to learn, and have the support of their families.

The buck stops with you when you're the boss. That means that if you are sick, you cannot do the work that needs to get done. So you need lots of energy to start a business.

You also need to be the kind of person who loves to keep learning—especially from mistakes. The hardest part of starting your own enterprise is having to live with those bloopers. But that's how you learn. The process of education never stops when you're operating a small business.

And when you're blessed with a family, it's vital to have their support. They'll also be affected if you leave the security of a regular job and paycheck. For that reason, you'll need to know if the family is also willing to make sacrifices.

Unless you have those three qualities—good health, a desire to learn from mistakes, and family support—you'll find it difficult to cope in the long haul.

❖ ❖ ❖

Prior to making a solo flight into your own business, follow the example of student pilots. They need to take lessons before going up alone. When it comes to making your solo flight, so do you.

You'll find the lessons you need in books and articles at your local library and on the Internet. But you must first determine if you have the qualities to succeed. So let's consider five main qualities:

1. Persistence
2. The ability to take the initiative
3. The ability to find satisfaction in creating something new.
4. Self-confidence
5. Knowing how to keep cool under pressure

You'll notice persistence tops the list. Many successful business owners struck out lots of times before hitting home runs. So take a personal inventory to see if you have already demonstrated those qualities.

Should you pass the inventory, take the second step, which is doing research. It also makes sense to read back issues of trade magazines in your field. You'll be informed about trends, buzzwords in the business you've selected, and problems you'll face. You'll have more credibility when you use some of those buzzwords at interviews.

Now you're ready to write a simple business plan. It's important to create one even if you're not looking for financing. Writing a plan will establish a route of getting from here to there. The importance of having a plan is summed up in the expression, "If you fail to plan, you are planning to fail."

❖ ❖ ❖

When you lose a job and create a new one, it's called "starting your own business." You're offering a service similar to the job you performed for you last employer.

You need to be patient in order to make it on your own. That's because you'll be working harder than ever. Does working long hours induce impatience in you? Then you had better think twice before attempting a solo flight.

The meaning of patience is clear. You have this quality when you can bear pains or trials calmly—without getting pissed off.

Let's assume you fit the definition. Then you'll be able to remain steadfast despite opposition, competition, and obstruction. You'll bump into them all when starting your own business. Problems never go away.

And you need to be patient while you're waiting for success. Most owners of new enterprises earn zippo at first and then take a modest personal income for a while.

Russian writer Leo Tolstoy put it very well when he wrote, "The strongest of all warriors are these two—time and patience."

❖ ❖ ❖

It's essential to make sure you've decided to become self-employed for the right reason. Your reasoning is right when you stick to your knitting. That means staying in the area where you have already worked.

Let's consider an example. If you're a lawyer with a big firm who decides to hang out your own shingle, you are making a solo flight for the right reason. You want your work to generate a bigger piece of the pie.

But if you're attempting to make it on your own just to try something new and exciting, you are making a solo flight for the wrong reason. And you might crash.

In order to stay airborne while taking the risk of self-employment, you must accomplish three things.

First, decide what kind of business you want to start. Second, take a personal inventory to determine if you have the background needed to pull it off. And third, interview a half dozen people who are doing the work you are thinking about. In that, way you'll learn how much of your desire is reality and how much of it is delusion.

Delusion is when you think you won't have to work so hard in a business of your own. Reality is working double the hours and twice as hard when you're doing your own thing.

❖ ❖ ❖

According to some retirement experts, some 20 percent of you who are at retirement age plan to start your own business. They suggest you think twice before taking a solo flight during retirement.

Many retirees have learned the hard way that launching a company late in life is the quickest way to blow retirement nest eggs. Most new businesses fail during the first five years of operation.

Before you accept an early retirement package in order to become your own boss, develop your new business idea on your current boss'ses time, and avoid using your retirement savings to start the new business or to cover your expenses. That will drain the retirement money you'll need when you're no longer working.

When the self-employed fail to generate the income they had expected, they lower their standard of living. How unfortunate. After all, a new retirement business is supposed to be a substitute employment—not a money drain.

❖ ❖ ❖

The suggestion that you need lots of money to start a business is a myth that needs to be debunked. A few hundred bucks is all it took to launch many new businesses.

Elmer Doolin is an example. The founder of Frito-Lay bought the recipe for Fritos corn chips for a hundred dollars. Doolin cooked batches at night in his mother's kitchen. He sold them from his car the next day.

Statistics show that many new businesses fail because of too much cash. And there's almost a direct correlation between starting with lots of money and going belly-up. A big loan can tempt you to start a business that grows too fast. Then you cannot handle it.

That is why it's easier to recover from an initial flop when you start on a shoestring because you haven't lost that much. And you'll be able to sleep at night without the use of prescription drugs.

Thus, the prevailing opinion that a lot of money is needed to start your new business is not always correct. Sometimes, less is best—and also a blessing.

❖ ❖ ❖

You can justify starting a business of your own for love or money. But the love needs come first.

Studies show entrepreneurs are motivated by the drive to create and to do something the way they think it should be done. That's the reason for considering only what you love to do. The money will follow.

When you plan to start your own enterprise, make a list of activities that you've always done well. Include achievements you didn't get paid for. Then build a business around the projects that have turned you on.

After you determine what you would love to do, take a reality check by planning your business on paper. A business plan should include a market survey, which is a quick way to find out if your idea is hot. If it is, keep your day job. Then you can hold on to your paycheck safety net while starting your business on the side.

Remember that entrepreneurs make solo flights so they can do things their own way. That's why you need to be sure to spend time analyzing what it is you love to do your own way. That's time well spent.

As Ben Franklin said, "Time is money."

❖ ❖ ❖

Because you're fifty and out of work and feel you'll never find employment in this sluggish job market, you figure now is as good a time as any to start your own business.

Besides, you have been dreaming about being your own boss for a long time. Just make sure you don't wake up to a nightmare. That could happen if you fail to talk over the new business idea with your spouse—your partner for life, for better or for worse. Remember?

You both need to be on the same page about a new business. You might be willing to make the sacrifices necessary for a start-up, but if your significant other isn't open to the idea, forget about it.

Should your other half give you the green light, keep three little words in mind: home-based business. That's how to keep your overhead low until you grow. Then you can move into an office and hire help.

When it comes to taking a solo flight, you'll sty airborne by getting clients or customers for your new business. That's the first step. You can take that step by applying the same networking skills you would use when looking for a job. Then if your business fails to takeoff, you can turn to those contacts for a job-finding campaign.

❖ ❖ ❖

Ah, the joys of home work. According to a study, people who work at home work fewer hours and earn almost 30 percent more than the typical American worker.

Another survey conducted by an industry association showed that working at home gives you four other advantages over commuting to the traditional office environment: you can eliminate the commute, become more physically active, keep a better home, and participate in more family activities.

As mentioned above, working from home means spending fewer hours on the job—about six hours fewer a week. And you can choose to work whatever hours you want. For example, an owner of a home-based business stopped working nine to five and conducted business during the evenings and on weekends.

But there's also a downside to working from home, whether it's telecommuting or conducting a business. While your quality of life improves, the stress gets worse. People who do home work do not miss the hassles of the office, the long commute, or their overbearing bosses.

But they do miss the financial security, the benefits, and especially the interactions with coworkers.

❖ ❖ ❖

Home offices are not always what they're cracked up to be, either for conducting businesses or job-finding campaigns. Many entrepreneurs who eagerly joined the home-office boom are now having second thoughts.

Worse than being alone is the fact that your dog barks every time you answer the phone. Or your wife asks you to pick up the dry cleaning as she leaves for work. It can be tricky to maintain a corporate image at home.

Yet executive suites can help you do it. That's why many people who run their own home-based businesses and job campaigns are fleeing to outside office space.

Job hunters who use executive suites are mostly higher-level businessmen and women with generous severance but no outplacement packages.

A job campaign conducted away from home gives you structure and some of the services lost with your job, and executive suites help higher-level job candidates maintain a corporate image.

Before executive suites became popular, business owners and start-up entrepreneurs were enamored with the idea of working from home while job hunters took it for granted that they had no other choice. Now they do.

Remember that the biggest disadvantage of working from home is being alone. You won't feel isolated if you job hunt in an outside office.

❖ ❖ ❖

After your job has been cut, that kindhearted company that booted you after years of loyal service will sometimes try to hire you back as a consultant. Nice maneuver on its part. The company gets your services again without having to pay fringe benefits, and you have even less job security.

While it could make sense to be an independent contractor in a mushy job market, you take several risks when a single employer controls your efforts:

1. You wouldn't be able to deduct business expenses like your home office because the IRS could try to put you into the employee category.
2. You'll run out of work when the assignment ends.
3. You'll remove yourself from the job market by suspending your search.

Diversifying eliminates those risks. While you're consulting for your former employer, try to find more companies as clients. That will give you several consulting gigs at the same time. As a result, you won't feel rejected when one of them ends.

So while you're deciding whether to interrupt your job campaign by taking on a consulting assignment for just one company, consider the advice of the economist Harry Markowitz: "Don't put all of your eggs in one basket."

❖ ❖ ❖

Business futurists tell us that the most exciting people will never join organizations. So when a cushy job with a corporation is not your cup of tea, you are a cut above the average employee. For that reason, organizations of the future will be run by the second rate.

When you desire to do your own thing someday, develop skills and services to sell to corporations. Then your job will become the job of finding customers for your own business.

While you're still employed, think about what skills you have to offer, and then develop a portfolio of those skills. You can add to your portfolio by taking on more tasks in your current job.

You can accomplish that by offering to train someone or learning the technical side of your job. That usually means computers. Then you'll be ready to volunteer the use of your newly acquired skills either on the job or to an outside group while doing your own thing.

You can also inventory your skills for your portfolio with a little help from your family, friends, and associates. Ask a dozen of them to tell you something you do very well. You might be surprised to learn you have hidden talents that are fit to be sold.

❖ ❖ ❖

According to small-business experts, the word "entrepreneur" used to apply to someone who started a business. But that was when you had to be especially innovative and take even more risks.

The same pundits say "entrepreneur" has a different meaning today because it applies only if you start something new. I disagree. The word's definition has not changed. When you organize, manage, and assume the risks of a business, you are an entrepreneur.

Although you're itching to become one because you're sick and tired of your job, consider the disadvantages. While successful entrepreneurs are richly rewarded, they are scarce. Over 90 percent of all start-up companies crash.

Failures happen because the word "entrepreneur" has become a glamorous one and because the lure of self-employment draws many people who really are not cut out for it. You have to wear all of the hats and figure out how to solve all of the problems. That's spreading yourself thin.

Do you still have an itch to do your own thing? Maybe you should lie down awhile until the feeling passes.

❖ ❖ ❖

A couple of ways to become your own boss include growing a business or buying a piece of someone else's. The second strategy is called "franchising."

According to franchise expert Robert Perry, an easy way to discover which franchises are better than others is to talk to a dozen of the company's current franchise owners, "You'll uncover the good and the bad news," said Perry in a printed report.

It's good news when franchise owners tell you they are meeting or exceeding income goals, have good two-way communications with the company, and receive prompt help and advice when it's requested.

You'll recognize the bad news when franchise owners you talk to complain about not making enough money, tell horror stories about a lack of support, and express bad attitudes toward the company.

"Just a single negative comment out of ten interviews should tell you something," Perry cautioned. So if you're thinking about buying into a franchise, experts suggest you think twice.

❖ ❖ ❖

The working wounded often think about business opportunities that include franchises. Buying into that kind of business can be risky.

A telltale sign that indicates you are about to buy into a high-risk franchise is when a company puts pressure on you to sign up immediately. You need to take a time-out to evaluate the situation.

Another revealing sign is when a company spokesperson tells you that the product will sell itself. Customers don't grow on trees. You need to see a written marketing plan that spells out how customers will be identified, contacted, and sold to.

And be alert to dangers when a franchising company has a post office box. When you sign on the dotted line, you need people to back you up. You'll breathe easier when you know there's an office with a staff inside it.

You'll recall that we spoke earlier about talking to a dozen of the company's franchise owners before making up your mind. In the event you're still interested after checking out the telltale signs, get a list of the company's franchisees.

And when you talk to them, understand some unhappy campers might be struggling because of their mistakes. Remember that you are buying into a business opportunity—not a business guarantee.

❖ ❖ ❖

Some infomercials claim you can get rich by buying a home-based business. There are legitimate business opportunities you can buy. However, lots of people lose their shirts after being deceived by promises that are farfetched.

The best home businesses are the ones you create for yourself—not the ones you buy in a box. Nevertheless, if you feel more comfortable having a blueprint, make sure the business you are buying is something you like to do, and confirm that your skills match what the business needs to succeed.

Many businesses you can buy involve selling a company's products or recruiting others to sell. So if you're considering a multilevel marketing business, you have to like selling, and you must be good at it. Remember that when a business claims "this will sell itself," run for cover!

Before buying any business in a box, investigate the company. The Federal Trade Commission, the US Postal Inspection Service, and your state attorney general can tell you about complaints against a particular company.

Above all, make sure there is a market you can tap into.

❖ ❖ ❖

When you are looking to buy a business in a box, avoid getting hoodwinked into joining one of those multilevel marketing (MLM) programs we just talked about.

MLM is a marketing strategy where you are offered the opportunity to go into business for yourself with the promise you'll make millions.

You are being lied to when an MLM recruiter claims anyone can be a good salesperson. Most of you are not—and never will be. Yet MLM recruiters insist that lacking sales experience is no problem because the company will sell you sales training devices. But motivational books, seminars, and CDs are the company's second product line.

In order to hit the jackpot, you must build a large network called a "downline" by recruiting terrific salespeople to go out and recruit other terrific sales people.

The majority of them flop. Winners succeed at the expense of others. They solicit friends and relatives who also lack sales experience, thereby setting them up to fail. By the time you discover MLM stands for multilevel monkey business, lots of folks will be mad at you

There are other ways to sell and make money. You'll find them in businesses where you do not take advantage of others.

❖ ❖ ❖

C H A P T E R   2 1

Advice for Women Only

How to Smash through the Glass Ceiling without a Head Injury

For women who interview, it can be tough out there. Some employers won't hire you if they feel your family will prevent you from working the hours a job requires. Others are afraid you'll get pregnant and not return after the baby is born. This issue is a dilemma for you and employers.

It's illegal for interviewers to ask personal questions like if you're married, if you plan to have children, how many kids you have, or who takes care of your kids.

But interviewers ask anyway. They need to know how well you can manage overlapping responsibilities of work and family. If *you* raise the issue, get out the tissue. You might not get to first base.

To hit home runs, think of your family responsibilities not as a need to be accommodated but as a reason to make businesslike inquiries into working conditions. Inquiries should be made only after you have sold yourself for the job. Then you can ask questions about what a typical workday is like, what the hours are, and if overtime, weekend work, or travel is required. That will also lay the groundwork for a good working relationship.

❖ ❖ ❖

Young women can make an interviewer's eyes glaze over by talking about their children at home. You need to focus on the job and what you bring to it. You won't advance your candidacy by mentioning family unless your interviewer brings it up.

Because some hiring managers—especially men—are prejudiced against hiring young women because they might become pregnant and leave, they'll ask about your martial status. Married women can explain they are a part of a two-income family devoted to their careers.

When you're asked if you have children, either tell the interviewer that you don't plan to manufacture any or say, "Yes, I do, and I assume you're concerned about whether I'm a dependable employee. I absolutely am. I'm committed to performing my duties and take every measure to make sure I can get to work."

And what if you're pregnant? Then volunteer your plans matter-of-factly.

There's no way to prevent interviewers from inquiring into your personal life. Your best defense is to prepare smart answers to dumb, illegal questions.

❖ ❖ ❖

Women who feel men have a better chance of landing a job they want should know that a study showed that women executives are superior to their male counterparts in many ways.

The study is based on evaluations of hundreds of men and women executives by their coworkers. Women outscored men in most categories, including the ability to meet deadlines, boost productivity, and generate ideas. The survey also indicated that women tend to collaborate more and compete less.

That information can boost your self-confidence at interviews, especially when you're asked questions about family matters. When competing against men for a job or promotion, talk about the benefits you offer as a female candidate. And if you're a working mother, be proud of it. You need to be extremely organized and productive in order to survive each day.

When you carry those skills over to your job, you can outperform men in numerous areas. Hiring managers would love to have somebody like you on their staff.

❖ ❖ ❖

The expression "glass ceiling" refers to females being held down in the workplace. You're prevented from reaching the top by an invisible glass ceiling underneath the real one. You can't see it, and your bosses don't talk about it. But try to get a promotion—and ouch! Your head cracks against that glass ceiling.

But you can almost hear the glass shatter on Wall Street as women with management skills are breaking through barriers. More women are winning top posts with mostly smaller money management firms that handle portfolios for people and companies with lots of money.

Women interested in the financial industry will probably achieve the most success on the buy side—managing money—as opposed to the sell side, which involves selling securities.

Why do men still dominate financial sales? The Wall Street culture is still very macho and cutthroat, and the old-boy network prevails. Women aren't comfortable pretending to be something they're not.

Young women with analytical skills might consider careers in finance. Managing money gives you a chance to be hired and promoted the old-fashioned way—based on your skills and abilities.

❖ ❖ ❖

You'll enhance your chances of breaking the glass ceiling—that invisible but real barrier between working women and top management—after you've mastered several critical business skills.

You must learn first how to play the game of politics. Instead of playing it as a vicious game, think of politics as managing relationships.

Next, you need to develop the ability to toot your own horn. If you want a higher-level job, begin to promote yourself by telling someone in charge what you want to do and the reasons why you can do it.

Finally, look for mentors and friends for support. You'll find them within your company and profession. Or if you're out of work, you'll find them through networking with former associates.

"In a dominantly male organization," says corporate consultant Stephanie Allen, "a powerful mentor can turn a glass ceiling into a glass elevator—right to the executive suite." The Denver-based consultant tells reporters that the glass ceiling is still in place but there are cracks in it.

So you'd better start telling yourself that it's not your gender but your experience that counts.

❖ ❖ ❖

At most companies, the biggest paychecks go to men. According to a New York–based Catalyst Survey, that's because men still hold almost 95 percent of the jobs with direct responsibility for corporate profits,

However, the study also showed that women are gradually gaining a bigger share of high-level corporate jobs, but not when it comes to the big position of chief executive officer.

Corporate boards want their CEO candidates to be experienced in profit and loss. Among Fortune 500 Companies in 2015, there are only twenty-three female CEOs. They include Meg Whitman of Hewlett-Packard, Phebe Novakovic of General Dynamics, and General Motor's Mary Barra.

The gap at the top is vast. According to the latest census statistics, women make seventy-seven cents on the male dollar. Salaries are split because of experience and a lack of salary-negotiating skills.

Women job candidates at any level should learn how to negotiate. Then after you land, find out what the guy sitting next to you makes. If it's more, request a salary boost.

❖ ❖ ❖

When you suspect the man sitting next to you gets paid more for doing the same work, don't just sit there—pound on your desk and ask for a raise.

Salary discrimination against women is a fact. The US Department of Labor reports that women who work full time earn salaries that are about seventy-seven percent of men's. That means that if you earn forty thousand dollars a year, the guy sitting next to you and doing the same work probably gets around ten grand more.

Before you walk off the job in a huff, understand that the Federal Equal Pay Act forbids discrimination in pay for similar jobs. Because discrimination is illegal, you have a right to pound on your desk and ask for that raise. But do your homework first. You need to prove that all women in your outfit who do the same jobs as men are paid less.

It's important for women to have equal pay. When you're paid differently for comparable work, you have less recourse to provide for yourself, your family, your education, and your retirement.

So the time has come for women to speak up by making their case and convincing the boss that they are as valuable as the men sitting next to them.

❖ ❖ ❖

A study by a couple of Chicago-based sociologists concluded what most women suspect: the size of your paycheck often reflects prejudice within your company. That's because men tend to dominate debates about wage surveys and job evaluations.

The sociologists, Professor Robert Nelson of Northwestern University and Professor William Bridges of the University of Illinois-Chicago, were quoted in the *Wall Street Journal* as saying their research clearly showed the old boy network was alive and thriving in the workplace. The professors say men will continue to get paid more than women unless policy makers and the courts step in.

There has to be a new understanding about the source of wage discrimination. Then changes have to be made. Gaps in wages remain despite the passage of the Equal Pay Act over fifty years ago.

So when employers point to market forces as the cause of pay differences between the sexes, you shouldn't believe it. But you should pound on your desk and ask for a raise.

❖ ❖ ❖

When it comes to women's salaries, there is some good news—according to a survey by *Working Woman Magazine,* women have pulled even or have passed men's salaries in some professions. Professions where women have cracked glass ceilings include advertising and health.

Female CEOs who work in advertising earn over twenty thousand dollars more than their male counterparts. Women dominate advertising because it's an industry where the idea is more important than gender.

Female physicists make roughly four hundred dollars more a month than their male coworkers, while women occupational therapists earn seven thousand more a year than male therapists.

But the survey also finds a surprising pay gap in the new Internet economy where men take home 15 percent more than women.

While the Federal Bureau of Labor Statistics says women still earn less than two-thirds as much as men on average, some experts contend the salary gap has been shrinking. The economy demands a high quality workforce that compels companies to hire based on merit rather than on gender or color.

❖ ❖ ❖

You've probably heard that over half of all new start-ups fail. Not so with small businesses owned by women. A Roper survey showed that women are highly motivated to succeed. Almost 60 percent of the women questioned have dreamed about going into business for themselves. The national study asked why they wanted to run their own companies.

Almost 50 percent of the women surveyed desired to be their own boss, and a little over 20 percent were looking for a sense of accomplishment. But only a few women said they were motivated to do it for financial rewards.

Maybe that's the reason businesses owned by women have higher than average success rates. In fact, women have outpaced men during the past fifteen years by creating twice as many companies.

Women-owned firms have created over ten million new jobs in the United States and employ more workers than the Fortune 500. Today, there are about eight million small female-owned businesses, according to The Center of Women's Business.

When it comes to starting and maintaining a business, women have it all over men.

❖ ❖ ❖

Not only are businesses owned by women burgeoning, but their sales and workforces are also booming. The reason for this phenomenon is that women are exhibiting a creative edge that seems to be driving their businesses toward spectacular growth. An ever-increasing number of women are successful in going into business for themselves because they take more risks than do men.

"Women also seek help from mentors and from resources like workshops," says small-business management expert Jane Applegate, "while a lot of men small-business owners I know would rather go down in flames than admit they need some help."

Today, there are almost eight million businesses owned by women, according to the SBA. That's over 28 percent of nonfarm firms in the United States. Interestingly, the US Census Bureau estimates female-owned businesses employ almost eight million workers. That's more than the entire Fortune 500.

When it comes to your job-finding campaign, why not make a list of women-owned businesses in your area and start knocking on doors?

❖ ❖ ❖

Women-owned businesses have become more significant players in the economy because they are displaying technical and managerial talents that have put them on the cutting edge of the business world.

Take Antoinette Alloca's Stamford, Connecticut–based technical writing and consulting firm. Her business grew rapidly after she creatively solved a key problem, says a report in the *Greenwich Times*.

Alloca couldn't afford to hire top sales people. So she began hiring older people who had been downsized by previous employers and offered them low salaries and high commissions. Her revenues grew from one million to twenty million in just several years.

According to a study by the Anta Borg Institute for Women and Technology, when it comes to technical talents, successful women in technology exhibit the same qualities of success as senior-level men.

Such expertise in women still surprises many men. It should come as no surprise that women business owners are displaying these technical and managerial talents combined with a creative edge that's been driving their businesses toward spectacular growth.

❖ ❖ ❖

Women in the workplace are stabbing each other in the back. That's the drift of a book by Judith Briles, who says that even though the practice is despicable and catty, women often sabotage each other in the workplace. Briles observed that more than 75 percent of the women surveyed had been undermined by another woman in the workplace.

Sabotage tactics include someone taking credit for your work, failing to give you important messages, betraying confidences, and passing on false information about you.

Attempting to destroy someone's career is not just an attribute that women possess. Men also do it, but men do not take it as personally because they're not as open with coworkers as women are.

Briles advises that women victims deal with sabotage by acknowledging what's happening and confronting the perpetrator. The author's advice isn't always easy for women to follow. Your parents said it's not nice for little girls to fight.

While business relationships differ from personal relationships, it's a fact that you need to be more direct in business. And you must also learn not to believe every woman is your best friend—or your opponent.

❖ ❖ ❖

"You've come a long way, baby" is not a politically correct phrase to use these days. But women have come a long way in business compared to where they were forty years ago. That's when Jane Friedman started in the publishing business. She rose to become Harper Collin's chief executive officer for ten years.

In the early days of Friedman's career, women could enter publishing only by holding small jobs in publicity but not in management, Friedman told the *New York Post*.

Friedman believes women have risen to top positions in many industries because they are nurturers by dint of their gender. What else do women offer that men don't? Women are more decisive than men, and they're extremely focused. Some experts say women have to be extra focused to make it in business because they have to work harder than men to get up there.

While business still has a way to go before achieving gender equality, nobody has to tell you about women who now hold very powerful positions in corporations, institutions, and government.

❖ ❖ ❖

Even though women speak twice as many words per minute as men do, they often hesitate when presenting themselves at interviews. Yet they still accuse people of not listening to what they have to say.

You've been conditioned to think you won't be heard, and therefore you speak accordingly. That means uttering more words each minute than do men. But when it comes to interviewing, your speech is typically more hesitant, polite, and apologetic than men's.

Ever notice how you often allow men to take the conversational lead in mixed company? It's no wonder that when you do get the stage, you're likely to fill sentences with false starts and qualifiers. For example, you might say, "Like, you probably won't like this idea, but here it is anyway." That creates the impression you're less capable than you are.

You can overcome this conditioning by jotting down a few notes about each point you want to make at an interview or business meeting. Then rehearse your material in conversation with friends.

You'll use words more effectively as a result, and you won't allow hesitation and those apologetic words to obscure your thoughts and speech.

❖ ❖ ❖

While women have made progress in the workplace, reforms for women didn't happen overnight. Several decades ago, more than four hundred midlife and older women from around the country met to launch a national membership organization called the Older Women's League (OWL).

At the opening session, participants were concerned about a lack of money and unequal treatment at work. They also bemoaned their invisibility in the eyes of the world. After all, gray-haired men were considered distinguished, while older women were regarded as—well, simply old.

Deborah Briceland-Betts, who was then the executive director of the OWL, had two big changes in mind that still haven't been realized some thirty years later.

First, women who choose to stay home to care for children or parents should not be penalized by pension or social security systems. And second, the salaries of men and women should be equalized in order to give women a chance at parity of retirement income.

You have the opportunity to help make those changes. One hundred fifty-three million American women are forty and over, and your new political power is gaining momentum.

❖ ❖ ❖

Although the workplace has become more casual as dress-down days have replaced traditional business attire, the more relaxed atmosphere is no excuse for avoiding manners.

Older men do not always catch the drift. That's because they're getting caught in changing times. Men are wrong to assume that you're grateful for their favorable assessment of your body or clothes when they say you look pretty, have nice eyes, or smell good. That was the custom a long time ago, even in the most impersonal situations at the office.

Men brought up in the old atmosphere sometimes assume that today's environment of business casual—where women have even greater sartorial freedom—means they can make even freer remarks. They're incorrect and might be whacked on the side of their heads with harassment charges.

At the office, put manners first. Business etiquette is based on common sense and common courtesy, and proper etiquette means following basic principles for everyday business situations.

❖ ❖ ❖

Part 3: Coping with the Hassles of It All

It's What You Think, Stupid

You can change your life by altering your attitude.
—Philosopher William James

THE ULTIMATE TOOL FOR MANAGING your career could be controlling your thoughts. Controlling what you think allows you to evoke positive emotions and make them work to achieve your goal.

You waste time by thinking about negative and gloomy things. And thinking that reaching your goal is impossible is a waste of prime thinking time.

You'll be ready for prime time when you use the technique that follows to break the self-destructive habit of negative thinking. The next time you're aware of thinking dark thoughts, just say no to yourself. Then switch your thoughts to a positive step you can take that's associated with your current situation—like writing your résumé, making a list of contacts, figuring out what you are best at, and thinking about what you want to do.

Switching negative reflections to thoughts about a positive activity will get you out of emotional slumps. Activity is the key. Psychologists recommend getting into action as a proven method of conquering depression that results from negative, or stinking, thinking.

Once you've tried switching your thoughts to a doable activity a few times, you'll develop the habit. And when you repeat a habit of choice, you will develop an appetite for continuing to choose positive thoughts.

❖ ❖ ❖

How you react to an event is not about what happened—it's about how you think about it and the action you take. So losing a job can be an experience that either crushes or blesses you, because nothing has any meaning except the definition you give it.

When you get canned, you are the one who decides how to feel and act. Your decision is based on your perception or understanding of the experience.

So your success in getting another job is determined by two things: what you think about it and what you do about it. You can either think that your world has come to an end or that a new world has opened onto exciting opportunities from which you can choose. It's your choice.

Why not decide to look at other career options where you can get a much better job than the one you've lost? When you change your angle of thought, your physical actions and behaviors also change for the better.

You might try adopting the viewpoint that being canned is a stroke of luck.

❖ ❖ ❖

Your attitude toward a situation means a lot. The mental position you take influences whether you fail or succeed. Industrialist Henry Ford had this to say about attitude: "If you think you can or if you think you can't, you're right either way."

The point of view you take toward circumstances such as your job or job hunt is also your reality. You can make the situation you're in work in your favor by thinking about it as an opportunity to transform yourself into the new person you've always wanted to become. For example, you can think about the networking piece of your job campaign as a chance to build a new support group.

You can also improve your attitude with the physical stance you take. One technique is to physically act as if you were feeling great. Another method for changing your physical attitude is to smile. It's hard to think negative thoughts when you're smiling. Go ahead—try it. Put a big goofy grin on your face and hold that smile as you think about your challenging job or search as a reason to develop a new side to yourself.

❖ ❖ ❖

If you're discouraged because you lost a job, remember that it's the stance, not the circumstance. Most of you do not deal with the stance—with your emotional attitude toward the situation. Instead, you blame the circumstance.

You tell yourself that the reason you're being clobbered is due to your age, sex, race, or appearance. You cannot not change fate. But you can modify your attitude about the situation. Successful people focus on their stance because the mental position changes their circumstance.

A couple of things will help you change your mind. A job offer does it every time. But you can't hang by your thumbs while waiting for one. The next best thing is to change your attitude. There's no waiting, and you have the power to control it.

When you study your achievements at work, don't think you cannot help a prospective employer because of your age, color, or appearance—that thought is unworthy of you. Holding on to a changed attitude will restore your self-esteem. Replacing negative thoughts with positive thoughts will also provide the energy you need for interviews.

Be that as it may, remember that it's your stance, silly. Not your circumstance.

❖ ❖ ❖

You can overcome negative thinking while putting some magic into your job-finding or selling efforts. All you have to do is use a formula that sales consultant Jeffrey Gitomer calls "AHA." AHA is an acronym that stands for attitude, humor, and action.

A positive attitude is not about thinking nice thoughts. It's a commitment to rededicating yourself each day to being positive, thinking positively, and speaking positively. A positive attitude makes you feel good about your self.

The *H*, or humor piece, is not about being funny. It's about finding what's amusing in most situations. Your ability to find humor will make others smile. When a prospect feels good in your presence, your chances of making the sale or landing the job will have increased a whole lot.

And action is waking up in the morning to a clearly defined set of goals, having a daily agenda, and following your game plan.

Aha! The attitude, humor, and action formula will help you whip the fear of failure and rejection by giving you the personality transplant you need.

❖ ❖ ❖

Think you have it bad? Your anguish over losing a job and being forced to look for work is practically a cakewalk compared to the economic and unemployment crises of the late 1920s. Norman Vincent Peale learned how to get through those tougher times.

The author of *The Power of Positive Thinking* told an interviewer, "Nothing was worse than standing on soup lines during the Great Depression." The late Reverend Dr. Peale said he saw formerly wealthy people waiting in those lines for their daily bread. You don't even have to stand in employment lines anymore.

There are three ways you can apply Dr. Peale's positive-thinking methods to your job-finding campaign:

1. Understand your situation will improve.
2. Assure yourself better times than ever will come if you have the will to survive.
3. Share your burden with others.

Dr. Peale believed that talking about your problems lightens your load. Today, it's called having a support network. Job finders suffering from the shock of being discharged are always advised to talk things over with loved ones and to join support groups for job finders.

Norman Vincent Peale's advice can help make your dog days of job hunting a more positive experience.

❖ ❖ ❖

You'll feel more positive when you act as if you're conducing a successful job-finding campaign. Dr. Norman Vincent Peale, who inspired millions to change their thinking and their lives, said he always used the "as if" principle in his life. "When you're feeling down, act as if you feel good," said Reverend Peale in a printed report. "By acting it, you become it."

No matter how bleak things may seem, you have options. Instead of blowing your brains out, you can blow them up. Dr. Peale taught that you can use your mind to think your way out of just about any situation.

The late reverend's philosophy is contained in *The Power of Positive Thinking*, which he wrote over a half of a century ago. His book was a best seller then, and it still is today.

You are using positive thinking principles when you let the issues surrounding your job or job campaign be your teacher and inspire you for positive change—and when you act as if the job you want is just around the corner.

❖ ❖ ❖

Stinking thinking is preventing you from making your dreams come true. When you tell yourself, "I'll never find a job," your thinking stinks. And when your self-talk says, "No company will hire me at my age," your thinking stinks.

You first need to change the quality of your thoughts in order to change your circumstances, because when you repeatedly tell yourself something, you start to believe it and therefore experience it.

Because positive thinking is the result of having confidence in yourself, you cannot just snap your fingers and say, "Okay, I'll start to think positively today." Self-assurance is the key. Without it, you can forget about trying to make your dreams come true. You've already rejected them.

Self-confidence encourages the positive thoughts that can make you feel so capable and motivated that any of your dreams can become possible.

You can develop self-assurance by taking a personal inventory of your strengths. Make a list of your best qualities. Confident people focus on what they do well. You used your strengths on past jobs and can repeat them again anytime. You can nurture self-confidence by reading your list frequently.

Positive thinking is made possible only by replacing your habit of stinking thinking with the positive thoughts that accompany self-confidence.

❖ ❖ ❖

Nobody says you have to feel good about interviewing. But you must have a positive attitude while doing it. How you feel before and after an interview does not affect the quality of your presentation effort. But a negative attitude gets you screened out.

Studies show that people are more inclined to listen and to act in your favor when you exhibit a positive attitude. Your disposition is reflected in your voice and body language. Prospects notice it.

That means that when you're communicating with sales prospects and prospective employers either face-to-face or by telephone, you must have a positive mind-set. When you are positive, your energy and enthusiasm and optimism come across in your conversations.

You'll have no trouble establishing the right mind-set when you understand that prospective employers couldn't care less about your career or the fact that you need a job right now.

What are important to prospective employers are their needs. You'll help them get what they want by enthusiastically matching what you offer to the job at hand. The enthusiasm you need will come naturally after you have given some thought to how your skills or what you offer can help future employers.

When it comes to finding the right job, the right attitude is a must.

❖ ❖ ❖

You must go into an interview with the attitude that you're going to win it. "Winning" means either becoming a candidate or receiving a job offer. So you need to be thinking, "I'm going to arouse this interviewer's interest so he'll want to hire me." That's the correct attitude.

In order to establish that attitude, you need to psych yourself up beforehand. If you walk into an interview with the attitude that maybe you'll like this company and maybe you won't, it's going to show through at the meeting.

So give yourself a pep talk just before an interview starts. You might tell yourself that you're about to make a presentation in a way that will motivate the interviewer to like you and to consider making a job offer.

People will like you when you come across in a positive way. And you'll give a positively excellent interview when you act as if you want the job, because you'll be enthusiastic about your background and how it can help a prospective employer.

Nevertheless, before you can persuade someone you are a winner, you must convince yourself first.

❖ ❖ ❖

There are no practice interviews. So you'd better think and believe you are going to win the next one. If you lack this kind of self-confidence, your job-finding efforts will be obstructed.

Trying to come across as a winner without sounding like a bragger often encumbers job candidates. While you need to present yourself with confidence, you won't want to sound too boastful about your abilities. After all, modesty is a reasonable trait. The poet Walt Whitman provided some insight into this dilemma when he said, "If you done it, it ain't bragging."

Psychologists tell us that modesty is often low self-esteem in disguise. Humility can erode your self-confidence. That's why a positive I-can-do-it attitude is crucial to your being hired.

You can develop a winning point of view by getting it straight with your-self that you have something to offer. Then be willing to say it to prospective employers.

What you have to offer is found on your résumé. Its bullet points show what you have done and the results you have achieved. You need to practice talking about them until your story is down pat.

Now you'll know and be able to express that you can do the job an in-terviewer wants done. If you are not thinking like an interview winner right now, don't leave home until you can change your mind.

❖ ❖ ❖

Interviewing is a mind game. Whether you give a good interview is all in the mind. To win, just know the rules of the interviewing game.

You do not play to win the job. Any self-respecting job candidate will become nervous holding on to that thought. Your goal for each interview is just to get the next interview. Usually, you'll interview with several decision makers at a company before getting an offer.

It also helps to look at an interview as a period of time for two people to decide if they want to work with each other, because interviewing, like any other business discussion, is give and take. You're not there to give a mono-logue about yourself. Interviewers do not want to be on the receiving end of a brain dump.

The purpose of interviewing is to exchange information with your inter-viewer. All you need to do is wrap your mind around this purpose instead of trying to remember a bunch of techniques.

In the process you'll discover what the interviewer expects you to ac-complish. Then you'll have your chance to demonstrate with brief statements how you can fit the bill.

When you consider interviewing to be a mind game, you'll understand that it's how you think about a job interview that determines its outcome.

❖ ❖ ❖

A nice phrase to keep in mind while interviewing is found in the opening lines of Johnny Mercer's song, "Accentuate the Positive": "You've got to accentuate the positive eliminate the negative."

While psychologists tell you not to stuff negative feelings because you need to work through things that bug you, analysis equals paralysis before interviewing. That's the time for quickly getting yourself up by accentuating the positive. Negative thoughts will tend to stay in the background as you focus on the positive ones.

True, it's not always possible to control bad moods. But you have the power to direct your thoughts, which can change your attitude. A technique for tapping into that power is making a gratitude list each day by writing down things for which you're grateful.

Even when your job has been robbed, there's always something to be grateful for. Perhaps it's the clean clothes you're wearing or the roof that's over your head. You can also be grateful for good health or for having a pet who loves you. Writing gratitude lists helps you to become grateful. Then an attitude of gratitude becomes habit.

So let the opening stanza of that old song be your guide:

You've got to accentuate the positive
Eliminate the negative
And latch on to the affirmative
Don't mess with Mister In-Between.

❖ ❖ ❖

When you face your job or career search with an attitude of gratitude, you are more likely to get what you want. People who are grateful for what they have are more satisfied with life. Therefore, they think more positively.

You have already experienced how things go well when you think they will. And when you expect the worst, that's what you get. You should expect the best in your job hunt by choosing positive instead of negative thoughts.

But seeing your glass half full is no easy task. American philosopher and essayist Ralph Waldo Emerson called thinking the hardest task in the world. It becomes easier to be a positive thinker when you at least acknowledge that you live in a land of opportunity and can take advantage of it.

Another inspirational writer, Claude M. Bristol, wrote in *The Magic Power of Believing,* "Positive creative thought leads to action and ultimate realization. But the real power is the thought."

You will have the power to think positively after you develop an attitude of gratitude.

❖ ❖ ❖

The slogan on the bulletin board outside New York City's Park Avenue Methodist Church mentioned earlier sums up what this chapter is all about: "Success is more attitude than it is aptitude."

Those natural abilities you were born with are your aptitudes. You need to use them to be successful. Experts say unused mental talents not only go to waste, but also often cause you to become anxious.

Discovering your aptitudes and deciding where they fit is only the beginning. As the slogan mentioned earlier indicates, it's your attitude—how you think about something—that determines your success. You don't have a choice of aptitude, but you can choose your thoughts and keep them positive. After all, you are what you think.

"Success is more attitude than it is aptitude" is a no-brainer because you become a winner by developing a successful point of view. Nobody has to tell you what happens when you change your mind from thinking failure to visualizing success. You will foster confidence in your ability to reach a goal that uses your aptitudes, and you will be blessed with a winning attitude to keep on keeping on.

❖ ❖ ❖

When no one compliments your work, do it yourself. You neglect to pat yourself on the back for a couple of reasons. It doesn't occur to you, and you tend to demand more of yourself than you would of others.

But as the days go on, nobody notices your job performance, and you are unacknowledged. Unless a career counselor is on hand to provide you positive feedback, a job campaign is thankless work.

That's why reinforcing yourself is necessary to survive any job or job hunt. It bolsters self-confidence, and mental health professionals say that self-reinforcement makes you feel secure. The time for this strengthening is right after your job has been snuffed out. Because that's when your self-esteem also went out the window.

Self-reinforcement empowers you to become more committed to your job search or current position because you tell yourself you did what was required.

The process of bolstering yourself begins when you write your résumé and then periodically review and update it. The résumé becomes your sales document containing your outstanding accomplishments.

Then whenever you go awhile without praise, you'll have all the material needed to compliment yourself. At least you'll know it's sincere.

❖ ❖ ❖

When you dwell on failures, you give legs to failure. But failure doesn't have a leg to stand on unless you lend it one of your own.

There is no such thing as failure when you look at an experience as merely something that didn't work out but might succeed the next time. It then becomes a learning experience.

Successful people admit to making mistakes. Everybody makes them. For the same reason, successful job candidates admit to making a mistake when asked about it at interviews. However, they also explain what they did to correct the situation and what they learned from the experience.

The only failures that exist are buried in your personality. I call them the Four *F*s:

1. Failing to have a job target
2. Failing to practice your interview presentation and telephone script
3. Failing to have a positive attitude
4. And failing to do your best

Americans classified as Four F by the Selective Service System are not acceptable for military service. Do you exhibit the Four *F*s just described? Then you would not be an acceptable job hunter.

Failure is not about having goofed while executing a project. It's failing to execute something in the first place. These failures are bad habits that are self-inflicted. You can root them out by changing your attitude from having failed at something to having grown through a learning experience.

❖ ❖ ❖

Negative attitudes ruin job campaigns. This is true no matter how good your qualifications look on paper. When you're reflecting anger, for example, your behavior can border on obnoxious.

While nobody wants to be an obnoxious job candidate, most people have negative thoughts that sometimes result in a display of an obnoxious trait. Yet you're not aware of how offensive behavior can undermine your otherwise sound job-hunting strategy.

There's no place for ordinary human imperfections at interviews—and especially not for showing anger and resentment about losing your job. You might not express your feelings verbally, but the indignation you feel can spill into the interview without your being aware of it.

So it's important to get the hostility out of your system before beginning the telephoning and interviewing phases of your campaign. Your anger can be vented to your career counselor, psychologist, personal trainer, priest, minister, or rabbi, or to a trusted family member or friend. Ask them to let you know when your attitude recovers.

Until then, work on selecting a job objective and write your résumé. But don't meet recruiters or go to job fairs and interviews until you feel confident and positive.

❖ ❖ ❖

A study in the *Journal of the American Medical Association* showed that people who had little control over their jobs "felt helpless and powerless." They were more likely to develop heart problems and high blood pressure.

When you hate your job—or lose it—you need to deal with sensations of anger and powerlessness so your health is not compromised. Try using your mind. Your head controls your body more than you realize.

Medical researchers now recognize what you think or feel will affect your body. For example, think back to a time you felt nervous because you had to give a speech. Your brain delivered information to various parts of your body, provoking your stomach to create butterflies, the back of your neck to become stiff, your heart to palpitate, and your palms to sweat.

You can use your mind to combat feelings of helplessness and powerlessness by simply making smart choices about what you think.

And when you act rather than being acted upon, you'll get back that sense of control.

❖ ❖ ❖

Whenever your courage needs a boost, give yourself pep talks and affirmations. There is a difference between the two methods.

Pep talks—brief statements that are charged with emotion—give you brisk energy for a short period. An example is when you tell yourself, "I'll knock 'em dead during this interview."

That kind of pep talk is like a quick shot in the arm. You will get its results quickly, and you will lose its results quickly. That's the problem with brief inspirational statements. Besides, if you don't really believe you can knock 'em dead, you won't.

But affirmations—longer statements asserting that a belief is true—give legs to pep talks. That happens because you state it in a forceful and positive way that dedicates you to the belief you want.

An example of an affirmation that will convince even you that you're going to knock 'em dead is, "I am relaxed while presenting my achievements exactly as I rehearsed in a way that matches the job I'm interviewing for and motivates the interviewer to want me as a candidate."

Philosopher William James said it best: "You can change your life by altering your attitude."

Affirmations and pep talks are your weapons against discouragement.

❖ ❖ ❖

You'll perform badly at interviews when you are overly concerned about doing well. A healthy concern is okay. That's because it encourages you to research, rehearse, and give the interview your best shot.

Nonetheless, it's unhealthy to think you absolutely must give a performance that's great. You'll work yourself into a panic if you do not perform as well as you think you must. So "must" is a dirty word. You almost always cause your own anxiety with the crooked thinking that starts with "I must."

So each time you think you must, change that "must" back into a preference. You would prefer to give a good interview, for example, but you don't have to. Nobody hits a home run each time at bat. You'll have other chances to step up to the plate.

You can strive for interview perfection but not self-perfection. Interviews will turn out better when you prefer to give a good performance without thinking you must.

❖ ❖ ❖

Have you ever heard of the "what-if" syndrome? It's thinking obsessively about something that may happen but probably won't. Job hunters with this syndrome have stress they can do without.

Any time you think "what if I'm turned down" or "what if I can't find another job like the one I left," you have the what-if syndrome. That kind of thinking gives you more stress to handle.

Of course you cannot eliminate all stress. But you can insulate yourself from extra stress by developing skills to cope with it. A powerful coping tool is trying not to connect your self-worth to how well you did or how prospective employers approve or disapprove of you.

If you're turned down for a job or think you gave a less than stellar performance during a job interview, you drag down your self-esteem when companioning with thoughts that cry "what if?"

While you might think an interview failed to go well or that a disagreeable interviewer didn't like you, chances are you're magnifying the problem. You create much of your stress by how you look at situations.

❖ ❖ ❖

How's this for a bumper sticker: "The next time the devil reminds you of your past, remind him of his future."

When you lose a job, devil thoughts invade and bulldoze you into the dumps. Hey, you need to be up in order to run an even halfway-decent job campaign.

Nobody has to explain how the devil's language reminds you of the past with self-talk:

- It says, "It was my fault."
- "I'm no good."
- "I'm too fat." (Or "I'm too thin.")
- "Oh jeez, I shoulda stayed in bed."

Stop bawling! The only past you should remind yourself about are the achievements you accomplished when you had a job. Then get those

achievements—the good things you accomplished and their results—
onto a résumé.

And do it right now. That's how to chase devil thoughts away. It's normal
to feel down after you've been forced out. But don't let negative thinking
knock you out.

Remember to hold this bumper sticker in your thoughts: "The next time
the devil reminds you of your past, remind him of his future."

❖ ❖ ❖

Negative thinking affects how you feel. It's average to entertain some gloomy
thoughts. "But it's really stupid to think you don't look very good today," says
Dr. Stephanie Gannon, the career psychologist mentioned earlier.

Gannon makes her point by explaining that if the government were to
plant a minicomputer into your brain and transmit negative messages about
you every ten seconds, you would march on Washington. "Yet you blithely
send yourself negative messages all the time."

You are your own worst enemy when it comes to feeling down in the dumps.
What you think is frightening or overwhelming is what you'll find stressful.

So the next time you experience anxiety, "observe what you might have
been thinking before you began to feel down," advises the career psychologist. Chances are that you put yourself down with a negative thought.

Countering negative thoughts with positive ones controls stress. So when you
feel down, build yourself up by mentally arguing against detrimental thoughts.

❖ ❖ ❖

Using Your Religion as a Powerful Job-Finding Tool

It's Okay to Ask God for Help in Finding a Job

Self-reliance, the height and perfection of man, is reliance on God.
—Ralph Waldo Emerson

When you have a religion, it can be used to help find a job. That's the good news from Dr. Joe Duffy, a career consultant and former Catholic seminarian. "Your faith can be a powerful job-hunting tool, even if you've been away from it awhile," said Duffy.

From his training at a seminary, the late Dr. Duffy developed a deep faith that job hunters can overcome obstacles by asking God to help. "You already have the spiritual faith it takes to help you through a job hunt," Duffy said, "but you don't realize it."

Many people leave their deep-rooted faiths in formal religious experiences during their teens but return to religion after raising families. "But your strong faith in a supreme being looking over you continues during those interim years," said Duffy. "You just don't reach out for it."

So whenever you're in a crisis, which includes the crash of a career, you're able to reach deep into the wellspring of faith and inspiration that's already there. But you must also focus on a job target while developing positive attitudes and not permitting yourself to be defeated. "You are never given problems you can't handle," Duffy said.

❖ ❖ ❖

God will help you find a job, but don't expect Him to just hand it to you. "God feeds the birds," as the old saying goes, but He doesn't scatter birdseed in their nests. As one of God's beloved creatures, you must take the initiative to get what you need out of life.

American statesman Benjamin Franklin put it another way: "God helps those who help themselves." You need to make the decision to be open to the job-finding experiences God will provide. But how can you be open to such God-given events when losing a job can make you feel depressed, downtrodden, and angry?

The remedy is to make a strong effort to be positive, upbeat, and trusting. You'll enhance your efforts to be open to God's ideas by joining a church group and becoming active in it. When you take the initiative to surround yourself with positive people, you're less likely to complain and more likely to make a positive contribution to society and to find steady employment.

So when you take responsibility for developing a more positive attitude, God will give you all the support you need.

❖ ❖ ❖

Job hunters who practice their religions are often enabled to use their beliefs to help them land. Joe Duffy, the career consultant and former Catholic seminarian you met earlier, observed that some of his career-counseling clients reached out to their faiths for various reasons. "Many who pray and meditate develop faith, hope, and a positive attitude," Duffy explained. "Others choose religion, frankly, as one of their primary networks."

Churches and synagogues offer more than just religious services to parishioners. You'll find religious organizations in your community that provide career services that include networking meetings, career advice, and help with résumés.

So why not look within your religious community for help? Members of a spiritual organization will also support you by providing some practical advice along with referrals to others who can help.

Your religion needn't be just for the Sabbaths anymore. It will become a powerful job-hunting tool when you discipline yourself to practice all of the elements of your creed—all of the time.

❖ ❖ ❖

It was Father William Thomas Cummings, a US Army chaplain who served in the Second World War, who told troops on Bataan, "There are no atheists in the foxholes."

And Dr. Joe Duffy, the career consultant who also studied for the priesthood, observed that there are also no atheists in the job market. "Job search clients often tell me they're not religious," he said, "then qualify it by saying they believe in a god or pray or meditate. I've never had anyone tell me they're an atheist."

Religionists agree that everyone has a deep-rooted sense of spirituality they can tap into. Some of you pray. Others meditate. Both are ways to reduce stress and anxiety while enhancing your positive energies. Through prayer and meditation, you can develop an inner sense of peace that will allow you to refocus on the job search and keep moving ahead.

While nobody knows when you'll be offered a job, turning inward gives you the faith to realize you will land—and that God is watching over you.

❖ ❖ ❖

You might have tried every job-hunting method in the book, but have you tried God? People suffering from life-threatening problems much bigger than the loss of a job often turn to God as a last resort, only to discover the truth in these words of a psalmist: "God is our refuge and strength, a very present help in trouble."

People who join Alcoholics Anonymous, for example, ask their higher power to help them stop drinking through AA's twelve spiritual steps. They can be applied to any problem, including to your failed relationship with the job market. You can take the steps piecemeal if you'd like. But the first three steps alone will do nicely.

The first step is to admit you're powerless over your unemployment situation and your life has become unmanageable as a result. You had no power to prevent the downsizing that cost you your job, and your life has become unmanageable because you haven't found work yet as the bills pile up.

Admitting you are powerless to help yourself means you're on the way to getting that power back. That's because you become willing to listen to God's guidance.

❖ ❖ ❖

The second step, which is coming "to believe that a power greater than ourselves could restore us to sanity," applies to job hunters who have been traumatized over the loss of their jobs. There's no need to let the word "sanity" freak you out. Sanity is defined as "soundness or health of mind." Your feelings of rage and anger and wanting to get even prevent you from thinking soundly and rationally enough to make plans for your job search.

Maybe you haven't tried God in the job-hunting process because you lost your faith and don't think it works, or you believe in God but think He doesn't believe in you. When losing your job causes your thoughts to scatter and groove in a compulsive way, it's a good opportunity to rediscover your faith.

After you come to believe a higher power can restore you to sanity, you'll be able to relax and have the peace of mind needed to make plans for moving forward. Then you'll be ready to take the third step, which is about letting go and letting God.

❖ ❖ ❖

With most religions, praying to understand God's will is standard operating procedure. Yet many of you have drifted in and out of jobs without giving much thought, let alone prayerful thought, to the work you were born to do.

You'll uncover God's plan for your life in the third spiritual step, which is deciding to turn your will and your life over to the care of God as you understand Him. This step doesn't require you to become a holy man or woman. It simply suggests you make a decision to let go in order to let God guide your efforts to solve your unemployment problem.

Should you consider yourself an independent person who relies on nobody but yourself, listen to what American philosopher Ralph Waldo Emerson had to say: "Self-reliance, the height of perfection for man, is reliance on God."

Let's say the G word turns you off. Then let "GOD" be an acronym for **g**ood **o**rderly **d**irection. God guides you with ideas, hunches, and intuitions. A spiritual writer in the Koran says that God best knows those who yield to guidance.

❖ ❖ ❖

CHAPTER 24

Best Ways to Cope with Rejection

Rejection gives you opportunities to learn.
—PSYCHOLOGIST ALAN PICKMAN

SIR WINSTON CHURCHILL SAID, "SUCCESS is going from failure to failure without getting discouraged." Chances are you won't get a job offer after the first interview. It usually takes lots of meetings with prospective employers before you get an offer to join a payroll. That's why your success—landing the job you want at a salary you deserve—requires "going from failure to failure without getting discouraged."

You don't have to like being rejected. Who does? But you'd better learn to live with it without being disheartened. Being turned down is a part of the job-finding and selling process. Hardly anyone makes a sale the first time out. It can take many "nos" before you get to "yes."

It's helpful to think of yourself as a product that needs to be sold. The place to sell is at interviews, and the more interviews you get, the sooner you'll land.

A successful job search depends on taking Churchill's advice about "going from failure to failure without getting discouraged." Are you still upset you haven't landed yet? Perhaps you haven't failed enough.

❖ ❖ ❖

Your feelings after being dumped at work are the same feelings you have after being dumped in a relationship. Everything is copacetic when you fall in love. But things turn bad when you're abandoned.

To make matters worse, the company who pushed you out often twists the knife by asking you to hand in your ID card. Then a security guard accompanies you to your office in order to make sure you don't take any of the company's articles while collecting your stuff. Rejection seldom gets worse than that.

On the subject of living through horrible experiences, former First Lady Eleanor Roosevelt wrote, "No one can make you feel inferior without your consent."

You won't consent to letting the bastards get you down when you consider being rejected as their loss. So when you lose a job or a job opportunity, it's someone else's loss, especially after you find the job that's waiting for you someplace else.

Jobs don't last forever these days, and you are not going to win every interview. Either way, being rejected is just a temporary inconvenience in your career.

When you affirm that nobody can make you feel inferior without your consent, you also gain courage and self-confidence. Mrs. Roosevelt also spoke about the benefits of stopping to look rejection and fear in the face. "Then you're able to say to yourself, 'I lived through this horror and can take the next thing that comes along.'"

❖ ❖ ❖

You procrastinate starting your job hunt because you dread pushing yourself into situations where you think you will be turned away. Nobody can blame you for not wanting to open doors only to see them slammed in your face. That kind of treatment would reduce the self-confidence you need to present yourself in the first place.

So why not look at rejection from another viewpoint instead of dreading it? It's hardly rejection if they did you a favor by kicking you out. Most downsizing victims find better careers or positions than the ones they lost.

A job campaign is about finding a position and a company that's right for you. The key word is "find" because you do the choosing. It's not the other way around. When you are the buyer rather than the salesperson, there is no risk of being rejected.

Many job hunters who preceded you found it helpful to go through their searches as a buyer or gatherer instead of a hunter. They gathered information about careers, companies, and jobs.

By following this technique, you'll have the business intelligence needed to make the kind of interview presentation that targets the prospective employer's needs. The job offers will take care of themselves.

❖ ❖ ❖

Job hunters who find themselves smack in the middle of the psychic jungle of rejection need to walk into the brick walls they know are there. The key to walking into those walls without injury is to understand that you need to be rejected before you are accepted.

Experts advise that you should not take rejection personally. When you are turned down, it doesn't mean you personally failed or have been rejected. It was your sales presentation that was given the thumbs down. You failed to convince the interviewer that you are a good match for the job.

You can depersonalize being turned down by thinking about people who take rejection as a part of their career, and then trying to imitate them. For instance, a big chunk of writing and acting careers consists of sucking up rejection.

Writers who can paper walls with rejection slips are eventually published when they keep submitting their work. And actors must attend lots of auditions before winning a part. In fact, up to 90 percent of an actor's job is "making the rounds" by contacting casting agencies and agents and auditioning before landing a role or commercial.

The numbers game you need to play to get hired is a lot easier, but the rules are the same for all careers. The more you submit, try out, or interview, the sooner you'll land. As the old Lotto commercial proclaimed, "You gotta be in it to win it." Poet T.S. Eliot agreed when he wrote, "For us there is only the trying. The rest is not our business."

❖ ❖ ❖

Rejection presents you with an opportunity to learn and improve your presentation. "While it's never fun or easy to hear you're not going to get the position," says psychologist Alan Pickman, "people need to keep in perspective that rejection is inevitable in the job search process." Even so, you'll find handling rejection takes some practice.

The first practice step is to understand it was not you personally who was rejected. Instead, your sales presentation was turned down because it failed to match the needs of your interviewer.

The second step is to use rejection as a helpmate. "Hopefully, with each rejection, the individual becomes a better candidate in the job search process," says Dr. Pickman. That's because you'll learn more about the marketplace and about yourself as a candidate by asking the interviewer why you failed to get an offer. Also ask how you could have given the winning presentation.

Not only will you get some good ideas that'll help you improve your personal presentation for the next interview, but you'll frequently smoke out an objection about your qualifications. That will give you the chance to re-present those qualifications your prospect missed the first time around in order to overcome the objections and to get the job after all.

Remember that rejection presents you with opportunities to learn. So milk them.

❖ ❖ ❖

When you are rejected after an interview, don't drop out, freak out, or go someplace to cool out. Rejection presents you with an opportunity to pick up new tricks and to be reconsidered.

You can keep the door open a crack by using the magic word, "why." With a big smile spread across your face, ask why you were not hired and how you could have given the winning interview.

Presenting your request sincerely is the way to pick up new tricks about how to improve your interview technique. You might also get tipped off about training you need before you can be reconsidered as a future candidate.

By refusing to give up after being rejected, you become a giant interviewer who will dwarf other applicants. Unlike your competitors, you will have used each rejection as an opportunity to learn about yourself and the job marketplace. That input will let you give a better performance at your next interview.

Meanwhile, you can keep your foot in the door of a company that rejected you by periodically following up with letters and e-mails or phone calls. That's how to show your interest in being considered for a job the next time around.

❖ ❖ ❖

Nobody says you must like rejection. But you need to deal with it by being tenacious in your efforts to get interviews. That means learning to take "no" for an answer and knowing who you are in a job-finding campaign.

You are a product or service that needs to be marketed and sold. The marketing piece includes the methods you use to be invited to interviews:

- Responding to classified ads and posting on the web
- Writing e-mails and letters to companies you target
- Following up your correspondence with phone calls to request meetings
- Networking with personal contacts—business, friends, and family
- Attending job fairs

The selling piece happens at interviews. People who sell for a living must see lots of customers before getting their first order. Your customers are the hiring managers at the companies to which you are applying.

Becoming tenacious at getting interviews with hiring managers is the result of using the self-marketing tactics listed in bullets above.

Some job hunters find it helpful to take a piece of their stationary and to fill it with the word "no." But make the last word in the lower right-hand corner a big "YES." Every time you're turned down for a job, circle the next no. And be grateful. It means you're getting closer to "yes."

In order to get a job offer, just hang in there by keeping on keeping on after being rejected.

❖ ❖ ❖

CHAPTER 25

Latest Ways to Beat Interview Anxiety without a Prescription

Never Let Them See You Sweat

Because you're so freaked out before your interview, I'll bet you would pay me to interview in your place. For that reason, it's more important to learn how to conquer anxiety than it is to develop interview skills. Anticipatory stress makes you forget about interview techniques anyhow.

Tension won't vanish by itself, so you need understand how to handle it. Therapists developed a useful strategy to help people with high anxiety conquer their fears of everything—and that includes stress associated with meeting people. The technique is called "systematic desensitization." After participating in situations you dread, starting with the least stressful and working your way up to the most stressful, you'll emotionally become less sensitive to your fears.

To apply systematic desensitization to your search, schedule your first interviews for the worst job opportunities. There's hardly any stress at all associated with interviewing for jobs you don't want. Besides, the more you interview, the easier it becomes.

Save the interviews for jobs you really want for last. Because you'll have been there and done that with low-stress meetings, you'll feel less sensitive about interviewing. Then you'll do very well with the biggies because your greatest fears have been curbed.

❖ ❖ ❖

Nobody ever gets nervous before interviewing. Not! It's normal to experience those interviewing butterflies but unnatural to deny them, says Jane Hodgetts, a career and life-planning consultant.

"Instead of trying to push away your uptight sensation—which most of you are inclined to do—just become aware of it," says Hodgetts. "Even acknowledge it, almost as if you were saying 'hello' to the uptightness."

To become aware of your feelings, Hodgetts advises closing your eyes and focusing on the place in your body where you feel the discomfort. This is also the first step to reducing interview anxiety. Just being with your stress and knowing it's okay to have it is a good way to relax. "It's like taking a deep breath and feeling untroubled as you exhale."

You might call the consultant's method a paradox. It's about changing the feelings that make you nervous by being with those sensations without expecting them to change.

When it comes to dealing with interview anxiety, Hodgetts sums it up this way: "Accept what is and don't push against it."

❖ ❖ ❖

Career experts and well-meaning friends have been giving you unrealistic advice about coping with preinterview stress. You've heard their nonsense before—just relax at interviews and be yourself. Yeah, right!

There's at least one career expert who debunks that unwelcome advice. Psychologist Stephanie Gannon says that getting anxious, even extremely anxious, before interviewing is perfectly normal. The Westchester County–based career psychologist speaks from personal experience. "Whenever I'm in a situation that provokes anxiety, I use nervous energy to psych myself up."

The energy method Gannon employs is focusing on a funny scene from a TV show. That's all she'll allow in her mind. "If another thought occurs to me, I just tell myself to think about it later. And right now, to think of what the actress did, how she accomplished the scene, and what was funny about it."

Dr. Gannon encourages her job-finding clients to not think at all about the interview. "Think about something funny, something you feel good about in your life." Then whenever stray thoughts enter your mind, command yourself to think about them later—after the interview.

When you practice the career psychologist's energy method to control preinterview anxiety, your stress will take a nosedive as your interview performance soars.

❖ ❖ ❖

Perhaps you're not comfortable going on interviews because you fear the interviewer will make you feel embarrassed or small. Maybe you feel anxious because you're thinking, "Gee, I'm not able to give a good interview."

You can easily overcome these fears by knowing the truth about them. As the Bible says, "You will know the truth, and the truth will set you free." (John 8:32.)

A truth that should put your mind at ease is that interviewers are not out to get you. They need to find out if you're the right match for the job. So chances are that you'll never be made to feel embarrassed at an interview.

Here's another truth to ease interview anxiety: preparation will enrich your interview performance. It was the English statesman and philosopher Francis Bacon who said, "Knowledge is power." The understanding you gain from background research—learning everything possible about the company and the responsibilities of the job—will give you the power that comes from being well prepared.

When you do your homework before each interview, you'll never fear being put on the spot, being embarrassed, or having nothing to say.

These truths about interviewing will greatly reduce your anxiety. As a result, you'll be more self-confident and in control.

❖ ❖ ❖

Interview anxiety is the feeling that you would rather jump off of a bridge than go to an interview. In spite of that feeling, by accepting the way things are, you'll be able to cope with a pounding heart, sweaty palms, and knocking knees. Those are the signals your body sends when it's time to be interviewed.

You must interview to get a job. That's the way things are and always have been. Your interviews will be vastly more successful when you anticipate and deal with the anxious feelings that spring up on interview day. Here's how to two-step the heebie-jeebies:

Step one is making a conscious effort to notice yourself getting nervous. Step two is gently acknowledging the uneasy feelings. But don't judge it by telling yourself, "I'm nervous, so now I won't be good." Or, "Why am I like this before an interview?"

By simply accepting the way you feel as normal and observing your rapid heartbeats and sweaty palms, you will restore your equilibrium.

Performers experience the same anxiety, but they know how to deal with fear because they expect it. To interview like a trooper, do not expect to displace anxiety. Acknowledge and deal with it instead.

You'll be able to trick fear by turning nervousness into productive elation. Apprehension will turn into excitement when you look forward to giving a performance and can't wait to do it.

❖ ❖ ❖

It's normal to feel queasy before interviews. After all, actors experience butterflies before going on stage. You'll defeat performance anxiety in the same way performers do. They learn their lines.

But when the show starts, actors forget the words and focus on their role. Your story needs to be rehearsed until you have it down pat. While interviewing, forget what you've practiced. The ideas you need to talk about will come to your mind automatically as you concentrate on the interviewer's questions and comments.

Actors also prepare mentally for their roles before the curtain goes up. Similarly, you need to get into the right interview mood in advance. You can accomplish that by substituting any thoughts of an upcoming interview with things that make you feel happy. That could be remembering a comedian you saw on TV, visualizing a relaxing scene, or remembering some music you love.

Either way, allow only those impressions to be in your mind. Whenever thoughts that irritate you come to mind, push them away. Tell yourself that you'll deal with them later.

But on an interview day, reflect only on the things that turn you on. And hold those thoughts.

❖ ❖ ❖

Nobody ever told you interviewing is going to be easy. Most job candidates get nervous before interviews. Don't worry about it. Even professional actors are anxious before going onstage.

You, too, can learn to live with performance anxiety by rehearsing for each interview. Experts say being prepared eliminates half of your anxiety.

Let's kick anxiety offstage by combining the four powerful techniques of preparation, moving, focusing, and listening.

Preparation. Anticipate questions you think an interviewer will ask. Especially the three toughest questions, which are, "Tell me about yourself," "What are your weaknesses?" and "Why is it taking you so long to find work?"

Rehearse the answers and how to present your background and achievements. Have at least six practice sessions by yourself.

Moving. You already know how exercise reduces tension. So just before entering an interviewer's office, get physical. You can take a brisk walk around the block or parking lot. That will relax your body and vocal apparatus.

Focus. Instead of thinking ahead about what you're going to say, focus your attention on the speaker instead. You won't be stuck for words after you've rehearsed what you want to say over and over again.

Listen. God gave you two ears and only one mouth. That means you need to listen twice as much as you speak in order to interview successfully.

So try these four techniques. "For us there is only trying," wrote poet T.S. Elliot. "The rest is not our business."

❖ ❖ ❖

You might recall that old TV commercial for an antiperspirant that ended with its various spokespeople saying, "Never let them see you sweat." That's good advice for interviewing. It's best not to let your prospective employer see how nervous you are.

Interviewers won't see you sweat when you understand it's only natural to feel anxious before interviews. It's anticipating an event that produces anxiety. This is worst than doing it. That's why actors get anxious while waiting in the wings.

Preperformance anxiety is overcome when the performance begins. By understanding that, you can learn to live with interview anxiety and then to conquer it. Your anxiety is nothing more than a rush of energy and excitement. That can help you rise to the occasion and give a better interview.

You don't have to be free of anxiety. A good performance of any kind is acting in the presence of fear. So just do it. Because feelings are not transparent, there's no way you have to let your interviewer see you sweat.

❖ ❖ ❖

Job hunters react differently to interview stress. Some of you are driven to a bout of dizziness. Others use the adrenaline rush to facilitate a brilliant interview performance.

Regardless of how stress affects you, it's something all job candidates have to deal with. And you don't have a lot of time to do it. The remedy for quickly managing stress before interviewing is to get physical.

You already know that exercise reduces tension. So here are a couple of quick fixes you can use on the spot. They will help you to relax just before walking into an interview room.

The first is to take a short walk around the parking lot. You can also get off of the bus a mile from the interview site and hike the rest of the way. Walking gives you the double benefits of having time to collect your thoughts and getting rid of nervous energy.

The second quick fix for diminishing unease is breathing deeply several times in the moments before you walk into an interview. Deep, slow inhaling and exhaling quickly reduces stress.

The quick fixes of walking and breathing will enable you to relax. That will increase your effectiveness at interviews.

❖ ❖ ❖

Why does interviewing give you the willies? Perhaps you've forgotten how to interview because the last time you had to pitch yourself was a long time ago. Relearning interview skills is no big deal when you understand that the more you do it, the easier it gets.

Your job is to just get out there and do it. Your skills will come back. No amount of acquired knowledge found in self-help books, career counseling, or classes will enable you to enjoy the thrill of knowing you gave a great interview. You can accomplish that only through practice.

Sure, you'll make a mistake or two at an interview. Nobody's meant to be perfect, and you can cover for any blunder in your follow-up letter. But you won't make the same boo-boo twice. That's how you learn.

Then each interview will get better and better. And with each interview, you'll be closer to getting a job offer.

So when the thought of interviewing gives you the willies,

Don't just sit there and become a dilly,

Go out to practice so you won't feel silly.

❖ ❖ ❖

The people with whom you interview could be as nervous as you are. They could be worried about making the right hiring decisions. Not an easy task. Hiring managers have not been trained in how to interview candidates. As a result, interviewers feel they're in the same pressure cooker that you're in.

The pressure will be released when both of you change your attitudes about interviewing. Instead of thinking you need to plead for the job, make each interview objective to help your prospective employer. Then show you've got the right stuff to fill the position.

This attitude adjustment will reduce your anxiety while relaxing your interviewer. You'll have taken the focus off of yourself and will be concentrating on an interviewer's needs. As a result, interviewers will like you more.

You gotta be liked before someone will hire you. Chemistry is even more important than the skills and experience you bring to the table. Ergo, being liked is the name of the interviewing game.

Once an interviewer likes you and is comfortable with you, she'll know that you'll fit in with the rest of the staff—and you'll be called back for another interview.

❖ ❖ ❖

If you compare going out on your first interview to bungee jumping, keep in mind these words by Mark Twain: "Courage is resistance to fear, mastery of fear—not absence of fear." Fear loses its grip on you when you understand its nature.

When you're afraid to fail, you procrastinate doing things so you'll not experience failure. And when it's change you fear, you stop trying new things.

Well, nothing in life seems as scary as facing your first interview. But when you need a job, you need to face that fear. You can do so by asking yourself what the worst that could happen is. You could blow the interview? So what! Your blunder would teach you a lesson that would make your next interview that much easier.

Eleanor Roosevelt knew this well when she said, "You must do the thing you think you cannot do." Then you'll be able to tell yourself that because you lived through a demanding experience, you can take on the next similar episode that comes along. "You gain strength, courage, and confidence by every experience in which you really stop to look fear in the face," said the longest-serving First Lady of the United States.

Your worst fears will not happen in the majority of cases. But when they do, you'll find them a heck of a lot easier to deal with than bungee jumping.

❖ ❖ ❖

CHAPTER 26

You're Either Too Young or Too Old

HOW TO HANDLE AGE, RACIAL, AND GENDER BIAS IN THE JOB MARKET

WHEN SATCHEL PAIGE, THE OLDEST rookie ever to play professional baseball, was asked about his age, he replied, "How old would you be if you didn't know how old you was?"

Paige never admitted his age. The pitcher was one of the greatest stars in the Negro Leagues for twenty-two years before becoming one of the first African Americans to make a breakthrough into the major leagues. So he wanted to keep playing baseball and enjoy his newfound fame.

A legend in his time, Paige was either in his early or late forties when he helped win the 1948 world series. The late pitcher is a role model for older workers. He overcame both color and age discrimination to illustrate that it's your skills—not your skin color or age—that count.

Your age should not embarrass you. Be proud of your maturity and recognize that age is an advantage. Like good wine, you have improved with age. And studies prove it:

* Senior employees are more dependable than their young counterparts because most of their family problems are behind and they have a better attitude.
* The turnover rate for workers age fifty and up is just 3 percent compared to over 10 percent for younger workers.

- Many older workers offer excellent customer service skills due to years of experience interacting with people and solving problems.
- With an aging population, customers appreciate dealing with a staff their own age.

Lots of companies who have caught the drift hire seniors to fill a range of technical and nontechnical positions. It's not how old you are but how old you look and feel.

It all comes down to what Satchel Paige understood so well: "How old would you be if you didn't know how old you was?"

❖ ❖ ❖

Another Satchel Page aphorism is, "Don't look back. Something might be gaining on you." When that something gaining on you is age, you still have time left to accomplish things.

Due to the increasing life expectancy, people are working longer these days. Some decide not to retire at sixty-five because they cannot afford to pack it in. Others want to continue working well into there seventies because they love what they do and want to stay productive.

Regardless of the reason you want or need to keep working, fretting about your age accomplishes nothing. Just ask senior citizens who have lived out most of their lives what they might have done differently. Nobody is going to say they should have spent more time worrying. Most seniors regret what they have not done, not what they have done.

You can gain confidence from the achievements of many seniors who have gone before you.

For example, Mary Baker Eddy began to publish *The Christian Science Monitor* when she was eighty-seven. Pablo Picasso was still turning out paintings at ninety. And Britain's Allan Stewart completed a bachelor of law degree at the University of New England at age ninety-one. Stewart said he completed a six-year degree in four years "because of [his] age."

So never let age stop your dreams. American poet Henry Wadsworth Longfellow understood this well when he wrote,

Ah, nothing is too late
Till the tired heart shall cease to palpitate.

❖ ❖ ❖

The appearance you project is important at any age. A forty-year-old job candidate is considered relatively young. "But if you are forty and out of shape or in poor health, you will have a problem being hired because you probably look decades older than you are," advises career consultant Steve Cuthrell.

On the other hand, says Cuthrell, a sixty-year-old person who is in good health and appears to have lots of vigor and vitality will have no trouble landing a position.

Nobody denies that age is a factor when looking for work. But it's only one of many factors. The most important ingredients are your achievements at work because they show what you can do for the company that is interviewing you for a job.

But if you lack energy at any age, you can appear older than your years. A remedy is to get a medical checkup and to start an exercise program.

Cuthrell sums up his advice about improving your physical fitness in order to appear more vigorous by saying, "The more energetic and seemingly unconcerned with age you are, the more vibrant interviewers will find you to be."

❖ ❖ ❖

Although your age is an issue in the interview process, don't let it bug you. "Job candidates find they're either too young or too old," says Steve Cuthrell. "Younger applicants are often told they lack experience and can be perceived as an embarrassment to older managers."

You can overcome the problem of being too young by highlighting your performance in summer jobs and in extracurricular activities during your high school and college years. "Stress the practical influence you've had on other employees," Cuthrell advises, "especially if you can prove you've supervised workers quite a few years older than you."

While looking for your first job, be careful not to land in a dead-end position. You need to look for opportunities where there will be some training and grooming for promotion.

Because of the need to single out companies that offer such opportunities, it can take longer for younger job hunters to land. In today's job market, "companies aren't stockpiling employees as they used to."

❖ ❖ ❖

It's no longer just the seasoned professionals who need to examine their careers. The younger workforce is now taking control over their destiny by identifying better career options.

That usually happens after you've paid your dues in the corporate world for a while. Sometimes you have no other choice. Company downsizings affect younger people, too, and the perception that it's easier to find a job when you're young doesn't always hold water. Sometimes you need more help to plan a career than your older counterparts.

There are many fields looking for young professionals. Software development, financial advising, and civil engineering are fast-growing fields. Others include database administration, information technology, and management consulting.

Younger workers can also consider smaller companies and start-ups where they can get the hands-on experience they may never get at large organizations. Sometimes it's a good idea to join a smaller company for a while just to gain experience. When you take a bridge job, it will help you get closer to your ultimate career goal.

❖ ❖ ❖

If life begins at forty, so does age prejudice. Although you cannot overcome it, you can deal with the maturity issue by understanding that age prejudice kicks in not because of calendar years but because of perception.

If you are over fifty and the person doing the hiring is half your age, there could be a big problem in the way the younger person perceives you. Outplacement consultant Steve Cuthrell suggests that job candidates need to be realistic. A young hiring manager might think of you as a father or an uncle. "If your age is a problem for that person, it's impossible to do anything about it."

Suppose you could force somebody to hire you. That somebody could feel uncomfortable about your age in relation to theirs. "That wouldn't be an effective relationship, and you wouldn't last very long," says the outplacement consultant.

You need a win-win situation for a relationship to work. That's why you're obliged to keep interviewing until you find an employer you can please. Job hunters need to take a good look at their relationships with each interviewer and recognize that they're either the right age or the wrong age—too young or too old. You can't win 'em all. So move on to the next interview.

The idea is to interview without thinking about your age. But proceed to show your capabilities and how they relate to the requirements of the position.

With that thought in mind, you can go in with your best shot. "If you're what they want, fine. If not, you wouldn't want the relationship anyway," Cuthrell says.

❖ ❖ ❖

The best way to buck the age barrier is to face it head on. While older job-hunters don't want to volunteer their age, they cannot lie about it either.

Of course, it's illegal for an interviewer to ask how old you are. Nevertheless, some of them do. If you're ever asked your age, it wouldn't be cool to try and finesse the question or to argue the point. What would you say? "Sorry, my lawyer told me not to answer that illegal question"? With that response, you can forget about getting a job offer. So admit your age, and then focus on the position and how you can help.

While the age element usually comes into play when you turn fifty, some experts say it kicks in five years before that. Either way, employers can be prejudiced about age for a variety of reasons.

For example, a perspective employer could think an older applicant will have increased insurance costs. You can explain that you don't need the same benefits as younger candidates, especially if you're covered by a spousal policy. Make that point when discussing salary.

The hiring manager might also feel that you have too much experience to accept a lower salary. You can explain that you're at the point in your career where you are determined to do something you really care about. Consequently, you can afford to worry more about the right job in the right company and less about salary.

You need to challenge stereotypes of older workers. The technique is to demonstrate at interviews how you've kept pace with technology, worked with younger workers, and embraced managerial changes.

❖ ❖ ❖

The good news for people over sixty is that you don't have to join the mothball fleet. After you retire or have to leave a job because of age, you still have plenty of years left. People live longer these days. That being the case, they need to find satisfaction and income during those years.

According to experts, you enjoy a second middle age due to this extended lifespan. It takes places between your half-century mark and the age of seventy-five. You can make it another growing period by asking yourself two questions: What work activities satisfy me? And what do I want out of life? Your answers can run the gamut from making more money, having leisure time, and contributing to society to having opportunities to develop and master a special area, developing a more spiritual life, or finding and living your true calling.

If you are satisfied with the way things are going in your current career, fine-tune how your time is allotted. But if you are dissatisfied because you find that most of your needs are not being met, you need to make changes by working with the two questions mentioned above.

That's how to create an even more satisfying career for the years ahead.

❖ ❖ ❖

Older job applicants find the playing field is not always level, despite age discrimination laws. However, there is a bright side. According to the late Dr. Lydia Bronte, the author of *The Longevity Factor: The New Reality of Long Careers and How It Can Lead to Richer Lives*, a major peak of creativity begins after fifty. That is one of the reasons why millions of older workers are finding jobs and changing careers. You might consider becoming a comeback kid at the company that cut your job by exploring part-time positions there. Companies still need to get the work done following a downsizing, so they often turn to people like you—and to staffing services—for help.

The many people you read about who keep working until the end demonstrate the truth of Dr. Bronte's concept of beginning another creative journey after you reach the big five-oh.

Pablo Picasso continued to paint into his nineties. Despite his arthritis, Pablo Casals remained a master musician until he died at ninety-six. Ninety-three-year-old Edward Gerjuoy continues to work at the University of Pittsburgh. The professor emeritus in physics and astronomy works weekdays from noon to 6:00 p.m. "Sometimes I'm the only one there on weekends," he told *USA Today*.

When you hit retirement age, you still have many years left. So pick a field and pick the job-finding techniques that appeal to you. Or pick up a paintbrush, a musical instrument, or a camera, and begin your life's next adventure

❖ ❖ ❖

Older workers who take joy in proving wrong the adage about not being able to teach old dogs new tricks find excitement in acquiring new skills. But too many of you are not getting a chance to share the excitement.

According to The Bureau of Labor Statistics, any worker on the rise can become history a little before reaching forty-five. This fact comes at a time when older employees are the fastest-growing share of the labor force. You'll recall that Astronaut John Glenn went back into space when he was pushing eighty.

Some of those corporate nincompoops who make hiring policies need to understand the truth about the value of older workers. Until the dawning of that day, you need to take control of your career as never before.

You can enhance your value at any age by learning new skills. Senior workers who offer skills that are in high demand will discover new opportunities.

For example, brokerage firms have learned that their clients enjoy having investment counselors whose life experience is etched on their faces. JPMorgan's CEO Jamie Dimon understood that well when he hired his seventy-eight-year-old father to join his firm's brokerage unit.

❖ ❖ ❖

You will face age discrimination sooner or later because aging affects everybody. And stereotypes of older workers guarantee that The Age Discrimination in Employment Act will continue to play a big role in the workplace. The legislation, which was passed over forty-five years ago, prohibits age discrimination in employment.

The law has helped older workers. Before it was passed, some classified ads stated that workers over thirty-five or forty need not apply. Yet lawyers agree that it's not easy for employees to win age discrimination lawsuits. While it's unlawful to fire you for age, courts have held that it might be okay to dismiss you for having too high a salary or pension.

Cases filed in court are mostly about age discrimination in firing, not hiring, according to the *New York Times*. That makes sense because when you apply for a position, you are usually not told why you weren't hired. But when you're fired, you can see if there was a pattern of age discrimination. You know how you performed and who else was let go.

Defense lawyers agree that many corporations that may have considered age in hiring, promotion, and firing decisions have now become more sensitive to the subject.

❖ ❖ ❖

Because members of special groups fear discrimination, you have most likely experienced this social evil. Most job candidates fall into categories if they're too young, too old, too fat, too thin, gray and balding, or pregnant women.

Discrimination pervades life, and your job-finding campaign is a part of life. But you can circumvent discrimination in the job market by avoiding the usual route of answering classified ads and posting on the Internet and instead selecting the networking or referral method of finding a job.

Friends and associates with whom you meet will instinctively refrain from referring you to any contacts who are likely to discriminate. Prejudice aside, networking is the major tool for getting hired.

A staggering 80 percent of jobs available to you are not advertised or published. You'll find them by developing a plan that allows you to be referred from one contact to the next. With this method, you'll always be passed on with a favorable reference until you meet your next job.

❖ ❖ ❖

As either a midcareer or an older worker, you hold a number of aces in your hand. You offer experience and wisdom that only comes with age, and older workers have proved they adopt better to changing conditions. Here are four ways to play your hand:

1. Upgrade your skills by taking college-level courses. Computer courses are always the best bet.

2. Stand out from younger employees by offering to work hours they don't want. This tactic works in service industries that need twenty-four–hour staffing.
3. Volunteer to do projects that are important to your boss and will allow you to showcase your talents.
4. Test the waters for an alternative career with temporary work. Temp workers constitute one of the fastest-growing segments of the labor market. That's because companies who downsize hate to add full-time workers who drive up salary and benefit costs. Besides, temping sometimes leads to a full-time gig.

There's another big ace you hold. Because older workers have no plans for advancement or to jump ship for more pay, you can be more advantageous than younger workers in terms of loyalty, dependability, and focus.

❖ ❖ ❖

Just because you turned fifty is no excuse to complain about being shut out of the job market. The expression "the older you are, the more difficult it is to land" is true only if you lack energy or have Dunlops Disease—a physical condition that is noticeable when your stomach dun lops over your belt!

Who wants to hire someone who looks like an old fogey? While you cannot change your age, you can change your image by getting in shape and learning new business methods.

You probably spent many years doing the same old job the same old way without learning any new tricks. The same old same old doesn't wash in today's job market. In addition to exercising and having a good diet, you need to understand technology. That's how to acquire an image that is vibrant.

You are showing a prospective employer that you have what it takes when you present yourself as a creative and aggressive candidate with a passion for life. You'll overcome calendar years when you keep in mind that it's not how old you are, but how old you look and feel.

❖ ❖ ❖

Instead of tormenting yourself about being too old to ever find a job, look for the silver lining—something hopeful in the midst of difficulty. Your age can be a valuable wake-up call that your thinking and health need to be upgraded.

You can consider age as wisdom and grace. Those qualities give you a leg up in the job market because companies need accomplished employees who are out of the box. You have to be older to offer that experience.

And the reason why you need to upgrade your health is a no-brainer. "The more energetic and unconcerned with age you are," says career counselor Steve Cuthrell, "the more vibrant interviewers will find you to be." So it's critical you look good when showing up for an interview.

Medical experts agree. Physical activity enhances your whole life. Exercising does more than just improve your physique. A healthy body influences how you look and feel.

So there's no need to freak out just because you're an older job candidate. And you won't panic when you take the advice of lyricist B.G. DeSylva: "Remember somewhere, the sun is shining, and so the right thing to do is make it shine for you."

The sun will shine for you when you do what you gotta do to look and feel good. Then let the interviews roll.

❖ ❖ ❖

When it comes to finding a job, your age is not a knockout blow. "How old you are is no more of an impediment than any other form of prejudice," says career counselor Bob Cuddy, "such as the schools you attended, your gender, height, or weight."

Age discrimination is out there because of stereotypes surrounding older workers. "You can overcome age prejudice by demonstrating you do not represent those stereotypes," says the Westport, Connecticut–based counselor who works with senior executives in transition.

Many employers perceive older people as disorganized, late for work, lacking energy and enthusiasm for what they're doing, and not hard workers. "You must demonstrate that you're not the kind of person who is looking for the easy way out, because that's what stereotypes are based on."

There is no need to try to hide your age. But you don't have to act it, either. Cuddy recalls someone saying that if you act your age, you're probably not going to do well in the job market.

You won't be discriminated against because of age when you come alive at interviews. That means demonstrating that you have energy by expressing enthusiasm about your work and career, what you have accomplished, and what you bring to the table.

❖ ❖ ❖

Older job hunters are taking the words of an economist to heart. Ernst Schumacher said, "Small is beautiful." In today's economy, small companies make beautiful job prospects.

Most of the senior executives Bob Cuddy coaches, are from large companies and they find positions with smaller corporations who employ between fifty and several hundred people. "When you go to those companies, you find that you can make a difference," Cuddy says. "You are a significant piece of the operation. And usually, that's very exciting for most people."

But when you have worked with a big corporation most of your working life, you'll need to adjust to the small-is-beautiful concept. That's because there will be less money in your paycheck.

Cuddy sums it up nicely when he says, "If you've been in the job market for a long time and really want to get some excitement out of a job, smaller companies are the place to go."

Small to medium-sized businesses look for candidates who offer experience. Older workers supply that know-how, and they enjoy the challenges and advancement that only smaller companies offer.

❖ ❖ ❖

A growing number of employers have discarded stereotypes about older workers. Experience is a hot commodity. Younger job hunters do not have your know-how. So companies want to hire people who can get right to work and to keep those employees who know the work.

But you need to keep your job skills state of the art. A big reason employees over fifty get dumped is because they don't. The key to keeping a job you like is a four-step process:

1. Identify the sills your company needs next.
2. Begin to learn those skills.
3. Tell those above you why you are good. Although you probably think everyone knows, most of the time they don't have a clue. And you could be bounced because the downsizing committee does not know what you have accomplished.
4. Determine what skills you can bring along to your next job. They are called "transferrable skills" and are the key to getting a better job fast. Some transferrable skills now in demand include training, analyzing, and coordinating.

The more talents you can offer to a prospective employer, the less competition you'll face for whatever job you want.

❖ ❖ ❖

According to a survey of over four hundred human resources professionals not many companies make active efforts to attract or retrain older workers.

The percentage of workers age forty-five and over has risen to about 40 percent. Yet a study conducted by The Radcliffe Public Policy Institute found that fewer than 30 percent of the companies surveyed made an effort to establish opportunities for advancement, skills training, or part-time work arrangements for senior workers.

"American companies cannot hope to stay competitive if they ignore the skills needs of such a significant segment of the workforce," said Paula Rayman, director of the Harvard University–based institute.

Raymond told *Modern Maturity* that the vocabulary, general information, and judgment of older workers "either rise or never fall before age sixty." Nevertheless, managers consistently make clueless hiring, promotion, training, and discipline decisions based solely on the age of the worker. But they are not totally at fault.

While studies show that older employees are reliable in a crisis, committed to doing quality work, and loyal and dedicated, senior workers are also perceived as unprepared when it comes to big changes in the workplace—especially changes involving computers and other technologies.

As a consequence, you need to become more proactive in order to compete in a rapidly changing job market by continually upgrading your skills, and especially your computer skills. Then you'll have earned the right to shout the truth about how dependable, knowledgeable, and experienced you are.

❖ ❖ ❖

The best way to overcome labels is by performance, said Colin Powell. The former secretary of defense and retired four-star army general recalled an early experience as one of the military's first African American officers.

When a superior told young Lieutenant Powell that he did his job very well "for a black officer," he was taken aback until he returned to the BOQ (base officers quarters) and began to think about it. Powell decided to perform his job better than any officer. He did. And nobody has to remind you of the results.

Powell was the first black officer, and the first officer who didn't attend West Point in order to rise through the ranks, to become chairman of the joint chiefs of staff.

You, too, can outperform the rest by consistently doing your best. Performance knows no prejudice. When it comes to using your skills, everybody is born equally. A study of almost two hundred seventy Harvard graduates makes the point.

The survey analyzed why some succeeded and others failed. People born to wealthy families did not do better than those from poor backgrounds. So the luck of the draw in how you were born does not apply to your success. Everybody has an equal chance in America.

It's how you respond to major setbacks in life that makes the difference. You have choices.

Colin Powell chose performance. You, too, can rise to the top by performing your tasks better than your coworkers.

❖ ❖ ❖

When a major New York bank started another round of job cuts, a department head turning sixty was forced to take a retirement package. Don had worked there for over a quarter of a century. "I was somewhat negative," explained the former banker, "because I'm old, was replaced by a younger person from a merger, and felt unwanted."

Don was concerned about ever finding a job at his age "until it was pointed out that [he had] experience and employers want [him]. And lo and behold it is true."

This advice enabled the downsized banker to feel confident during interviews. "After that, I could just sell myself because my skills were what hiring managers wanted," he said. Don also discovered he was able to get other work without any problems by being positive about his age.

Don landed a similar job with another bank where he replaced a man in his late twenties. The hiring manager felt the younger worker didn't have enough experience for the job. So she upgraded the salary and title of the younger person's low-level position in order to bring Don aboard in a senior management job as vice president in charge of a department.

Don discussed his major takeaway from the experience: there's no need to be despondent over age when you work on the positive part. That means expressing all of the experience you've had. Prospective employers will respect you for that. "At all times, keep your head up. And if you're a senior, it's great."

❖ ❖ ❖

Don was employed in his new job for five years when his bank was acquired by a larger financial institution in another state.

He was offered a position at the company's new headquarters. But Don decided against relocating his family and took a severance package instead. Then he began to showcase his years of experience in another job-finding campaign. Don was then sixty-five.

The senior job hunter learned a couple of lessons from his previous job hunt. First of all, hiring managers respected him for his age. And second, he offered the experience only a senior candidate can offer. "When you sell all of the experience you've had in the field you're looking to work in, it can be done," said Don. "And I know it can be done."

When Don was doing the hiring and the shoe was on the other foot, he asked younger applicants how much experience they'd had. "Now, as an older job candidate, I walk into a room and interviewers ask what I would do in a particular situation."

Don landed as the head of a department with a major New York brokerage firm. He considers himself well paid for doing the same work with the title he requested. "And they wanted me because of my experience. I'll be sixty-six next year."

❖ ❖ ❖

Older workers feel there's discrimination no matter which way they turn. "There's not only age discrimination in the workplace, but there's also wage discrimination," says career specialist Anita Lands, "because older workers come with higher price tags."

Although age discrimination exists, there's no need to let that fact paralyze you from action and kick you out of the game, Lands advises. Instead of beating your head against the corporate wall, go after small- to medium-sized companies. Small companies are growing, so they need to hire experienced personnel.

You can value the fact that as an older worker you come with experience, training, and knowledge—and a wonderful work ethic. "It's important for you to value this within yourself," advises the New York City–based career specialist. "Because if you do, so will the world. And if you don't, the world will act accordingly."

❖ ❖ ❖

A study proves there is age discrimination in hiring. The American Association of Retired Persons (AARP) mailed pairs of résumés and cover letters from equally qualified older and younger job seekers to over eighteen hundred companies and employment agencies.

The applicants were fictitious job hunters who applied for the same positions to test for bias in hiring. Each had ten years experience. But from the date of their college graduations, employers could surmise that one applicant was over fifty-five and the other was around thirty. The findings suggest thousands of incidents of discriminatory treatment, the AARP reports.

For example, a hiring manager telephoned a younger applicant to express interest. But the same manager sent a letter to the older applicant saying they had no positions that matched his experience.

Older workers should modify their résumés. Take out information that would date you. The year you graduated from college can be eliminated, and if you worked for other companies before spending a quarter of a century at your current job, chop off the first ten years of your experience.

Employers consider the past ten years of experience to be the most relevant.

❖ ❖ ❖

Aristotle said, "Education is the best provision for old age." You need to follow the ancient Greek philosopher's advice and update your skills in order to find a new job or keep the one you have.

You are competing for available slots not only with younger workers, but also with a huge amount of workers your own age. According to government statistics, people approaching the fifty-five to sixty-four age range are the fastest-growing segment of the workforce.

Speaking of the overall importance of acquiring knowledge to succeed, Aristotle also said, "Educated men are as much superior to uneducated men as the living are to the dead."

As you grow older, keeping your career alive should include knowledge of The Age Discrimination in Employment Act. The statute protects most employees over forty from discrimination that's age related. Violations come in the form of being passed over for promotion despite nice job evaluations or being told you're overqualified for a job, which could mean the boss thinks you're too old.

When you believe you've been the victim of discrimination in the workplace, look up your state's human rights commission on the Internet and fight for justice.

❖ ❖ ❖

There has never been a better time for older executives to offer their skills to the job market. According to a survey conducted by the Pew Research Center, more than three-quarters of today's workers expect to work for a salary after they retire.

Most of those surveyed said they wanted to continue working not because they had to, but because they wanted to. You need to keep that in mind when you're worried about not finding work because of age. As the study indicates, there's no need to look at your calendar years as a barrier.

Older workers are a tremendous and largely untapped source. A large number of new and fast-growing small companies are eager to tap into your background. So you can wear your age as a badge of honor that younger small-business owners will appreciate. Many of them grumble about not being able to find seasoned candidates who are willing to work for less money.

You'll identify small company prospects by networking among your friends and business associates and responding to job listings in newspapers and postings online. You can also contact staffing services—temporary employment agencies—that specialize in your field.

Just make sure you are at the top of your game. That means being as much on the cutting edge of technology as your younger counterparts are.

❖ ❖ ❖

Baby boomers are bouncing all over the workplace. Boomers born right after the Second World War range in age from almost fifty to over sixty-five. They've seen computers shrink the world and the number of jobs as many occupations have disappeared into third-world communities where labor is cheap. What's a baby boomer to do?

As you grow older, you need more jobs, not fewer. Because you're expected to live well into your eighties, you need to keep on truckin' in order to exist. For most of you, it will be a working retirement. Oh, stop groaning! There is some good news here.

Studies show training keeps you feeling young. If you're ready for a change, you'll have the time of your life. Areas of opportunity for retired boomers include project assignments for executives and managers, consulting engagements, accounting during tax season, researching, and retail sales,

Now is the time to prepare for a working retirement. Be as up to date with computer skills as recent college graduates are. Computers are required for practically any field you choose. And expect to become freelance talent for hire.

❖ ❖ ❖

Baby boomers who are not ready for pasture are fighting back. Many have sued their current and former employers for age discrimination. And that has spawned lots of litigation.

Under federal employment law, you can sue at age forty. But it's no easy task. The US Supreme Court has ruled that you need to prove with a preponderance of evidence that age was the reason for discrimination. Because the burden of proof has been increased over the years, it's harder to prove an age discrimination case unless you live in a state that has stronger protections for older workers—like New York, California, and Michigan, for example.

Advocates for age discrimination say illegal bias is the result of deeply held prejudices by employers that young people are more energetic and cost less to employ than older workers. While that might be true in some cases, many claims are unfounded because they arose from legitimate efforts by companies to reduce costs by cutting jobs.

Corporations also save money by firing executives who make six figures and replacing them with younger workers for much less money. There's nothing illegal about that.

While it might be risky business to sue the bastards, you're definitely at risk in the job marketplace if you've failed to keep up with technology. It can be wiser to invest your money on courses that can help you get reemployed than on costly legal fees you might not recover.

❖ ❖ ❖

Corporations still win the vast majority of age discrimination cases. Even though congress and the White House outlawed age discrimination almost fifty years ago, courts have chipped away at the law. This has helped corporate America to defend itself in two ways. Courts have raised the burden of proof, and they've limited an employee's use of certain evidence that often ties in with age.

Judges have held that while it's unlawful to fire you for age, it may be okay to can you for having too high a salary or pension. Paradoxically, that comes with age. Gotcha!

It's also a fact that employers still prefer to hire younger workers to older ones with compatible experience. That's why most cases under the Age Discrimination in Employment Act of 1967 are about discrimination in firing, not hiring.

Let's assume you're justified in bringing a lawsuit for age discrimination because you've noticed a pattern of unequal treatment. You're in an awkward situation. The already high cost of litigation that has tripled over the past ten years discourages employees who think they're victims from bringing a suit.

You need to try to find a lawyer who will represent you on a contingency basis. That means your attorney agrees to accept a percentage of your settlement only if you win. Or you can join a class action lawsuit brought by other workers in your company who have similar claims.

❖ ❖ ❖

You can stop thinking about the years after you turn sixty as those dreaded wind-down years. Many of you are not only finding jobs, but are also pursuing new careers.

In fact, senior citizens have become the largest segment of the job market. Some seventy-five million baby boomers born during the boom after the Second World War have saturated the job market. They range in age from a tad under fifty-four to sixty-eight.

People are living longer due to the miracle of modern science and medicine. I'll bet your grandparents don't even look like grandparents anymore. Grandmothers are turning blond instead of gray.

So you might as well take advantage of the opportunities offered by your senior years. Connecticut-based columnist Dee Maggiori calls them icing on the cake. "The trick is to enjoy all it offers with grace, humor, and gratitude."

You can be grateful for your older years by considering them a precious gift. There's no need to live a boring and inactive old age when companies, and especially small- to medium-sized organizations, need the years of experience and expertise you offer.

❖ ❖ ❖

CHAPTER 27

How to Overcome Ten Job-Search Barriers

We are made strong by what we overcome.
—American nature essayist John Burroughs

Barrier #1: When You Stutter

Job hunters who stutter have a double whammy. You need to find a job, but you're terrified to interview because of your affliction. Nobody blames you for not wanting to struggle with words. And who can blame an interviewer for being uncomfortable watching you do it?

Your stutter has demeaned and humiliated you. Although your parents might have taken you to a psychiatrist who prescribed tranquilizers or beta-blockers, nothing worked. So you stopped trying. There was no hope then. But there is hope now.

That's the word from stuttering expert Dr. Martin Schwartz, a psychiatrist and speech pathologist who explains the condition. "The reason you struggle with words is your vocal chords lock and air required for speaking cannot pass."

How to Overcome the Stuttering Barrier

The New York City–based doctor has developed a method that enables you to unlock the vocal chords when you speak. He says "the passive airflow technique" has helped over 90 percent of the patients who have studied and practiced it.

Dr. Schwartz has written an excellent book that explains the method. It's titled *Stutter No More*. If you feel stuttering has been holding

413

you back, consider putting your search on hold while investigating help that's available. A good way to start is to call the stuttering hotline at 1-800-221-2483.

❖ ❖ ❖

BARRIER #2: WHEN YOU'RE TURNED DOWN
Being rejected can certainly let the air out of your balloon. A turndown affects your self-confidence and can lead you to believe that you have failed. But where is it written that life is hassle free or that interviews must be conducted in a user-friendly environment? Nowhere!

How to Overcome the Rejection Barrier
You'll shove the rejection barrier out of the way by making an effort to do three things during your search:

First, anticipate being turned down a lot. Rejection comes with the territory. As with any kind of sales, you'll find more rejection than acceptance during your search.

Second, make an effort to anticipate the high doses of anger that you can experience following rude behavior from nasty people.

And third, make an effort not to gripe about being rejected or to churn it over and over mentally. When you feel resentful and frustrated, chewing the cud only makes things worst. Instead, let negative feelings motivate you to work tenaciously toward your goal of finding a job.

As you can see, effort is the key to overcoming the barrier of rejection. Making an effort is also linked to your successful ability to withstand frustration.

Those are the reasons why your struggle can be the key to almost any emotional problem surrounding your job campaign.

❖ ❖ ❖

BARRIER #3: WHEN ASPECTS OF JOB HUNTING CAUSE ANXIETY

Anxiety is often caused by the anticipation of having to write and perform. You're required to do both activities during a job search or sales campaign, like it or not. You must write résumés, follow-up letters, and various kinds of e-mails, like it or not. And you must perform during interviews, networking meetings, and while telephoning, like it or not.

While you might never get to like it, there's no need to be dismayed. It is possible to look for work while retaining your peace of mind.

How to Overcome the Anxiety Barrier

The challenge of overcoming tension produced by your job hunt lies not in learning to avoid anxiety, but in coping with it.

An effective coping technique is to make it your intention before each activity to try to do your best, not try to be perfect. That intention will make your energy positive, and it will work for you.

Positive energy is initiated and shaped by your own will to do your best. As with any project, anxiety is the enemy only at the beginning. Then, on a regular basis, you can challenge and check a feeling of unease with a will to do your best. That's how to turn anxiety into a helpmate.

❖ ❖ ❖

BARRIER #4: WHEN NERVOUS HABITS HINDER YOUR PERFORMANCE

Lots of you have nervous habits. Even movie stars do. It's reported that Madonna plays with her jewelry, Kirstie Alley flicks her hair, and Matt Dillon taps his fingers. But they don't show their habits while they're on camera. Oops! Your nervous habit is showing. And it will drive interviewers nuts.

This is true even when you're not aware that you jiggle your legs, twist your ring, or play with your hair. Psychologists say habits are satisfying and calming but hard to control. In fact, habits performed for years can kill your career. How? Instead of listening to what you have to say, listeners will pay attention to the quirky things you do

How to Overcome the Nervous Habit Barrier

Although voluntary nervous habits like nail biting, hair twisting, knee bouncing, and hand wringing are hard to control, you can break them. But involuntary habits—like Tourette's Syndrome and other uncontrollable body movements—call for professional help. What follows are two ways to break a voluntary habit cycle:

One method is to do something else in place of your ugly routine. So instead of biting your nails, spend money on a manicure. And instead of picking your cuticles, use a presentation binder at interviews to occupy your hands.

Another method is to understand and accept the fact that your anxiety will increase during times of stress. Those are the times to take a time-out to meditate or breathe deeply until feelings of uncertainty pass.

Sometimes, controlling a habit can be as simple as remembering not to bounce your knee, play with your jewelry, or flick your hair.

❖ ❖ ❖

BARRIER #5: WHEN YOU FEEL BURNED OUT

You do not get burnt-out by doing too much. Burnout is caused by working at something you don't want to do. It's like moving forward on one leg while trying to pull back with the other. You're split physically and mentally. That can make you feel anxious and drain your energy.

Comedian Jimmy Durante described the sensation when he sang, "Did you ever have the feeling you wanted to go when you still had the feeling that you wanted to stay."

Psychologist Dr. Abraham Low gave a name to that feeling: "being in duality." That's having a double character and not being able to make a decision.

How to Overcome the Burnout Barrier

The late neuropsychiatrist offered this four-step remedy to help his patients make up their minds: Think. Decide. Plan. Act.

So **think** about the kind of job you like doing. **Decide** if there are jobs out there that will offer you the opportunity to do it. **Plan** a strategy for your search. Then **act** on your self-marketing plan.

Remember that burnout is caused by doing something that's not for you while wishing there was something else you would rather be doing. You'll avoid burnout by following Dr. Low's advice to think, decide, plan, and act.

❖ ❖ ❖

BARRIER #6: WHEN YOU PROCRASTINATE

Procrastination is the feeling that you must write the perfect résumé or give a flawless interview that will knock 'em dead. You think these things must be done so perfectly that you put off doing your job campaign.

Psychologists say that trying to do things perfectly means you're afraid of failing. Therefore, you avoid change until success is guaranteed. Of course, there are no guarantees in the life of a job candidate—or in life, period. So you've put yourself into an emotional tailspin with thinking that's self-defeating. It's your thinking that's got you stuck.

How to Overcome the Procrastination Barrier

You need to change your thinking by deciding to go for progress instead of perfection. You already know that nobody's perfect. That is why finding your next job doesn't depend on writing a perfect résumé or on giving a perfect interview. The secret lies in just making a start at what bugs you.

To help get your thinking unstuck, make "progress, not perfection" your motto for the duration of your search.

So make a little start at something each day, and begin right now by setting several doable goals that can be accomplished today. For instance, start writing a job objective for your résumé and make a couple of phone calls.

That would be progress—not perfection. And that's a powerful thought that will help remove the procrastination barrier from your work life.

❖ ❖ ❖

Barrier #7: When You Isolate Yourself

A few job-search clients I've coached felt so ashamed about losing their jobs that they isolated themselves. They didn't want family, friends, or neighbors to learn about their fate.

Depression is a cause of isolation. A panic disorder is another. Regardless of the reason, isolation is an unhealthy behavior because being isolated keeps alive the negative feelings that caused you to withdraw in the first place.

How to Overcome the Isolation Barrier

You need to take care of yourself emotionally after losing a job or else you'll run a high risk of burnout. Self-care can be administered in a variety of ways.

One of them is to understand that you won't be stigmatized when you lose your job these days. Then you can feel free to allow family and friends into your life. Because those with whom you have a bond know you the best of all, they'll be able to provide valuable input about your campaign and personal issues, too.

Another method of emotional self-care is to make use of the naturally occurring therapies that surround you. They are the activities you like doing that reduce stress. So find some recreation. The word "recreation" breaks down to "re-create."

You can re-create yourself through exercise. It's a plus to do it with others. That's because you'll become a part of another social environment whose members share the same goal of maintaining their health and bodies in order to reduce the stress.

Never underestimate the importance of caring for yourself emotionally. Find something new and different. You'll grow when you pick up new ideas along the way.

❖ ❖ ❖

BARRIER #8: WHEN YOU HAVE A RÉSUMÉ BLOCK
A résumé block is the same as a writer's block. It can be a psychological hurdle to get any piece of writing started. Perhaps you're concerned that you don't have much to say on a résumé, that you haven't accomplished much, or that you lack some skills. Or perhaps you fear that your résumé will look thin or unimpressive.

"All of you have done things in your jobs," says psychologist Alan Pickman. "You've completed tasks. And have used certain skills to achieve them." What you've achieved in your jobs will certainly be enough to fill a résumé of two pages—or to at least occupy a page and a half, which is the minimum length for a résumé.

That's easy for the career psychologist Pickman to say. But what if your psychological block is an inability to uncover those achievements?

How to Overcome the Résumé Block
Not to worry, advises Pickman. "Sometimes it takes an outside perspective to help discover your successes." Outside help can come from a career coach or from feedback from valued friends and colleagues.

At the same time, you need to decrease the concern that putting something down in a résumé is like setting it in stone. A résumé is a work in progress. You can make changes to it as your search unfolds.

Pickman puts it this way: "It's always a good idea to revise your résumé along the way as you get clear about what you're looking for."

❖ ❖ ❖

BARRIER #9: WHEN YOU'RE A WORKAHOLIC

You'll know you're a workaholic if you look forward to Monday mornings the way most people look forward to Friday afternoons. And when interviewers ask, "What are your weaknesses?" you play it cute by telling them you're a workaholic.

You might think the interviewer will jump for joy at the prospect of having a workaholic on board a reduced staff. In reality, prospective employers will know you won't be a good fit.

Workaholics set poor examples. They don't delegate responsibility and are not team players. In fact, workaholics can be sick cookies. The obsession with work causes them to ignore core responsibilities like family and friends. Some pay a price with heart attacks or sicknesses. Others eventually snap.

How to Overcome the Workaholic Barrier

Lessen your addiction to work by reducing the number of hours you work. Then plan to be more productive in fewer hours.

Once you get used to doing more in less time, take five-minute rest periods every half hour or so. You can exercise, do deep breathing, or take short walks during the breaks.

Thomas Edison said, "There is no substitute for hard work." While the inventor's advice applies to everyone, workaholics must learn to disengage from their hard work for short periods during the day.

A final thought—get a life! Find something other than work that you'd like to do. Then do more of it.

❖ ❖ ❖

BARRIER #10: WHEN YOU HAVE INTERVIEW PHOBIA

Interviewing would be a snap if it weren't for the other person sitting across from you. After all, you give a perfect interview while taking a shower. The trouble starts after you leave home.

Your nervousness is set in motion when you start to speculate about what might go wrong during an upcoming interview. Now you know the truth: interview phobia is a social disease that's similar to social phobia. Social phobia is being anxious and fearful of being judged by others.

How to Overcome the Interview Phobia Barrier
Don't worry about it. Murphy's law says, "Anything that can go wrong will go wrong." Guaranteed. You need to accept that fact and understand that for every mistake, there is a remedy.

For example, what if you forgot to say something? If it's really important, the interviewer will ask you about it. If she doesn't, include what you forgot to say in your follow-up letter or e-mail.

Maybe you're concerned about mixing up your words. A simple way out is saying, "Excuse me…let me back up." Then start over. Or try to inject humor. You might say, "Sorry, the teeth I rented are a little loose." Interviewers will relate to that because everybody fumbles words sometimes.

❖ ❖ ❖

CHAPTER 28

How to Get Support for Your Search

SELF-HELP FOR JOB HUNTERS

> This is not the time to be alone.
> —RANDY PLACE

IT MAKES NO DIFFERENCE WHETHER you got shafted or volunteered to leave. It's a difficult time in your life either way, and you need to kick-start the momentum you lost after your job ended. Your career can be reestablished in a shorter period of time when you seek the support of your spouse, partner, family, and trustworthy friends.

Because job hunting is a lonely task, this is not the time to be alone. You need to reach out for advice and encouragement. But try not to overdo it by advertising your situation to the community or to fellow workers. You need to use a networking approach that's more selective.

Consider your spouse or partner to be your best friend. This is a time when relationships are usually strengthened because family members need each other during the time it takes to find a job—and job finding is full-time work.

You need to support yourself by spending up to twenty hours a week on your job-finding campaign and on making contacts, doing research, and following up on leads.

❖ ❖ ❖

Even if you are offered a severance package that includes career counseling and office support, do not become complacent. You—not some outplacement company or a career consultant who is assigned to handle your case—are responsible for landing a job.

But career counseling makes your job hunt much easier. That holds true unless you're assigned to a wacko PhD or to a recent college graduate with a master's degree in counseling who never had to look for a job in the business world.

It's your task to select a career consultant with business experience. That person can help you get more control over your job campaign by showing you how to avoid the mistakes most people make during the first two days after being terminated.

Some employees blow their stacks at the executive doing the firing. Nice going. They've just ruined a reference. Others panic and become a nuisance with cries for help to friends and business associates. Well they can cross those names off their network lists.

There is a right way of telling contacts about your plight so they can help. A good career consultant with a business background will know how to support your search by showing you the right way to conduct it.

❖ ❖ ❖

When you're offered outplacement as a part of your severance package, grab it. An outplacement service helps you find another position by providing career counseling and office support.

Attitudes toward outplacement can vary. Some of you are ready to roll as soon as you initiate a relationship with the outplacement firm, while others are suspicious. You have reason to be. The service will not place you in a job or even guarantee to help you find one. Nor can an outplacement firm specify the time it will take for you to land.

So what is the value of professional help? You'll find a job in less time than you would if you searched on your own. But you need to be selective when choosing an outplacement firm. Some of the bells and whistles—such as psychological testing and TV equipment—offered by some are not surefire signs of a can't-miss firm.

The most important factor is the career counselor to whom you'll be assigned. Be sure to meet with that person before you sign on and to qualify the potential career advisor by asking four questions:

1. How many years have you been a career counselor?
2. How much experience have you had advising candidates in my field?
3. Are you willing to meet with me at least once a week?
4. Are you available by phone and e-mail if I have questions between counseling sessions?

Some outplacement companies limit the number of times a counselor can see clients. That's why you need a seasoned counselor who can advise you on a weekly basis and will be willing to provide assistance between meetings.

❖ ❖ ❖

At career seminars I hold, job candidates show particular interest in how others cope with their problems. You can understand the reason why that would be of interest. People who share a common experience like losing a job can help each other without using a psychologist, an employee assistance program professional, career counselor, or social worker.

You may have feelings after being terminated that you cannot express to your family or even to a counselor. Some experts say it can be more fruitful to talk to your peers. Nothing beats sharing your feelings, problems, and how you cope with others who are in the same boat. Self-help groups are available to assist a variety of people from alcoholics, atheists, and arthritics to war veterans and job hunters.

Check out your local paper. Churches, synagogues, colleges, and universities may offer job-hunting support groups in your community. You can also check out The Self-Help Clearing House online, which will refer you to local support groups. Most groups charge minimum fees and have a career counselor on hand.

It might come as a surprise to know that even when a counselor is not available to lead a group, you will be able to come up with more ideas about dealing with job-hunting issues than some trained professionals would. That will enable you to pass on practical advice to new members.

Scientist Frank Oppenheimer summed it up nicely when he suggested, "The best way to learn is to teach."

❖ ❖ ❖

When you're still looking for work after spending a year in the job market, there is nothing wrong with you. But there is something wrong with the way you're conducting your search. "There's an awful lot of tricky things that may come up," says career consultant and author Kate Wendleton, "and people can't be objective by themselves."

The surest way for inexperienced job hunters to discover what's wrong is to reach out for support. You can see a career counselor privately or join a job-finding support group. That's much less expensive than ongoing counseling.

If you decide to choose private counseling, hire a career advisor who only charges by the hour. "And that way you can see if you're getting your money's worth," says Wendleton. "And if you don't like it, you just don't go back."

But some job hunters choose to go it alone. Solo job campaigns work when you have a lot of contacts, know where you're headed, and are highly in demand. "But most people need some coaching throughout their job search," advises the career counselor.

Statistics indicate that the majority of job hunters who receive coaching throughout their searches land faster and at higher rates of pay than those who choose to go it alone.

❖ ❖ ❖

Job hunting is an art. You'll master the art of running a successful job-finding campaign by learning a combination of tested and proven job-hunting techniques. You learned and absorbed them as you read this book. You can also visit your local library and online bookstores, join a job-search support group, or see a career counselor.

If you enjoy working alone, you'll find many excellent books and articles on the web that describe job-search strategies.

If you prefer working with others, support groups, which can be found in the basements of churches and synagogues, can give you experience in applying search strategies with your peers. They will give you helpful feedback in return. Most job-hunting support groups offer weekly meetings, charge modest fees, and have a career counselor on board.

Because it costs a lot more to work privately with a career counselor, select one who charges by the hour like doctors and psychologists do. Then you'll know if you are getting your money's worth. If not, don't go back.

Your job-finding campaign will work best when you follow some of the strategies that have worked well for millions of job candidates who have gone before you.

Some choices are outlined above. In a nutshell, read all about it, share your job-search experiences with others in a group setting, or get private coaching.

❖ ❖ ❖

Epilogue

I LEAVE YOU NOW WITH timely advice from Frank Mauser, my late friend and trusted advisor. During our last lunch together in New York, Frank handed me a folded piece of paper on which he had written these words:

THE SECRET

* Begin where you are.
* Do what you can do gracefully.
* Step out in faith.
* Expect God to help

The paper outlining the secret is quite faded after being tacked to a bulletin board in my officer for twenty years. However, I'm able to see it every day. And whenever I apply its four principles to problematic situations, good things happen.

You, too, can expect nice things to happen with your search and career when you follow the secret's four easy steps.

Begin any project right from where you are—from the step you need to be on today. Then do what you can do gracefully by simply doing your best. That means aiming for progress, not perfection, and being grateful for whatever progress you make—even if it's just a little. That's how to attract awesome events into your life.

Now you can step out in faith, knowing you've done your best on that step and can do no more. And voilà! You've earned the right to expect good things to happen—especially when you expect God to help.

One of my job finding-clients who worked with the secret knew this well. In response to my asking him how he felt, George replied, "I'm better than good—too blessed to be stressed."

May all your endeavors be blessed.

Ransom (Randy) Place

Randy Place

Greenwich, CT
September 2015

About the Author

RANDY PLACE IS A JOB-FINDING and executive coach, writer on career topics, broadcaster, and host of www.yourcareerservice.com. For twenty-three years, he helped thousands of employees who had been let go from JPMorgan Chase find jobs.

And he coached executives at CBS Television, Pitney Bowes, and major outplacement firms in New York on job-finding techniques, communications skills, and selling strategies.

An accomplished seminar leader and speaker, Randy has designed and presented workshops on interviewing, telephoning techniques, job-search writing, and sales training nationwide.

Randy's groundbreaking nationally syndicated radio series, *Your Career Service,* has been heard on over two hundred radio stations across the United States. And his articles on career topics have appeared in the *Wall Street Journal's National Business Employment Weekly.*

A former broadcast journalist in New York, he has also been a commercial spokesperson for an array of national and regional advertisers.

In addition, Randy was a sales executive at NBC Radio and the New York City sales manager for syndication at Wolper Productions.

He holds a Bachelor's in Sociology and Broadcasting from Syracuse University, and a Master's in Journalism from New York University.